S0-FAJ-639

WORDS
FOR THINKING
AND THOUGHTS
FOR MEDITATION

WORDS

FOR THINKING

AND THOUGHTS

FOR MEDITATION

---

366 Daily Devotionals

Paul Krebill

Copyright © 2004 by Paul Krebill.

ISBN :   Softcover   1-4134-5206-X

Used by permission. All rights reserved. No part of this book may be reproduced
or transmitted in any form or by any means, electronic or mechanical, including
photocopying, recording, or by any information storage and retrieval system,
without permission in writing from the copyright owner.

Unless otherwise noted, scriptural quotations are from the New Revised Standard
Version Bible, copyright 1989, Division of Christian Education of the National
Council of the Churches of Christ in the United States of America. Used by
permission. All rights reserved.

This book was printed in the United States of America.

To order additional copies of this book, contact:
Xlibris Corporation
1-888-795-4274
www.Xlibris.com
Orders@Xlibris.com
23980

CONTENTS

PREFACE

Readers will find in this volume of meditations three hundred and sixty-six daily devotional readings. Each day's reading includes a scripture reference, a short prayer, and a brief meditation. These can be used privately, in the family, or in a small group setting. One can begin using this volume on any day on the calendar. It is my hope that these words of faith may stimulate thinking and meditation for the reader's devotional time each day of the year. Throughout the year various questions and concerns are addressed from the point of view of traditional Christian faith.

This volume had its beginning with the devotional readings which I wrote for the congregation of St. Andrew Presbyterian Church in Billings, Montana during my twenty-five year ministry in that parish. The encouragement of many of those original readers, and especially the gentle urging of my wife, Doris, have motivated me to make this 366 day devotional book available to a wider readership.

I wish to acknowledge the untiring assistance of Harriet Whearty and Pat Fink, whose secretarial support made the original devotional readings available to the congregation of St. Andrew Presbyterian Church. More recently I have been assisted by Mary Lensink, Janice Peace, George McClure, Ray and Harriet Whearty and Lindsey Zent, who have helped me bring this volume to its final form. Finally I am indebted to Faith K.Kelly of *Designs by Faith,* for the cover photograph taken at Westminster Spires Camp on the Beartooth Highway of Montana

—Paul Krebill, Bozeman, Montana
February 2004

JANUARY

JANUARY 1

THINGS ARE THE SAME, THINGS ARE DIFFERENT

And the one who was seated on the throne said, "See, I
am making all things new."
—Revelation 21:5

READ: Revelation 21:1-6

During the holiday season did you take time to think? Or
were you too busy with a thousand details? Did you think about
the year which has just ended? How is your world different at the
threshold of another twelve months? How is your world the same
as it was last January? Perhaps things are both the same and different!

New Year's resolutions seem to arise out of these two questions.
How do I want to change my life? I am still the same person as I
was a year ago, but now I see some changes in my life I would like
to make. Some circumstances cannot be changed, but other factors
can be made different. In many ways I really do want this new year
to be different for me. And yet it has been frustrating in the past to
face up to the fact that broken resolutions insure sameness for the
new year, much as I don't want that.

It is the vision of Christians that God is the one who promises
newness of life. "And the one who was seated on the throne said,
'See, I am making all things new.'" (Revelation 21:5) The closer
we live to God and God's will for our lives, the more we are able to
draw upon God's power to enact the changes God wants in our

lives. The more God's power infuses our life situation, the newer our life and our new year will be!

PRAYER: O Lord of the New Year, giver of newness, grant me power to change the things in my life that you and I know need transforming. Through Christ, the transformer of life. Amen

~ ~ ~ ~ ~ ~

JANUARY 2

REGRETFULLY YOURS

Have mercy on me, O God, according to your steadfast love; according to your abundant mercy blot out my transgressions. Wash me thoroughly from my iniquity, and cleanse me from my sin.

—Psalm 51,1,2

READ: Psalm 51:1-10 and John 21:15-19

One of the most poignant scenes of regret in the New Testament is the account of the risen Christ asking Peter three times. "Simon, son of John, do you love me more than these?" As readers who know the story of Peter's past sin, and as people with painful memories of our own transgressions, we can read between the lines and feel the regret which Peter must have had when the risen Lord confronted him with that penetrating question. He had not shown his love for Jesus when he denied knowing him on that fateful night of Jesus' arrest and trial. John tells us of Peter's confession, his repentance, and of Jesus' forgiveness.

As you review the old year in your life, what are your regrets? The most difficult regrets to deal with, are those resulting from our own sin and failure to obey Christ. The first step in allowing God to dissolve our regrets is to give up scape-goating. So easily do we place blame outside ourselves by saying or thinking, "So and So, made me do it." Peter could not do that in Christ's presence.

Neither can we. Honest admission of our failure opens the way for Christ's forgiveness, to our turning around, and to the washing away of our iniquity.

When we say to God, "I am regretfully yours, O God, forgive me," then we can receive God's forgiveness And following such forgiveness comes God's command to us, as it came to Peter. "Feed my sheep . . . Follow me." (John 21:17, 19) In that precious moment in Peter's life he was given a profoundly happy new year!

PRAYER: Forgive me O God, for all that I regret. Through Christ may I be given a truly new year! Amen

~ ~ ~ ~ ~ ~

JANUARY 3

LIFE'S GAINS AND LOSSES

Blessed be the name of God from age to age, for wisdom and power are his. He reveals deep and hidden things; he knows what is in the darkness, and light dwells with him.
—Daniel 2:20, 22

READ: Daniel 2:1-6, 16-23

As we enter a new year and look back upon the old year, it is wise to for us to count our losses and gains, and to contemplate the meaning which last year has had for us. What has been my learning experience? How do the preceding twelve months add up to for me?

In the story of Daniel, the king had a dream which troubled him deeply, so much so that he couldn't sleep. He needed to understand the meaning of his dream; and so he asked Daniel to give him its interpretation. Daniel sought God's wisdom so that he could correctly understand the king's dream.

For each of us to make an honest assessment of life's gains and losses, we, like Daniel, must seek the wisdom and perspective of

God. Think of what you have lost in this past year. Perhaps you have lost a loved one. Other serious losses may have been in your own health or in your relationships with friends and loved ones. Material losses may also have been significant. The loss of a job has been a serious loss for many. What have been your gains? Helpful insights, perhaps, or new relationships, new responsibilities, or possibly new possessions.

Instead of taking such gains for granted, or aimlessly fretting over losses, why not present your life's gains and losses before God in prayer, and ask for God's wisdom to interpret these events or circumstances in the light of God's intention for your life. "He controls the times and the seasons . . . . It is he who gives wisdom and understanding." (Daniel 2:22—The Bible in Today's English Version, American Bible Society, New York, 1976)

PRAYER: Help me, O God, to understand the losses and gains in my life in the light of your wisdom and from your perspective. In Christ. Amen

~ ~ ~ ~ ~ ~

JANUARY 4

STOP LOOKING—AND LIVE

And why do you worry about clothing? Consider the
lilies of the field, how they grow; they neither toil nor spin.
—Matthew 6:28

READ: Matthew 6:25-34 and Matthew 11:28-30

As you look ahead, are you anxious about what might happen? Do you find yourself wondering where you will be twelve months from now; what crises will have shaped your life in the coming year; what changes will occur. If you are so inclined you can imagine many unfortunate developments, and you can work yourself into a frenzy worrying over what might happen. It doesn't do us much good to play the "what if" game. But it is a human tendency.

Jesus must have known that we normally have anxiety over the future, and that we can so easily become first-rate worriers. There is nothing worse than pacing the floor waiting for the arrival of an over-due loved one. The tendency is to imagine all sorts of dismal scenarios. But Jesus said, "Therefore I tell you, 'Do not worry! . . . But if God so clothes the grass of the field . . . will he not much more clothe you?"(Matthew 6:25, 30) This does not mean we ought not to have reasonable concerns in questionable circumstances, or should not act responsibly in whatever situations emerge, in the misguided belief that God will take care even if we mess up. However, it does mean that worrying and fretting do not do any good at all; and in fact sometimes our anxious fears make matters worse.

In place of worrisome anxiety, Jesus offers us a healthy dependence upon God to lead us through the next twelve months—as God has led us in the past!

PRAYER: O God, help me to consider the lilies of the field and your care for them. In Christ. Amen

~ ~ ~ ~ ~ ~

JANUARY 5

HOW CAN I BE HAPPY?

For the grace of God has appeared, bringing salvation to all . . . Grace be with all of you.
—Titus 2:11, 3:15

READ: Acts 3:1-10

She was lying in a hospital bed after having been flown in from an outlying community. Facing open heart surgery the next day, she hastened to assure the visiting chaplain that "she believed in God" although she rarely attended church. "Just sort of got out of the habit," she confessed. As the chaplain prepared to leave her bedside, she asked, "Would you pray for me?" Like most people today the religious issue in her life was not whether or not God exists. Her problem was one of fearfulness, anxiety, and guilt. Her religious issue was her need for God's grace in time of her need.

"Life's been pretty good to me," he said to an old friend over coffee one morning at the local café. "But ever since I sold the business and the kids moved away, I can't seem to find much to enjoy. Even hunting and fishing have lost their appeal. How can I be happy again?" He also, like so many, needed God's grace and salvation for life's fulfillment.

"Ever since I was a child, I have been a loser. I was always chosen last for sports teams at school. 'D's and 'C's were my grades most of the time. My sister got the 'A' grades in the family, and my dad never let me forget it. Life's a drag." She told her counselor during the very first hour. Another case of someone needing God's grace and salvation to feel better about herself.

This is what the Christian faith is all about: God's gift of happiness, God's grace by which we are made able to feel good about ourselves. That's what the word "salvation" means!

PRAYER: Dear God, by your grace and salvation may I receive the gift of happiness! In Christ. Amen

~ ~ ~ ~ ~ ~

JANUARY 6

ARE THINGS GETTING BETTER OR WORSE—OR WHAT?

> And he has put all things under his feet and has made
> him the head over all things for the church.
>
> —Ephesians 1:22

READ: Romans 8:18-30

Florence and Madge were engaged in a dismal conversation one morning over coffee. "What's this world coming to? The kids are all on drugs, and more and more people seem to be messing up their lives," Florence complained, not for the first time.

To which Madge added, "I just heard from my niece who told me that she had left her husband because he had been beating on her, and he beat on their little girl as well."

"It was never this way when we were kids," Florence said, adding, "And then there's the ever present threat of a terror attack. I sometimes think God must have given up on us as a lost cause."

"Oh no," Madge hastened to say, "I believe it will all finally come out all right. But, meanwhile it is pretty bad, I have to admit."

What do you think? Will God come to our rescue? Or are we merely on the down side of a cycle? People used to think that things were getting better day by day, and that perfection was just down the road. Life could become perfect, if you just educate people to a better way. Reacting against such a rosy view point, many writers and playwrights gave us very dismal stories, believing that despair was the only reasonable response to modern life.

The Bible assures us that God is ultimately in charge, and that "all things work together for good for those who love God, who are called according to his purpose."(Romans 8:28) This means that in every event God is at work seeking to bring about God's will, which is ultimately good; and that those who love God and want to serve God's purposes will grow in their understanding of what God is doing. Finally Christ will be seen as Lord of all things. Certainly there is mystery here; but more important, there is faith in the future in this Christian conviction which can carry us through a great many disturbing circumstances.

PRAYER: O God, help me to know that you will guide the future as you have the past. In Christ. Amen

~ ~ ~ ~ ~ ~

JANUARY 7

WHAT IS TRUE, WORTHWHILE, AND RIGHT?

Pilate asked him, "What is truth?"

—John 18:38

READ: John 18:33-38 and Mark 12:28-34

A group of parents had asked to address the school board to present a request. The gist of their request was that they wanted the schools to teach values to the children, so that they might grow up knowing right from wrong. One of the school board members jumped in with, "Whose values? Who's to say what's right and wrong. It's a matter of where you're coming from."

Another board member countered: "Yes, but we are talking about the morals and ethics which our churches teach, which we all grew up with."

"Yes, but which church are you going to follow? They all have different ideas; and besides a lot of children are not in any church and those things don't apply to them," the first board member retorted.

Many today do not believe that there is a final authority on matters of truth and goodness, but that each person should come to his or her own decision. Often this position is reflected in the statement, "If it feels good to you, it is OK." However, the Christian does not believe that the true and the right change according to who is thinking about it. Rather, we believe that God's word of truth and goodness comes to us through Christ, and that God is the ultimate authority over what is right and wrong. However, there are never simple answers such as a list of "do's" and "don'ts" to solve all our questions. When Jesus was asked about what is good, he summed up the matter by saying that we should love God and our neighbor.

If we do this, we will have values of the true, the worthwhile and the good, by which to live and to teach our children.

PRAYER: Help me to discern day by day what is right according to your will, O God. In Christ. Amen

~ ~ ~ ~ ~ ~

JANUARY 8

HOW CAN I GET ALONG WITH OTHERS?

The commandments . . . are summed up in this word,
"Love your neighbor as yourself." Love does no wrong to a
neighbor; therefore, love is the fulfilling of the law.
—Romans 13: 9,10

READ: Leviticus 19:15-18 and Matthew 7:12

Throughout the teaching of Jesus, getting along with others is matched with getting along with yourself.

From this rich vein of ore, the Golden Rule has been refined: "Do unto others as you would have them do to you!" In Jesus' summary of the law the second of his two chief commandments is: "Love your neighbor as yourself." When Paul summarizes the commandments this is the only one he uses. Very important this must be! "If you want to answer the question of how to get along with others, you must turn to yourself and ask. "How do I feel about myself?"

When we do not get along with each other, and treat others badly, the cause most often lies in the feelings we have about ourselves. If you feel unworthy, or guilty, or deprived, anxious or uneasy about yourself, you will find it difficult to reach out to others in positive, helpful, and loving ways. Similarly, when others treat you poorly, the cause may very well be their own lack of self-esteem.

Not only does Jesus advise us to love ourselves, so that we get along with others, but he provides the way to gain self-esteem. This is salvation: realizing that God loves us as we are, forgives us when we admit our failings, and gives us grace to set forth on a new life pathway. When I know that God accepts me, then I find that I can love the one whom God loves—myself! When I feel OK about myself, I can relate to others in a positive and loving way. That's getting along with others!

PRAYER: Thank you for your promise to love me, O God. Transform my relationships so that the Golden Rule applies! Through Christ. Amen

⌐ ⌐ ⌐ ⌐ ⌐ ⌐

JANUARY 9

POOR SOUP

> But Jesus, perceiving their thoughts said, "Why do you think evil in your hearts? For which is easier to say, 'Your sins are forgiven,' or to say 'Stand up and walk?'"
>
> —Matthew 9:4,5

READ: Matthew 9:1-8 and Proverbs 24:8,9

My mother had a phrase she used to refer to a man who had a "down in the mouth" look about him: "Poor Soup," she would say, and not too sympathetically at that. Obviously what such a man thought about himself was evident in how he appeared, and my mother picked up on that. When you harbor negative thoughts about yourself or your world, it will show through. Our thoughts have a way of determining how others will relate to us and at least in part what will happen to us.

When Jesus healed the paralyzed man in Matthew 9, he was aware of the influence of thought upon action. Jesus addressed the man first on the level of his inner attitude. "Take heart, son; your sins are forgiven!"(Matthew 9:2) When the paralytic was given this transformation of thought and attitude, he became able to walk! The gift of Christ changed both his thinking and his physical ability. Now that he was forgiven he could walk!

On the other hand, Jesus saw in the faces of the teachers of the law the negative thinking when he said, "Why do you think evil in your hearts?" (Matthew 9:4) Because these people thought ill of Jesus in the first place, they missed seeing the power and love of God expressed in Jesus' healing of the mind and body of the paralytic man.

When we get into a "poor soup" frame of mind, we may very well miss the helpful, loving action God offers to us. We can get so caught up in self-pity, or in scornful thoughts, that the lifting power of Christ doesn't seem to phase us.

PRAYER: Change my thinking, O Lord, that I may look up and grasp your love for me in Christ. Amen

~ ~ ~ ~ ~ ~

JANUARY 10

CUSTOM BUILT AND ONE OF A KIND

> For by the grace given to me I say to everyone among you not to think of yourself more highly than you ought to think, but to think with sober judgement each according to the measure of faith that God has assigned.
>
> —Romans 12:3

READ: Romans 12:1-16 and Proverbs 23:14

"How am I doing?" "How do I look?" "What's the competition up to?" "Who's ahead?" We live in a very competitive society In this competitive environment we judge ourselves in comparison to others, as if life were a race to see who is ahead. The object of our running the race seems to be to gain enough advantage over others, so that we can think more highly of ourselves. Our lives become affected by this kind of competitive thinking when winners think more highly of themselves than they ought to, and losers develop unduly low opinions of themselves.

Paul urges us to allow God to change this kind of competitive thinking when he wrote: "Do not be conformed to this world, but be transformed by the renewing of your minds, so that you may discern what is the will of God—what is good and acceptable and perfect." (Romans 12:2) How we think about ourselves should take into account what unique gifts God has given to each of us individually. Our own self-evaluations should be directed toward understanding how well we have accepted and made good use of God's gifts. Because God's gifts to me are different from what God has given others, I cannot get into the comparison business. Each of us is custom built by God. Each of us is one of a kind. It does not matter if someone else seems to have a talent I do not possess, or has a life style I may be tempted to envy. How am I doing with what God has given to me? How well am I living the way God wants me to live? These are the questions I must ask as I evaluate myself.

PRAYER: Thank you, God, for your gifts to me: my life, my strengths, my interests, my friends and associates. Let me discern your intention for me, for my life is filled with such gifts. Let me do well as I seek to follow your will for my life. In Christ. Amen

~ ~ ~ ~ ~ ~

JANUARY 11

WHISTLING IN THE DARK

Finally, beloved, whatever is true, whatever is honorable,
whatever is just, whatever is pure, whatever is pleasing,

whatever is commendable, if there is any excellence and if
there is anything worthy of praise, think about these things
—Philippians 4:8

READ: Philippians 4:1-8 and Proverbs 24:3,4

One's work environment can surely make a difference in how
well one works. When the room is pleasant, well lit, with adequate
space, as well as having a touch of attractive decor, the work done
in it will be of better quality. Today's text would be a good motto
for architects—think on these things and you'll design a better
building!

As with buildings, so with lives. If one wants a productive and
enjoyable life, its foundation must be placed upon some positive
thinking. Thinking about what is good and true, helps bring about
the good and the true. Thinking beauty precedes the creation of
beautiful art and music.

While it is true that one can be caught in terribly unfortunate
circumstances in which it is cruel to preach "think nice thoughts
and you'll be all right," it is also true that merely changing one's
circumstances will not necessarily change one's spirit. Paul is urging
the Christians in Philippi to stretch forward toward God's goodness
and righteousness, knowing that the attainment of the Christian
life depends upon how fully we take hold of what God is giving us.
Paul declared "I press on toward the goal for the prize of the heavenly
call of God in Christ Jesus." (Philippians 3:14)

There is something to be said for whistling in the dark. When
life is overshadowed by difficulties it helps for God to lift our
thoughts into the sunlight above. Like an airplane emerging above
the clouds into the dazzling brightness of the sun our lives brighten
when we look above the clouds to God.

PRAYER: Lift me, O God, when it is gloomy. Put a new set of
thoughts in me, through Christ. Amen.

⌐ ⌐ ⌐ ⌐ ⌐

JANUARY 12

YOU ARE WHAT YOU THINK

Let us not become conceited, competing against one
another, envying one another.

—Galatians 5:26

READ: Galatians 5:16-6:10

There is no area in our lives in which our thoughts determine
what happens, more directly than in interpersonal relationships.
What you think about yourself will affect what others think of
you, and thus influence how they will respond to you. If you think
you are of little value, you may well find that others treat you as
though you didn't matter much. If, on the other hand, you have
an inflated view of yourself, and tend to be puffed up, others will
react to you negatively. Superior attitudes on the part of some
members of a group can destroy the group itself.

Paul is struggling with the problem of how the church ought
to deal with those who have done wrong. He warns that those who
approach the wrong-doer must do so humbly, knowing that they,
too, could be in the same position. Rather than with a superior,
self-righteous attitude, the church should gently deal with those
who have made mistakes in their conduct. Such humility is not
self-effacing but it is unwilling to be judgmental. This kind of
honest view of oneself on the part of each member of the group
helps to build and maintain fellowship.

In this well-known passage to the Galatians in which the
concept of reaping what you sow is put forward, one sees a very
direct application of how one's own self-image determines how
one's interpersonal relationships will be carried out. To insure good
relationships, "Live by the Spirit, I say, and do not gratify the
desires of the flesh." (Galatians 5:16)

PRAYER: Let me think honestly about myself, O God, so that in humility I know my need for you and seek to love others as you love me. In Christ. Amen

∼ ∼ ∼ ∼ ∼ ∼

JANUARY 13

BE STILL AND KNOW

> Have you not known? Have you not heard? Has it not been told you from the beginning? Have you not understood from the foundations of the earth?
>
> —Isaiah 40:21

READ: Isaiah 40:21-26 and Genesis 1:1-3

Have you ever thought that the year ought to begin in September instead of January—at least in the Northern Hemisphere? September is when we get things started: school, clubs, many cultural activities and many other programs in society. So why not begin the year in September! But, let's look at this in another way. Now, in the middle of an active winter program, it is a good time to do as the Psalmist suggests, "Be still and know that I am God." (Psalm 46:10) Now is a good time to stop, take stock, and start again on a renewed footing.

This is a time to think about a new beginning which comes as a result of God's gift of Jesus Christ which we have celebrated during the Christmas season just past. The coming of Jesus was such a radically new beginning that the Western world reset its calendar to begin with the birth of Christ. In many ways we reset our inner calendar on the basis of our experience of the coming of Christ into our lives again during this season. The Christmas season has a way of reuniting us with our families and loved ones, and of lifting our minds to higher levels of thought and resolve. We have become aware of God's abundant blessing in our lives. And so, what better time to restart our lives for another year!

During the first month of another new year it is fitting to turn our attention to the God who established all the universes, and whose creative love has brought each of us into being.

PRAYER: As a new year begins, O God, cause me to be still and to know that you are God! In the name of Christ whose birth we have celebrated anew. Amen

~ ~ ~ ~ ~ ~

JANUARY 14

BEHIND THE UPS AND DOWNS

But we must always give thanks to God for you, brothers and sisters beloved by the Lord, because God chose you as the first fruits for salvation through sanctification by the Spirit and through belief in the truth.
—II Thessalonians 2:13

READ: II Thessalonians 2:13-17

Life has its ups and downs. We have heard that often. It remains accurate. Changes come, sometimes bringing to us painful disappointment, or confusion of purpose and direction. The circumstances of ones's employment may change suddenly. New assignments, a new supervisor, or different co-workers, perhaps even job termination. One's family make-up may change with the departure or addition of a family member. Perhaps now one is alone; or maybe an aged parent has moved in for care. You never know what a phone call will bring, perhaps announcing some disturbing news. Or even more unsettling, is waiting for a phone call which has been expected but does not come. In its place, disappointment spreads throughout one's mind and heart.

The Thessalonian Christians were waiting for the return of Jesus. When this did not happen as they anticipated they were becoming disappointed and downcast. Paul wrote to encourage them by saying in effect, *In the midst of your disappointment, remember that God chose you from the beginning as his own. Let your life be guided in God's truth and lifted up by his Spirit.*

When change and disappointment come into your life, remember that behind the ups and downs there remains the steady, certain fact of God's loving call to you to be God's own person. With this realization that you have belonged to God from the beginning, you can make a new beginning in your life in the midst of its ups and downs.

PRAYER: When life has some downers for me, help me to remember your love and your call to remain faithful. Help me to pick up the pieces and begin anew. In Christ. Amen.

⌐ ⌐ ⌐ ⌐ ⌐ ⌐

JANUARY 15

WHEN IN DOUBT, READ THE DIRECTIONS

In the beginning was the Word, and the Word was with God, and the Word was God. All things came into being through him and without him not one thing came into being.

—John 1:1,3

READ: John 1:1-13 and Psalm 111:10

Changing circumstances in life often require major decisions in order for us to keep on course. Sometimes these occasions are turning points when we are persuaded to change our goals and alter our directions. Such periods of major change can open the door to doubts, and previously held values may come under question. A person may have been in a job with the goal of making as much money as possible. But when the job situation changes, the opportunity to consider other goals may present itself. For example, one may come to doubt the value of money for money's sake and begin to think in terms of one's own family needs. Such a consideration might lead to the decision to spend more time at home with the family.

When life changes bring doubts, and new directions appear to be called for, it is good to remember where the "directions" came from. That is, the instructions for the effective operation of ones own life! As with any appliance such directions come from the manufacturer, who is God, who brought us into being in the first place. What better source for the operation of our lives than the Inventor! "In the beginning was the Word" (John 1:1) by which everything came into being. The Psalmist said, "The fear of the Lord is the beginning of wisdom."(Psalm 111:10)

PRAYER: When I must make big decisions for my life, O God, my Maker, help me to read the directions first! In Christ who is the Word. Amen

~ ~ ~ ~ ~ ~

JANUARY 16

GOING TO JAIL OR PASSING GO

He is the beginning, the first-born from the dead.
—Colossians 1:18

READ: Colossians 1:15-23 and Mark 1:1-3

In the game of Monopoly it is a very good and necessary thing to pass "GO" and to collect one's salary, especially after having made some costly mistakes or having had some bad luck. But it is not good to turn up the card which says, "Go to jail, do not pass Go." In a way, a summary of the Christian Gospel might be given in these terms. Instead of going to jail for your mistakes, you can pass GO and have a chance to begin again. This is what the resurrection implies. Paul assured the Colossians that Christ is the one who at the beginning is raised from the dead and offers the opportunity for a new beginning after mistakes have been made and admitted.

When you have been traveling along the wrong road and discover your error, and you turn around to get on the right road, it is a good feeling to go past the point of your wrong turn and finally to start on the right road.

The Gospel gives us that good feeling! The opportunity to get back on the right road and to start in the direction God has mapped out for us. That's why Christ is the Good News!

In quoting Isaiah, Mark uses the imagery of the highway to show that Jesus' coming requires the removal of crooked and uneven roads, so that the highway of life can be straight as Christ leads us. Let the new beginning of this season help you straighten your pathway, and move you in a different direction from your earlier mistaken course!

PRAYER: Help me, O God, straighten my pathway and help me to follow the way Christ leads me. In the name of Christ. Amen.

~ ~ ~ ~ ~ ~

JANUARY 17

A NEW NAME ON A WHITE STONE

And I will give a white stone, and on the white stone is written a new name that no one knows except the one who receives it.

—Revelation 2:17

READ: II Corinthians 5:11-19

The astounding declaration of the New Testament is that through Christ each of us can become a new person! "So, if anyone is in Christ, there is a new creation: everything old has passed away; see, everything has become new!" (II Corinthians 5:17) How we wish for that! To be able to discard the old habits and behavior patterns; to be able to feel good about ourselves again; to gain new skills in relating to others; to have some way of dealing meaningfully with problems in the world around us. These constitute nothing less than transformation from one person to another, it would seem. Yet, this is what Paul declares Christ will do for one. Many persons who work in Rescue Missions are living examples of persons who by the power of Christ have been transformed from hopeless addicts to productive citizens.

If the power of Christ can work such dramatic changes in others, certainly we can pray for his power to replace our own weaknesses. The Christian faith puts us on a course of life which follows the death-resurrection cycle. We are invited to confess our sin, to throw away our old ways, and to be given new ways of living.

Sometimes major changes in life precipitate name changes. Teen-agers often let childhood names go and take on their given name. Sonny becomes Sam. Dolly becomes Dorothy. Marriage traditionally provides a name change for the bride. Sometimes in psychotherapy a person may decide that changing his or her name will bring about an important step toward mental health.

Revelation speaks of writing a new name on a white stone that no one knows except the one who receives it. This is symbolic of the gift of transformation which Christ offers to those who will accept it.

PRAYER: O Christ, take away the old stuff in my life and give me new life! Amen.

～ ～ ～ ～ ～ ～

JANUARY 18

MOVED TO A NEW ADDRESS

I will write on you the name of my God, and the name
of the city of my God, the new Jerusalem.

—Revelation 3:12

READ: Colossians 3:5-11

We use the term "where I am coming from" to denote more than mere location. This phrase refers to our set of values, attitudes, and experiences which determine how we speak, act, and relate. If I show anger at a certain event, it may very well be due to my experience with that sort of situation earlier in my life. How I make my decisions is determined by where I'm coming from—what my convictions, opinions and prejudices may be.

A symbolic place name for where we are coming from as Christians is "The New Jerusalem." Having given our lives to Christ we have been given a new address—new place to come from. So our actions, attitudes, values and decisions will be radically different because of where we are now coming from, now that we belong to Christ.

Paul describes how we shall be different in the Colossians passage noted above. He contrasts the ways of those who come from God's city as having put on a new nature, replacing the old.

Next time you use the phrase, "that's where I'm coming from," stop and think about the fact that as a Christian you are coming from a new address, The New Jerusalem," and thus you will be acting out of love and justice, with Christ's concern for the world in your mind and heart.

PRAYER: Move me, O God to a new address, to the New Jerusalem, where Christ is, and let me "come from there" in my future actions! Through Christ. Amen

~ ~ ~ ~ ~

JANUARY 19

A NEW SONG

And they sing a new song before the throne and before the four living creatures and before the elders. (Only they) could learn that song.

—Revelation 14:3

READ: Ephesians 4:17-24 and Psalm 30:1-5

You could tell a lot about a person if you knew what song he or she were singing. You sing one kind of song when you are down and depressed—some form of the blues; and another kind of song when you are up and joyful. It says something about our society when you listen to popular music. So much of it is sad and yearning. Some is angry and violent. So little is free and easy. What does that mean about us?

When you have been given a new nature, a new hope in Christ and a new name and place to come from, you will sing a new song! Being a Christian can make a difference on an emotional level. Christ's transforming power should make you want to sing a joyful song. Like the exuberant love song you sing when you are in love, so you ought to feel a joy and sense of bliss as a result of God's powerful changes in your life. You simply can't celebrate Christmas without singing the carols. Easter makes us sing hymns such as "Jesus Christ is risen today, Alleluia!"

We have inherited a singing faith from our Hebrew ancestors. We have their hymn book, the Psalms, which give us ample evidence of songs and music as an authentic response to God's grace on the part of his people in both Old and New Testaments.

"Sing praises to the Lord, O you his faithful ones!" (Psalm 30:4)

PRAYER: O God, you have given me newness of life. Help me to sing a new song of praise. In Christ. Amen.

~ ~ ~ ~ ~

JANUARY 20

FROM RANGELAND TO DOWNTOWN

So come, I will send you to Pharaoh to bring my people, the Israelites, out of Egypt.

—Exodus 3:10

READ: Exodus 3:1-10

In the summer of 1984 in the mountains of western Montana, two extremely private and isolated men living completely separated from civilization, suddenly gained national notoriety. They were Don and Dan Nichols, a father and son, who came to be known as the "mountain men." After abducting a young woman and subsequently killing one of the men who tried to rescue her, the Nichols became fugitives as they continued their wilderness life-style by moving from one hidden camp to another in the densely forested mountains until they were finally apprehended. In a "20/20" interview Don Nichols said that he had wanted to stay entirely free of society, and that it had been his aim not ever to have an address, because "once you have an address, all the trouble begins," he said.

Strangely, the public was not entirely negative in its treatment of the two Nichols. Perhaps it was the "mountain men's" intentional un-involvement to the "nth" degree which caught the imagination of modern, stressed out people! We don't like the hassle which society imposes upon us either.

Moses as a young man was uninvolved with the major issues of his time. A sheepherder for his father-in-law, he spent his time away from civilization on the open range much of the year. He had killed an Egyptian who had been mistreating one of Moses' fellow countrymen, and now Moses was a fugitive. However, one day his life was turned around. He met God; or rather God searched him out and asked him to lead the Israelites out Egypt, through the wilderness, and into the land of Canaan. Suddenly Moses was involved in society "up to his ears!" From that time onward he would be known to the world. His life became public, significant and important, one which accomplished great things for God.

Much as we'd like to remain out on some isolated rangeland or up on some mountain, God wants us downtown, so to speak, to get involved in some way by which to make a meaningful contribution to our world in the time given to us. Just as God called Moses to get involved, Christ called his disciples to follow him and to get involved. Do you hear Christ's call to you? Christ will transform us into workers for God, if we will let him.

PRAYER: O Christ, help me to become involved meaningfully for God in my world! Amen

~ ~ ~ ~ ~ ~

JANUARY 21

CURRENCY EXCHANGE

After this he went out and saw a tax collector named Levi, sitting at the tax booth and he said to him, "Follow me."

—Luke 5:27

READ: Luke 5:27-32

Levi was a man much taken with money. He loved it, and tried to get as much of it as he could. In his job as tax collector for the Roman government he ran what might be called a currency exchange as he collected funds from the Jews in their own coinage and turned it into tribute money for the Caesar in Rome—and into profit for himself. Luke tells us that Levi himself was exchanged in a manner of speaking, from service to Caesar and self to obedience to Christ. It was a currency exchange from Roman to Christian! An exchange symbolized in his name change from Levi to Matthew.

Direct, personal contact with Jesus precipitated a change in Levi's life from a devotion to money to a commitment to Christ instead. He was changed into a new person whose first loyalty would now be to the mission of Jesus in the world. Matthew responded to the call to be one of the twelve disciples in Jesus' inner circle.

From our own lives we know that certain life events can contribute to such an exchange of currencies—values—in our lives. Perhaps a serious illness, or the death of a loved one, an accident or some form of reprieve in which we sense that we have been given a new chance at life. The birth of a first child often re-arranges the priorities of the parents. Meeting the one whom you will eventually marry can do that too.

In a Christian sense the most significant transformation of values comes when one commits one's life to Jesus Christ and to his work in the world. That is a very basic exchange of currencies in one's life—from service of self to following God's intention for one's life as revealed to us in Christ.

PRAYER: "Take my life and let it be, consecrated, O Lord, to Thee!" Through Christ. Amen

～ ～ ～ ～ ～ ～

JANUARY 22

A FLASHING LIGHT

Now as he was going along and approaching Damascus,
suddenly a light from heaven flashed around him.

—Acts 9:3

READ: Acts 9:1-9

A flashing light in the sky or anywhere else is a sign of something very important. It may signal disaster or tragedy as an ambulance rushes by. Danger may be its message when it is on a highway department barricade at a washout or a sharp curve. A flashing light can change the course of your journey when the light blocks the road ahead. In comic strips of an earlier day, a flashing light bulb over a character's head indicated a sudden burst of insight, or a new idea!

The flashing light in Saul's case signaled both a change in the course of his life, and a radical change in thought. One of the most difficult transformations for us is to change our theology—how we think about God. Saul held so tenaciously to his Hebrew theology that he fanatically went about persecuting those who believed differently. Having sought extradition papers from the High Priest in Jerusalem he was on his way to bring back those in Damascus who were honoring Christ. Then a flashing light confronted Saul. In time, as a result of his meeting Christ in that moment, he became a convinced, active, and influential Christian—a complete change of mind—a new direction for his life—a new name, from Saul to Paul!

So powerful is contact with Jesus Christ that even our minds can be changed. That's a major accomplishment for most of us. We are usually somewhat stubborn about our beliefs and value judgements. Christ's powerful transformation will change our minds and alter the course of our lives. That is always difficult, because it feels so risky. But with Christ all things are possible. Consider the changes you want him to effect in your life and dare to open yourself to the changes God wants for you. Then hope for a flashing light!

PRAYER: Oh, Christ, change me at those points where you know I need transformation. Amen.

~ ~ ~ ~ ~ ~

JANUARY 23

FROM SICKNESS TO HEALTH

> Thus says the Lord of hosts: Return to me says the Lord of Hosts, and I will return to you says the Lord of Hosts.
>
> —Zechariah 1:3

READ: Luke 8:1-3

By the time we meet Mary of Magdala in the New Testament, she is a changed person! More is said of the "new Mary" than of the old. This we know: She has become a full supporter of Jesus' ministry through her presence in the group which followed him, and in this capacity provided for the needs of Jesus and his disciples, which she did by using her own resources. We are told that formerly Mary had been plagued by seven demons. That could mean physical, mental, or moral problems, either very acute, or chronic, or both. Whatever her problem, she was cured of it through her contact with Jesus; and now she is an active supporter of his cause. Christ has turned her life around and brought her from sickness to health.

When one is ill of mind body or spirit, the vital presence of a person who is strong and well, and who is loving and caring can play a major role in one's own return to health and strength. When life seems to be torn apart in too many directions, or when physical disease threatens our well-being; when we fear for our own personal future, or are aware of our own spiritual or moral weakness, the loving, caring, strong presence of Christ in our lives can very well turn us around and put us on the road to health of mind, body, and spirit!

PRAYER: O Christ, come near to me when I am ill in mind, body or spirit. Bring your healing presence to me and help restore me to physical health, mental balance, spiritual vitality, and moral strength. Amen

~ ~ ~ ~ ~ ~

JANUARY 24

FROM NIGHT TO LIGHT

> Thus says the Lord God: Repent and turn away from your idols; and turn away your faces from all your abominations.
> —Ezekiel 14:6

READ: John 3:1-21

One of the most intellectual conversations reported of Jesus is his discussion with Nicodemus, a Pharisee and a teacher. John, who gives us the story, makes very sure that we are aware that the conversation took place in the dark of night, when Nicodemus would not be seen talking with the "outlaw," Jesus. This serves as a metaphor for the fact that Nicodemus, like all Israel, was in the dark about the truth of God and the Kingdom of God. However, contact with Jesus brought Nicodemus into the light and changed his life—from night to light! So much so that he became a supporter of Jesus defending him before the Jewish officials. Later he prepared the body of Jesus for burial, by providing expensive spices. Jesus changed Nicodemus so that he became aware of the truth of God and began walking in it.

In a day when so many of us know so much, and when scientific exploration is our principal tool for gaining knowledge of the truth, we may very well remain in the dark when it comes to spiritual truth. Some years ago the televised movie, "The Day After" showed expert knowledge of what a nuclear war would do to the world, but the movie displayed utter ignorance of the spiritual reactions and realities of such a supposed scenario. Like Nicodemus, we are experts in some matters, but often are kindergartners in the things of God. Jesus changes that, and shows us the truth of the spiritual side of our lives. Let him bring you from night to light.

PRAYER: O Christ, show me the truth of God and of God's kingdom. Amen.

~ ~ ~ ~ ~ ~

JANUARY 25

FROM FEAR TO COURAGE

Let the wicked forsake their way, and the unrighteous their thoughts; let them return to the Lord, that he may

have mercy on them, and to our God, for he will abundantly
pardon.

—Isaiah 55:7

READ: John 21:15-19

Peter, the Rock! The early church recognized Peter as a man of
supreme courage. His bravery for Christ led him into conflict with
the people of power in Rome. As a result, Peter was crucified.
Earlier, however, Peter had not been so brave. In fear for his life he
claimed not to know Jesus on the night of Jesus' arrest and trial
lest he be implicated and arrested. It was his confrontation with
Christ after the resurrection which turned Peter around from fear
to courage. From the time of Peter's life-changing experience with
Jesus Christ after the resurrection Peter carried the Gospel into the
waiting and sometimes hostile world of the Roman Empire.

Christ gives us the courage, when ordinarily we are fearful. Many
a cleric has been afraid to speak the truth when the prevailing
government has held the power of life and death over him. However,
exceptions outshine the rule. In the early 1980's Archbishop Romero
of El Salvador courageously spoke out against the official repression of
his government against the poor of his land. For his courageous stand
he was murdered—martyred like Peter of old.

We may be afraid to speak in public, or to make a personal
contact of some kind for Christ and the Christian way, or to hold
fast on some moral issue, but our fear can be replaced by courage
after our lives have been empowered by Jesus Christ. How many
Christians over the centuries must have endured great pain and
humiliation with a steady hand and heart, because they held in
their minds the image of Christ on the cross! When you are afraid
to do the right thing, think of Christ who changes fear to courage
in us by doing the right thing for us!

PRAYER: O Christ, still my fears, infuse my mind and body with
courage, so that I can be a good disciple of yours! Amen

~ ~ ~ ~ ~ ~

JANUARY 26

FROM SADNESS TO JOY

For godly grief produces a repentance that leads to
salvation and brings no regret.
—II Corinthians 7:10

READ: Acts 22:6-16

Paul writes to the Corinthian Christians declaring that sadness
can lead to a change of heart, which leads to salvation. Perhaps he
is thinking of his own life story. Three times the book of Acts tells
of Paul's conversion story. There was a sadness when Jesus in a
vision asked Saul why he was persecuting him. There followed a
change of heart—indeed a complete change in the direction,
purpose and activities of Saul of Tarsus. So great was this
transformation that he changed his name to Paul. A 180 degree
change, we would say—from killing Christians to making
Christians—from a theology of works to a theology of grace.
Salvation now, he saw, comes from faith in God's love in Christ,
rather than from a meticulous following of the law. From sadness
to joy!

We want that for ourselves. We want our resentments, our
vengefulness, or our bitterness to go away, for these make us sad.
But how? Like Saul, meeting Christ can turn us around. What we
are doing for our own self satisfactions and our efforts to try to
prove ourselves worthy of God's love, can be replaced by a new
direction in life—the joyful following of Christ, sharing his love
with others.

PRAYER: O Christ, meet me on my road of sadness, turn me
around and put me on a joyful path. Amen

~ ~ ~ ~ ~ ~

JANUARY 27

HOLDING ON TO THE ETERNAL

Because we look not at what can be seen but at what
cannot be seen; for what is seen is temporary, but what
cannot be seen is eternal.

—II Corinthians 4:18

READ: II Corinthians 4:16 to 5:5

A very talented high school student working at a menial job in
a drive-in cleaning chickens was asked how he could settle for such
work. His answer was that while doing such mindless work he
could ponder so many profound things. Robert Louis Stevenson
has a story of a hired man who worked in a cow barn. When he was
asked how he could stand such a job day after day, his reply was:
"He that hath something beyond, need never be weary."

As you look ahead do you feel like you must face an endless
succession of meaningless days in which to become weary? What
will be your day to day problems which lie ahead. How long will
things last? What major appliance on which you depend is due
soon to break down?

While it is true that the visible things of this life deteriorate,
we deteriorate physically and become weary as we grow old, Paul
points out that we can be growing spiritually as our inward self is
renewed daily. The beauty of some older persons is to be found in
the unseen spiritual resources in their being. While earlier beauty
may have been mainly physical, beauty in later years is interior—
spiritual What is the eternal dimension in your life? Is that aspect
of your life growing? Are there unseen glimpses of eternity which
provide you with an inner joy, even though the outward visible
elements in your life are becoming more and more wearisome, or

perhaps painful? The Christian faith can provide you with such an eternal quality. Pray for it!

Prayer: Help me, O Lord, to grasp the permanent, unseen and eternal truths and thoughts, feelings and perceptions which make up real life. In Christ. Amen

~ ~ ~ ~ ~ ~

JANUARY 28

MEETING IN ETERNITY

And this is eternal life, that they may know you, the only true God, and Jesus Christ whom you have sent.
—John 17:3

READ: John 17:1-8

One of the most painful circumstances in human life is the separation from loved ones which we must endure from time to time. Whether such separation is due to death, or moving away, or because of some other disruption of relationship the pain of being apart from one another is difficult to bear. Often lovers who must be away from each other for long periods of time console themselves by saying that the same moon will shine upon each one at the same time. Such separations are especially devastating in times of war when a husband, or a wife, a father or a brother have been shipped overseas to a war zone. Such separated loved ones try to find ways to console each other.

At the end of Jesus' time with his disciples he experienced the human pain of impending separation, when he prayed the prayer recorded in John 17. He found similar consolation in referring to God as the common reference point to unite him with his friends forever. For the disciples to know God, and for Jesus to know God, placed them together in an eternal fellowship with one another and with God.

The eternal dimension of life takes on new and profound meaning for us when we affirm that "in eternity we shall meet again!" For the Christian the farewell at the grave side of a loved one is not forever. It is for the time being, until we are re-united with each other in God's eternal presence.

Space, like time, does not limit the Eternal One. Thus, when we are separated from one another by time or distance in life, we may find relief from the pain of separation by joining with our loved ones in the eternal dimension—in God's presence!.

PRAYER: Draw me, O God, into your loving presence, and may you also invite those whom I have loved and lost, so that we may be together again. In Christ. Amen

~ ~ ~ ~ ~

JANUARY 29

AN ETERNAL PACT

Those who eat my flesh and drink my blood have eternal life, and I will raise them up on the last day.
—John 6:54

READ: John 6:52-71

Some years ago one of the world's most famous magicians made a pact with his associate in which he promised to communicate with his associate after his own death. While stories of such mysterious happenings abound, there was no report that the famous pact was ever fulfilled. It is, however, intriguing to think about possible contact with those who inhabit eternity. While in the White House, Mary Todd Lincoln confided in a friend that she often visited with the child whom she and her husband, the President, had lost. So painful was the death of her boy, that she found solace in his mysterious presence. Without such a conjecture death frequently appears too final for us to comprehend. Perhaps it is a proof of the reality of eternal life that our minds naturally seem to gravitate toward some mystical relationship between those who have died and those of us who remain here for a while longer.

Jesus must have been thinking of just such a concept when he announced to his disciples that the bread and the wine of the Last Supper provide access to eternal life for those who partake of them in the manner Jesus sets forth. Jesus made a pact with his associates at the Last Supper in which he promised that he would be with them in some sense each time they ate the bread which is his body, and drank the cup which is his blood. We believe that in the sacrament of communion Christ is mysteriously present at the table when the elements of the Lord's Supper are partaken by the communicant. This is the New Covenant into which Christ entered with his faithful followers of all generations.

Thus, it is through Communion that the Christian is transported beyond the border of physical reality into eternity, partially now and fully later on, as promised by Christ. Through Holy Communion we are invited into Christ's presence with all others of his people past, present and future!

PRAYER: We pray for your presence, O Christ, in the Sacrament and for fellowship with the Saints of all times, Amen

~ ~ ~ ~ ~ ~

JANUARY 30

TIME IS OUR ENEMY?

As long as the earth endures, seedtime and harvest, cold
and heat, summer and winter, day and night, shall not cease.
—Genesis 8:22

READ: Genesis 1:1-5

Time is sometimes regarded as our enemy with its restless

movement. It never stops and is always hastening on to some deadline, and then on to another deadline a few hours ahead. Usually there is not enough time to do all the tasks we have set for ourselves, or for all the duties others have assigned us. It is the rapid lapsing of time which makes it our enemy. For some people, however, time hangs heavy on their hands when there is nothing to do, no one to seek, no visitors expected, just three meals a day and fitful sleep at night. Walk through the corridors of any nursing home to see those for whom the enemy is too much empty time.

While time is the measurement of days according to the rotation of the earth, and the span of months according to the movement of the earth around the sun, the Bible sees time and its changing phases as a gift from God to us. According to the Genesis story of creation, God provided us with day and night, among the very first acts of creation. A little later in Genesis the story of Noah and the flood has among its conclusions the assurance that God will continue to provide us with a stable clock and calendar. And come to think of it, what a jumbled mess things would be if God had not established such stability of days and seasons.

You can't change the steady progression of hours, but you can thank God for such an ordered life, and ask for his help to order your use of time prudently.

PRAYER: O Creator God, I thank you for time and its orderly movement. Help me to make good and effective use of the hours and days you give me in a way that fulfills your intention for my clock and calendar. In Christ. Amen

~ ~ ~ ~ ~ ~

JANUARY 31

LIFE'S LITTLE DAY

So teach us to count our days that we may gain a wise heart
—Psalm 90:12

READ: Psalm 90:1-12

A wise and seasoned pastor near the end of his long years in the ministry spoke to a group of young seminarians about the life and work of a minister and gave them something to ponder when he said that for every book one reads there is another book which one will not have time to read—because of spending time on the first one! "So be selective about what you spend your time reading," he advised. That insight from a man close to end of his ministry came as a shocker to those young students who assumed an endless span of years ahead of them. Time is as the older person advised. It is limited, and there will be an end to it. We must not live as though we, like God, have all the time in the world.

The Psalmist declares that a thousand years in God's sight are but as yesterday when it is past. Time is not a measurement appropriate to the Timeless One who stands beyond time. God existed before creation and will continue forever and ever, long after our little day is ended. Forgetting that our days are numbered puts us in danger of wasting what time we have, and of failing to do the things we know God wants us to do.

PRAYER : O God, help me to remember that I am finite with only so many days left to live. And make me a much more prudent user of my time, much more ready to do what you require of me, while there is still time. In Christ. Amen

FEBRUARY

FEBRUARY 1

WHAT YOU SEE IS NOT ALWAYS WHAT YOU GET

For you are like whitewashed tombs, which on the
outside look beautiful, but inside they are full of the bones
of the dead and of all kinds of filth.

—Matthew 23:27

READ: Matthew 23:25-28 and Exodus 20:1,16

A group of university students were caught bearing false witness when they lied about their age claiming to be high school kids in order to buy cheaper ski lift tickets available to high schoolers. They not only bore false witness, but they defaced themselves by misrepresenting their identity in claiming to be younger than they were. How common this is in our culture. Politicians arrange for photo opportunities in order to present false and misleading images of themselves to the voting public. Buying votes through false advertising. Amid all the glitter and seductive coating in modern life what you get is not always what you see. Let the buyer beware! And the voter as well.

The Christian has a significant contribution to the surrounding culture at this point. We can be real! We can be honest about who we are and how we present ourselves to others. We can bear true witness. Jesus pointed this out in the negative when he challenged the duplicity of the Pharisees by saying that they pretend to be righteous when in fact inside they were anything but good. In contrast, true followers of Christ are open about themselves and their short-comings, sometimes at great personal risk. But in so doing we help to lay a firm foundation for honest interpersonal relationships.

In a real way the Christian who is honest about the witness he or she bears, contributes to justice in society, just as a true testimony does in a court of law. For the sake of society, let's be real, true, and honest!

PRAYER: Help me, O God, to present the real me to others. Through Christ. Amen

~ ~ ~ ~ ~ ~

FEBRUARY 2

CRIME DOESN'T PAY

> You must no longer live as the Gentiles live, in the futility of their minds. They are darkened in their understanding, alienated from the life of God because of their ignorance and hardness of heaart.
> —Ephesians 4:17, 18

READ: Ephesians 4:17-25 Philippians 4:8 and Exodus 20:15

The British crime novelist, P.D. James, explains and defends the murder mystery by pointing out that since the murderer is always caught, the story declares that crime doesn't pay, and so murder mysteries are, in effect, moral statements. Such stories stimulate one's fascination with death and violence, and are popular because of such evil stirring in the human heart. Similarly, the daily news keeps bringing us reports of violence in families, on the streets, and in the lives of both rich and poor alike. It would appear that society is always on the verge of destructive violence—the dark side of human life.

However, as Christians we are encouraged to think about what is pure, and honorable, true and good. Our conviction is that ours is a moral universe and that it does make a difference how one acts.

God is the source of what is good, and true and right. Whatever or whoever opposes God alienates people from the life of God's way. Our task is to help turn society toward what is good and right, true and beautiful. We can do this by concentrating our attention and thought upon God, who is the source of truth and righteousness. By so doing we function as the leaven in the loaf, the salt of the earth, the light not under the bushel, as Jesus said.

Perhaps P.D. James carries this light into the darkness by her exposing the murderer by the end of each mystery story. Let us be willing to expose the evil in our society by allowing the light of Christ to shine into the dark corners in the world around us.

PRAYER: O God, help me to be a leaven in the loaf through concentrating my thoughts on you. In Christ. Amen

~ ~ ~ ~ ~

FEBRUARY 3

MERE MORTALS, THAT YOU CARE FOR THEM

Then God said, "Let us make humankind in our image, according to our likeness.

—Genesis 1:26

READ: Genesis 1:26-28, Psalm 8:3-9 and Exodus 20:13

As various sciences have grown in their understanding of human behavior many of our emotions have been explained in physiological terms. Depression is thought by some to be a combination of genetic make-up and body chemistry. Anger is traced to the endocrine glands. Some people have referred to this approach as "rat psychology." The Psalmist, however, sees the human being as "a little lower than God." Genesis says of the human being that he or she is created in the image of God. (Unlike rats or cats) Could it be that the latest frontier in psychology, shame, might not yield to merely physical understanding, but rather to an understanding of ourselves as children of God? Scientists now wonder what shame is, trying to discover what gland, so to speak, it comes from. Perhaps we must look to God's intention for us and our failure to conform.

The Biblical understanding of human life is that each of us is responsible to God. We sense separation from God to the extent that God's intention for each of us is not matched by our behavior. When we do not live up to what God intends, might it be shame that we feel? When we are truly ashamed, we tend to hide from God, and in doing so our shame deepens. The ancient story-tellers of Israel understood shame when they told us that Adam hid from God after he disobeyed God's command in the Garden of Eden. In Christ our shame is lifted, when we allow Christ to reconcile us to our Creator, through God's own love for us. Furthermore, we can lift the prevailing evaluation of human life to its God-given position—"little less than God!" Indeed—"in God's image." Not merely like rats and cats! If nations could begin to regard all people in such a light, think of the efforts to relieve human suffering which would be launched!

PRAYER: Oh, Christ, lift my shame, and may I help in the lifting of all your children. Amen

~ ~ ~ ~ ~ ~

FEBRUARY 4

LIKE A STONE CHIMNEY STANDING

The grass withers, the flower fades; but the word of our God will stand forever.

—Isaiah 40:8

READ: Psalm 103:15-18 and James 1:9-11

After a devastating house fire which destroys an entire structure, one often can see the stone chimney still standing when everything else has been reduced to ashes. The Old Testament in two different places refers to the word of God as lasting forever, and we might add—like a stone chimney still standing. A house fire challenges our sense of security. In what do we place our trust? In things made by human hands? James talks about wealth and reminds us that God will lift up the poor and bring down the rich. This may be an exaggeration. But James is advising us that God does not regard wealth or the lack of it as a significant basis for judgement. He will deal with each of us on issues far deeper than our statement of net worth.

Yet we are seduced into thinking that a well stocked portfolio and an ample bank account will give us ultimate security. The word "securities" is even attached to such holdings. We live in a time when life savings can be quickly diminished by a long and serious illness, or when major shifts in the stock market can turn security into paper. As a nation we are tempted to evaluate our security only in military terms, while failing to provide adequate education for our young. If tragedy hits like a house fire, what will still be standing when the smoke dissipates? Will our security have been placed in God's wisdom and truth, in a life devoted to God's service?

It is the message of the Bible that a life spent in service to God's word and will, shall be secure—like a stone chimney still standing.

PRAYER: Let me put my trust in you, O God. May my security be my holding on to your Word. In Christ, the Word made flesh. Amen.

~ ~ ~ ~ ~

FEBRUARY 5

THEY MADE ME DO IT

For I know my transgressions, and my sin is ever before me.
—Psalm 51:3

READ: Psalm 51:1-5 and James 1:12-16

Scapegoating is a very common trap. We so easily fall into the habit of always blaming someone else for the difficulties we get our selves into. This can spoil relationships within a family when each blames the other for failures of one kind or another. "It's your fault that I did this." The government is a favorite scape goat. "Our company is experiencing serious loss because of government restrictions and requirements."

There is a more deeply disturbing scape goating going on when we blame God for our failures. This can lead to a life of bitterness. It has become popular in some circles to assign human foibles to the work of Satan. When someone falls into serious failure it is sometimes blamed on the work of the Devil. This in a curious way lets the sinner off the hook, so to speak. Billy in the Bil Keane's cartoon, "Family Circus," has been shown to have a ghost-like Devil hovering over him as he excuses himself to his mother. "The Devil made me do it."

James asserts that one is tempted by one's own desire; and that this leads to the sin which motivates us. Owning up to our own failures, admitting our own part in the problem, identifying our own mistakes and bad judgement, is the beginning of wisdom. Only when one confesses one's own sin and gets over blaming others, God, or Satan, can one begin to deal with one's own failures and foibles. Perhaps the most classic wording of such confession is that of the fifty-first Psalm: "For I know my transgressions, my sin is ever before me."

PRAYER: Make me honest and open about my shortcomings, O God. Forgive me the sin which is in me, through Christ. Amen

~ ~ ~ ~ ~ ~

FEBRUARY 6

SAFE IN PORT

O give thanks to the Lord, for he is good; for his steadfast love endures forever.

—Psalm 107:1

READ: Psalm 107:1-9, 29-31 and James 1:17-18

Winter driving can make one extremely thankful to be home. After miles of snow packed roads, and blowing snow, there is no more welcome sight than home. The overwhelming sense of thanksgiving and relief which comes at such a time is what one ought to feel constantly toward God For it is God who gives us every good gift. This is James' message. All good comes from God. The Psalmist uses the phrase: "He brought them to their desired haven." (Psalm 107-30)

When we talk of prayer, we quickly assume prayer to mean asking God for things. Much of our praying ought to be thanking God for every good gift. James affirms that our origin is in God, so that every moment of life is a gift from God. Whatever is good in your life comes from God. Think of it! How that can change your attitude toward others in your family, toward your acquaintances, and even to strangers. Whatever is good about all our relationships, is a gift from God. The pleasant voice of the person at the check-out counter; the loving words of a parent or spouse; the gleeful appreciation of a child; the gentle countenance of the aged. Whatever is good is from God. Because God is good, and his love is eternal.

PRAYER: O God, open my eyes to the goodness all around me, and remind me that these are gifts from you, carriers of your love into my daily life. In Christ. Amen

~ ~ ~ ~ ~ ~

FEBRUARY 7

MIRROR, MIRROR ON THE WALL

> Happy is everyone who fears the Lord, who walks in
> his ways.
>
> —Psalm 128:1

READ: Psalm 128 and James 1:22-24

There is nothing like looking into a mirror to jolt you into facing reality—especially in the morning. Unlike romantic art, the mirror—and the camera—do not tell lies. James uses the idea of a mirror to describe what happens to one who hears the word of God. The true revelation of God's word shows us ourselves as we are. There is no proof of the truth of the Bible better than the way in which it tells the truth about ourselves. What better look in the mirror than Paul's words of self understanding: "I do not understand my own actions. For I do not do what I want, but I do the very thing I hate." (Romans 7:15)

James goes further with his reference to the mirror. He talks about looking in the mirror, seeing oneself in stark reality, and then turning away from the mirror and doing nothing to change one's reality. That, James says, is like hearing the word and not doing what the truth of God requires in your life. Perhaps this is why church is an unhappy experience for some people. Really seeing oneself is uncomfortably real.

Is your experience in worship or Bible study like looking in a mirror and seeing yourself? It should be. That's the point at which some could quip, "Now you're meddling, preacher!" When you read the Bible or hear the Word preached, paraphrase the little poem: "Mirror, mirror, on the wall. What must I do first of all?" Hearing the Word and doing the Word makes for the most effective worship and Bible study experience in our lives.

PRAYER: Help me, O God, to see myself more clearly. Through your Word, show me what changes in me you want. By your Spirit, transform my mirror image. In Christ. Amen

~ ~ ~ ~ ~

FEBRUARY 8

INSIGHTS WHICH INCITE

> But they were insistent and said, "He stirs up the people by teaching throughout Judea, from Galilee where he began even to this place.
>
> —Luke 23:5

READ: Isaiah 49:3, Luke 23:1-5, and John 18:33-38

The first Christians had very little political power. They did not occupy the seats of the wealthy or the prominent. They were "nobodies," and yet through that early group of followers of Christ the world was turned upside down. Even though these early Christians did not make up the important elements of society, their influence eventually made a great deal of difference for all of history to follow. As Luke reports the trial of Jesus before Pilate, he tells about the way Jesus seemed to start riots through his teaching. In John's study of the same trial Jesus reveals to Pilate that, "My kingdom is not from this world." (John 18:36) His Influence and power would be different from that of a politician or military ruler. The power of Jesus in the midst of an alien society was that of a catalyst. His teaching changed dramatically the outcome of the conflicts and the intermingling of all elements of society.

Ever since Jesus' time the insights he provides have incited people to "riot" as Luke reported. From his very teaching we know that "riot" is not the right word for it. Rather, it is transformation and reconciliation which have been brought into the world by the Christian message and its insights.

To be a Christian is to be a loyal subject in a kingdom which is not of this world. It doesn't matter how much power or wealth you have, as a follower of Jesus you are given the capacity to be a catalyst by which God brings about his solution to problems both personal and world-wide. Let yourself be led by this new king whose kingdom is not of this world, but who promises to change this world.

PRAYER: O Divine Master, let me be your agent of transformation in the world around me! Amen

~ ~ ~ ~ ~ ~

FEBRUARY 9

PICKLES AND ICE CREAM, AND SLIPPERY STEPS

> You are the salt of the earth; but if salt has lost its taste,
> how can its saltiness be restored? It is no longer good for
> anything but is thrown out and trampled under foot.
> —Matthew 5:13

READ: II Corinthians 5:16-21

Salt changes slippery steps to safe steps, milk and cream into a frozen dessert, and it keeps vegetables and meat from spoiling. These are metaphors of what we as Christians ought to be doing in society. Helping to make society safe; keeping back the forces which would bring decay and rot, and helping to turn life into a tasty dessert, so to speak. We are to be Christ's catalysts—preservers— for he came to save the world from ruin and spoilage.

During the Dark Ages the Church and its Christian monasteries were the institutions which helped to preserve language and culture. After the breakup of the Soviet Union the churches were called upon in a number of instances to do human service work, which had long been denied them. In Hungary, after the collapse of the Communist government, clergy and others in the churches provided some of the needed leadership to build a free society. In all these examples we see the Christian church serving society as a catalyst which saves the best aspects of culture and social life.

In an even more critical way the Christian influence in Eastern Europe is keeping violence from erupting in some instances, thereby saving lives. The example of Martin Luther King Jr. and the Civil Rights movement in this country helped to steady the freedom movement in East Germany, keeping it from violence. Again the catalytic influence of Christian faith is at work saving the world.

As Christians, we are called to provide the catalyst of love and non-violence in every circumstance we encounter. Like the salt which preserves meat and makes pickles tasty, we must help make our society a better place—more tasty and free of spoilage!

PRAYER: Help me to be the salt which preserves the good in all of life around me. In Christ. Amen.

~ ~ ~ ~ ~

FEBRUARY 10

ENJOY!

God saw everything that he had made, and indeed, it
was very good.
—Genesis 1:31

READ: Read Song of Songs 2:8-15; 4:8-15 and Romans 14:19-23

In the broadest sense Song of Songs helps us to celebrate the physical and the sensuous aspects of our experience as human beings. Taste, touch, smell, sight and hearing are God-given delights for which he has created stimuli to excite and to please us. If you take seriously the text in Genesis 1:31, God is excited and pleased by what he has made for us, and for himself. Mountains, streams, sky and trees and grass; beef-steak, perfume, the aroma of coffee; the beauty of the human body both feminine and masculine, the cool drink of water, the sound of music—all are gifts of God and all are good.

Of course, the danger of letting the sensual take over, must be avoided. You ought to eat only so much beef-steak. The Bible does not answer this danger by making us turn away from physical experiences. Rather, it is the counsel of the scriptures to put the sensuous in proper proportion to the rest of life, and to respect the desires and needs of those around us. Our enjoyment of the physical should not cause pain and suffering to others. Moderation in what we eat could mean that those who do not have enough to eat will have more—if we take steps to see that our resources are shared with others. Piano playing in a thin walled apartment needs to be modified, lest our sound intrudes upon our neighbor. Our enjoyment should be experienced within the larger context of the good and the well-being of all human society. My freedom as a Christian must be governed by love—God's love for me and my love for my neighbor.

PRAYER: Thank you, God, for the pleasures of your gifts to my five senses. Guide my enjoyment by your love. In Christ. Amen.

~ ~ ~ ~ ~ ~

FEBRUARY 11

IT'S GOOD TO HAVE THINGS PROPER

Do not be deceived; God is not mocked, for you reap whatever you sow.

—Galatians 6:7

READ: Galatians 6:7-10

"Proper" is an old and quaint term; yet there is something in it to be reclaimed. There is a kind of satisfaction in knowing that things are as they should be—proper! At least for some of us there is pleasure in straightening things. When a picture is hanging crooked, there are some who are unhappy until it can be adjusted to assume its proper position.

Living a proper life has fallen out of fashion as our society has come to question what is right and good, trading such concepts for lifestyles based on one's own whims and passing fancies. Paul reminded the Galatians that there is an underlying order in the universe. Cause and effect operate in the field of human behavior, and so it matters how you act. The cultivation of desires and lusts which are contrary to God's intention for your life will lead to the perversion of God's hopes for you. Personal freedom carried out without regard for what is appropriate to the order of things as God has created us, is often destructive of one's own future, and that of others. In the extreme this truth is tragically evident in drug induced deaths among popular entertainers. So also with the abuse of one's body by eating too much of the wrong foods. What you sow is what you reap. It is an orderly universe under God. It is good when things are proper.

The happier part of this lesson from Galatians is that when one cultivates those aspects of life which are in line with God's will, one's life flowers with his blessings. A proper planting brings an appropriate harvest of good.

PRAYER: Help me today to give my attention to what is good in your sight, O God, so that there may grow in me a harvest of good. In Christ. Amen

~ ~ ~ ~ ~ ~

FEBRUARY 12

A GOSPEL PLAQUE

So we have known and believe the love that God has
for us. God is love and those who abide in love abide in
God, and God abides in them.

—I John 4:16

READ: I John 4:13-21

"Smile! God Loves You!" These words can be found on many Gospel plaques which you can buy in religious bookstores and at souvenir counters as well. For less money you can buy Gospel Pencils or Gospel Buttons which say the same thing. While these items speak the truth, they replace an earlier generation of plaques which made a more profound affirmation, which comes directly out of the New Testament: "God Is Love." On the surface, the newer plaque appears to say the same thing, but when you really think about it, the statement from I John, "God is love" goes a great deal deeper.

When we understand love to mean whatever is good and true, whatever is harmony, beauty and peace, whatever is justice and righteousness, we then identify God as intimately involved in all of life. Thus the love of God is expressed in the beauty of a sunset, the just court decision, an arms limitation agreement, the honesty and integrity of a responsible employee, the working together of persons with varying opinions, and wherever God is in some sense involved and present. It isn't just that God loves; the Gospel affirmation is that God IS love.

The Creator who established the universe and placed humankind over it as God's agent and steward, continues to work for peace and perfection in the world. Love created— Love redeems—Love brings perfection. This is what it means to say that God is love, a much more profound declaration than merely to say that God loves me. This makes living in this world much more secure—knowing that the essence of God is love.

PRAYER: Thank you God, that you are love, and that such love covers everything! In Christ. Amen.

~ ~ ~ ~ ~

FEBRUARY 13

TOO GOOD TO KEEP

> For we cannot keep from speaking about what we have seen and heard.
>
> —Acts 4:20

READ: Acts 4:13-22

An upset mother complained to her small child's public school teacher "Have you been teaching Bible stories? My child comes home telling me stories from the Bible she has picked up in your class."

The teacher replied, "No, we don't teach Bible stories, but I notice from time to time that some of the children are telling such stories to each other. Stories which they have heard in their Sunday Schools."

This incident reminds one of the words of the Psalmist: "O Lord, our Sovereign, how majestic is your name in all the earth! You have set your glory above the heavens. Out of the mouths of babes and infants." (Psalm 8:1,2)

The stories of God's people in the Bible do indeed have a power all their own. They are too good to keep. Hearing them we want to share them. But often our lives are jaded by too much input, from TV, and other media; or we have become so worldly-wise that the simple, direct message of God's love doesn't strike a nerve in us as once did, when we were children.

Maybe that is one reason why Jesus lifted up a child as an example of faith. "Unless you become like children . . . . ," he said. It may strike us as quaint that Bible stories should be big news among the little ones in the elementary school classroom. But then, why not? The Bible is big news—good news—news which is too good to keep!

PRAYER: Dear God, make us children at heart again, so that we may become overwhelmed by the great good news we find in the Bible. In Christ. Amen

~ ~ ~ ~ ~ ~

FEBRUARY 14

BE MY VALENTINE

Be subject to one another out of reverence for Christ . . . .
Each of you, however, should love his wife as himself, and a
wife should respect her husband.
—Ephesians 5:21, 33

READ: Song of Songs 6:2-10 and Mark 10:6-9

Carefully nailed to a power pole on a busy street corner was a small sign with hand-printed words: "Sean, Come home. Love, Mother." What a poignant story of family separation that weathered sign conveys. A run-away boy, and a heart-sick mother. The personal columns of big city newspapers tell of marriage break-ups and estrangements: "Come home. All is forgiven." The disintegration of the modern marriage and family in our society has been the subject of serious study and much concern. Lives embittered by such alienation, and disenchanted with broken hopes have become jaded, so that Valentine's Day has become a celebration to avoid. And at first glance, the words of Song of Songs sound naive and out of date. But let's hear it for old values of romance, marital bliss, and family solidarity!

What we do in our family life and marriage is serious business. It takes work to build a family unit which withstands the rigors of modern, fast-paced pressure. There is a place for the romantic affirmations of love we find on Valentines. These can be the cement that holds family members together. Valentines can be the applicators of such needed glue!

The Christian is made more capable of loving his or her family members because of the family of faith into which Christ has called and loved each of us. Let Christ's love for you inspire your love for each other.

PRAYER: Help me to love as you love me, In Christ. Amen.

~ ~ ~ ~ ~

FEBRUARY 15

LOVE AND MARRIAGE GO TOGETHER

And the man and his wife were both naked, and were not ashamed.

—Genesis 2:25

READ: Song of Songs 4:1-7, 5:10-16, Genesis 2:21-25, and Ephesians 5:1-5

Passages from the Song of Songs have long been the source of nervous snickering in Sunday School classes, when curriculum and teachers have dared to consider them. This book has been pointed to by those wanting to combat book censoring in schools and libraries: "If you ban 'such and such' a book, you'll have to ban the Bible!" Our Victorian heritage has made the words of Genesis 2:25 anything but true. We have allowed the sexual aspect of human experience to become perverted by misuse, disuse, or over emphasis. The results in our society are far more serious that mere embarrassment. Sexual abuse, pornography, promiscuity, and sexual dysfunction, as well as minor 'hang-ups" make up some of the bad harvest from the bad seed of poorly conceived ideas and values of earlier generations, perpetrated often in the name of religion.

Fortunately many in our time have been helped to shed negative connotations of human sexuality and are more ready to read and receive God's Word through The Song of Songs, than were their parents. God wants us to celebrate human love physically as well as spiritually, and to understand sexuality as a gift of God's creation. Other passages in the Bible, like the Ephesians verses for today, help us further to understand that relationships in this regard are essential and appropriate only in marriage. Like the old song: Love and marriage go together like a horse and carriage."

PRAYER: Help me, O God, to live and love as you intend for me—appropriately and meaningfully. In Christ. Amen

~ ~ ~ ~ ~

FEBRUARY 16

BETWEEN ME AND THEE

I will put enmity between you and the woman . . . .
And the Lord God made garments of skins for the man, and
for his wife and clothed them,
                                        —Genesis 3:15,21

READ: Genesis 31:43-50 and Romans 7:14-25

In former times many church youth group meetings were closed with the Mizpah Benediction: "The Lord watch between me and thee while we are absent one from the another." (Genesis 31:49 King James Version). What we didn't know at the time was that the phrase was originally meant to keep Jacob and Laban from doing harm to each other. Genesis 31 tells the story of Jacob's stormy departure from his in-laws, and of the truce they reached at a place called Mizpah. In the earlier chapters of Genesis human enmity is symbolized in the clothing people were given to cover their nakedness, thereby keeping themselves separate from each other. Genesis points out that before the intrusion of sin into human life, the man and the woman were unclothed and unashamed. But now, after the entry of sin into the human situation, our broken relationship brings shame, embarrassment, enmity, and all manner of human problems, much like the ugliness which existed between the woman and the snake in the same story!

Our most difficult struggles lie in the area of human relationships: between parent and child, between spouses, among neighbors or co-workers. On a larger scale the enmity between races, and between religious groups, among nations and political ideologies come immediately to mind as areas in which we struggle.

When we take the Genesis story in its deepest meaning, we recognize that human sin—the desire to break away from God and from each other—is the most painful aspect of our human condition against which we struggle. The message of the Bible is that only in Jesus Christ is to be found the forgiveness and reconciliation needed to solve this painful human struggle.

PRAYER: O Christ, bridge the gap between "me and thee." Amen.

~ ~ ~ ~ ~ ~

FEBRUARY 17

AMID THE BRAMBLES AND THE THISTLES

And to the man he said, "Because you have listened to the voice of your wife, and have eaten of the tree about which I commanded you, 'You shall not eat of it,' cursed is the ground because of you; in toil you shall eat of it all the days of your life; thorns and thistles it shall bring forth for you: and you shall eat the plants of the field."

—Genesis 3:17,18

READ: Mark 14:34-36

Our recognition of Jesus' complete humanness is most evident in the story of his struggling prayer in the Garden of Gethsemane. He did not want to endure the humiliation, pain and destruction of the cross, praying that it be avoided. We can identify with the struggle he was enduring in that moment. We struggle against physical hurt, and whatever else in our life imposes physical limitations upon us.

The ancient creation story symbolizes the physical restraints upon humankind by its reference to our labor against adverse conditions to raise the food and fiber we need to survive. We must work amid the brambles and the thistles. One can expand the idea of brambles and thistles to include every physical obstruction to a long and productive life. Germs, bacteria, viruses, cancers, as well as all kinds of human diseases which attack the body and mind. We struggle against disease and decay which are aspects of our own human limitations.

The key to Jesus' own victory over such physical odds was his submission to the will of God and his closeness to God throughout the struggles of his life. In 1820 Henry Lyte wrote, "Change and decay. In all around I see. O Thou, who changest not, abide with me." Perplexed and distraught by the realities of human life, with its physical diseases and limitations, we can look from the finite to the infinite to find strength to work around the brambles and the thistles.

PRAYER: Not my will but yours be done in my life, O God. In Christ. Amen

~ ~ ~ ~ ~ ~

FEBRUARY 18

TEMPUS FUGIT

By the sweat of your face you shall eat bread until you

return to the ground, for out of it you were taken; you are
dust, and to dust you shall return.

—Genesis 3:19

READ: Ecclesiastes 3:1-15 and Hebrews 9:27-28

Perhaps the most real fact of life is that time flies; and the
older one gets the faster it flees away. This is a profound human
limitation which has a far more pervasive effect upon each of us
than we would imagine. Because of the time limit put upon each
of us we continually struggle against time in order to get everything
done, and to make hard choices about what we can and cannot fit
in. A sign of this continuing effort is the fact that as the day wears
on we become more tired; and eventually we fall into bed
exhausted—"from dust to dust!"

This time limitation takes on a mystical dimension when one
thinks about "time travel" which has intrigued people all over the
world and throughout the years. This thinking has given rise to
theories of reincarnation, science fiction stories using time machines,
spiritualism's seances, and various ghost stories. We wish we could
live in another time, visit with our forebears of a century long since
past, or with our descendants in some far off future. We would like
to skip back and forth in the calendar of time, but we are bound to
our own span. With the Psalmist we cry: "The days of our life are
seventy years, or perhaps eighty, if we are strong; even though their
span is only toil and trouble; they are soon gone, and we fly away."
(Psalm 90:10)

But with Hebrews we proclaim joyfully that, "Christ having
been offered once to bear the sins of many, will appear a second
time . . . to save those who are eagerly waiting for him." (Hebrews
9:28)

PRAYER: Make me patient. May I be a wise user of my time. In
Christ. Amen.

~ ~ ~ ~ ~ ~

FEBRUARY 19

THE POOR IN SPIRIT

Blessed are the poor in spirit, for theirs is the kingdom
of heaven.

—Matthew 5:3

READ: Matthew 5:1-3 and Psalm 57

The poor in spirit, according to the late William Barclay, the Scottish Biblical scholar and teacher, are those who realize their own utter helplessness, and consequently put their whole trust in God. "Foxhole Religion" was a term used in World War II to describe the emergency faith of soldiers in fear for their lives. While such new-found faith was frequently ridiculed by those of more long-standing faith, the first of the Beatitudes makes us see the possible validity of such faith under fire. Jesus is saying that it is a happy condition when a person knows his or her desperate need for God. When one's own resources have run out and one is "up against it," then to know what it means to depend utterly upon God, is sheer joy. At first this sounds unreasonable. If one is in that much trouble, surely there is little joy about that. However, what Jesus is pointing to is the all-sufficiency of God's power and love for us, which we discover when we let go of our own attempts to bail ourselves out.

Happiness is to know that God cares about you so much to want only good for your life. In the midst of life's problems and set-backs, it is a comfort to know that God wants a better life for you than you have imagined for yourself. You must nevertheless be realistic enough to recognize that the accidents and mistakes of life as well as war and violence run counter to God's will for your life. To pray for help in times of trouble, anxiety, fear and pain is to align yourself with the One who wants the best for you. Indeed the One who is at work seeking to bring that about!

PRAYER: I need you, O God. I've tried it on my own and it doesn't work. I give you thanks for your redeeming work on my behalf. In Christ. Amen

~ ~ ~ ~ ~ ~

FEBRUARY 20

THEY THAT MOURN

Blessed are those who mourn, for they shall be comforted.

—Matthew 5:4

READ: Matthew 5:2,4, and Psalm 51:1-12

In T.S. Eliot's play, *The Elder Statesman*, Lord Claverton is the elder statesman. Having suffered for many years from guilt for some early misdeeds, finally toward the end of his life he is able to confess his sins to his daughter. Happily he experiences the joy of new life as a result of his disclosure. Happy are those who are sorry for their sin!

This is the second Beatitude of Jesus. In it he shows us that true happiness comes when we let go of our self-justifying rationalizations, and stop hiding our mistakes and ourselves from God; when we admit to God that we are truly sorry. What a good feeling to get it off your chest at last! That is the joy referred to in this Beatitude.

It takes emotional energy to "keep the lid on," so to speak, and to figure out ways of fooling yourself into thinking you are better than you really are. It is tiresome to hold up a false face, to carry on an act, trying to save yourself. Jesus' words take on new meaning in this context: "Come to me, all you that are weary and are carrying heavy burdens, and I will give you rest." (Matthew 11:28)

PRAYER: O most merciful God, soften my hard heart and make me pliable to the Spirit's convicting. Help me to look at myself honestly and to tell it to you! In Christ, the Agent of your forgiveness. Amen

~ ~ ~ ~ ~ ~

FEBRUARY 21

THE MEEK

Blessed are the meek, for they shall inherit the earth.
—Matthew 5:5

READ: Matthew 5:2,5 and Psalm 37:4-11

Some words have a way of wearing out, losing their meaning. Some words change meaning over time. "Meek" is one of those words. Jesus is not referring to sickly self-effacement, nor to ineffective, cloying weakness—meanings with which this word is often associated. What meekness refers to here is the gentle spirit, the selfless courage of conviction, the person who does not claim power or greatness, but rather acknowledges God as the source of personal identity and strength.

To be able to deal gently with others, to stand firm in the face of evil, and to acknowledge God as the One who is good and just, is to be happy with life, to feel blessed. The prophet Micah summed it up in his advice, "to do justice, to love kindness, and to walk humbly with your God." (Micah 6:8)

There is something curiously reciprocal about this. When you are happy in your relationship with God and accepting of yourself, which is what "Blessed" means, than you can be meek. Happiness produces meekness and meekness results in happiness!

PRAYER: Most loving God, I affirm your acceptance of me, your redeeming love in Christ. I thank you that through your love I can accept myself and love others. Give me gentleness and meekness! Amen

~ ~ ~ ~ ~ ~

FEBRUARY 22

HUNGER AND THIRST AFTER RIGHTEOUSNESS

Blessed are those who hunger and thirst for righteousness, for they shall be filled.

—Matthew 5:6

READ: Matthew 5:2,6, and Amos 5:14-15, 24

Do you want goodness and justice to be done so badly that "you can taste it?" If so, you will be filled with happiness, knowing that God, the source of all goodness and justice, has made the way very clear for such a way of life. You will know that God is bringing righteousness to the world partially now, and fully at the close of time! This is what Jesus is saying to us in the fourth Beatitude. You'll be made happy to know that your craving for goodness in the world is being satisfied by God.

Ours is not a perfectionist religion which lays upon each the impossible task of living perfect lives. We are not judged on the basis of how much goodness we have, or the degree of righteousness we have achieved. If that were so, we would be continually frustrated and never pleased with ourselves. Guilt would be our daily dose, and we would always be anxious about our salvation. The good news is that it is our earnest desire for goodness and justice that counts. The extent of its accomplishment in our lives will vary according to the circumstances and realities in which we live. But, if we truly want goodness, it is the goodness and justice of God which will be infused into us and provide us with eternal life. What bliss!

PRAYER: May your justice and goodness, O God, fill the world and my life, in Christ. Amen

～ ～ ～ ～ ～ ～

FEBRUARY 23

RELATIONSHIPS REDEEM

> The disagreement became so sharp that they parted company; Barnabas took Mark with him and sailed away to Cyprus.
>
> —Acts 15:39

READ: Acts 15:36-41 and II Timothy 4:9-11

In a discussion between two young fathers concerning child-raising problems, one said that he had learned in a psychology course that the child's personality was set in the first three years and after that you couldn't expect much change. The other countered, "That may be so, but I am a firm believer in the power of relationship to further shape a child's life." He was right. How often a meaningful and supportive relationship can change us for the better, no matter our age.

A study of the relationship of the young apostle, John Mark, with the two older associates, Barnabas and Paul, is revealing. Mark had traveled with Paul and Barnabas from Jerusalem to Antioch; and then had accompanied them on a missionary journey from there. Something must have happened to cause Paul to break his relationship with Mark; for he refused to take him along on his succeeding missions. So sharply did Barnabas disagree, that the two older men argued and then separated, Barnabas taking Mark, his cousin, with him. If neither men had kept a relationship with Mark, we most likely would never have heard of him again. But, we learn that ten years later Paul regards Mark as a useful associate. Mark's reputation had been redeemed, largely due to the support Barnabas had given him.

We have it in our power to help redeem those around us through supportive, affirming relationships we can establish with them. Think of the young lives which have been lifted out of oblivion by Big Sisters or Big Brothers through that most helpful program of advocacy for deprived youth. We can do that for the children in our families, and for the youth and adults in our circles of acquaintances who need our support and love!

PRAYER: To whom are you sending me, O God, to whom would you have me offer a loving relationship? Help me to fulfil your hopes for such relationships in my life. In Christ. Amen.

~ ~ ~ ~ ~

FEBRUARY 24

WRITING OFF THE DIRT

And Jesus said, "Neither do I condemn you,. Go your way, and from now on do not sin.

—John 8:11

READ: John 8:1-11

We do not know anything more about the woman in this story; but it would be reasonable to guess that from the time of this incident, her life was lived in a moral manner. Jesus' relationship to her that day must certainly have redeemed her life from sin. We do not know what it was that Jesus wrote in the dirt beneath her feet, but the net effect of the writing would have been the re-writing of her story. Had he condemned her, she may not have changed at all; had he failed to condemn her sin, she probably would not have changed her ways. But, as it was, he loved her and accepted her as a child of God; he had compassion for her; he did not excuse her wrong-doing—he condemned it. He wrote off the guilt, but did not condemn the woman while still condemning the sin itself. And who knows? Maybe some of the Pharisees learned to be a little less judgmental that day!

What does this mean in our day? It means that we are not to be soft on sin and wrong-doing, as some are tempted to be these days. God is still offended by acts which are deceitful, violent, hurtful, and vain. So should his followers be, as well. But, on the other hand, God is fair and loving beyond our best imagining; and we must try to approach God's level of justice in interpersonal relationships. The insight which sent the Pharisees away ought to sober us as well. Only those of us who have no fault at all, are invited to condemn!

Understanding ourselves as forgiven sinners goes a long way to prepare us to enter into redemptive relationships with each other.

PRAYER: Forgive my sin, O Christ. I thank thee for thy continuing love—*despite*! Amen.

~ ~ ~ ~ ~ ~

FEBRUARY 25

SIMPLY DIFFICULT

In everything do to others as you would have them do
to you, for this is the law and the prophets.
—Matthew 7:12

READ: Matthew 7:1-12

There is a danger in trying to reduce the Christian Faith to a short formula, as some do when they say: "My religion is the Sermon on the Mount." The scripture noted for today comes toward the end of the Sermon on the Mount. Interestingly, Jesus himself uses this statement in verse 12 as a summary of the religion of his ancestors. But, does this simplify things as much we think? "Do unto others as you would have them do unto you." Those words are deceptively simple. However, at the same time, they are surprisingly difficult ones to follow. We so normally treat others more destructively and hurtfully than we want them to treat us.

There are some popular misconceptions of this formula. "You

scratch my back; and I'll scratch yours." It is not Jesus' intention to make this statement a plan for manipulating others into serving us. "Do to others, as they do to you." Again, Jesus' intention is not to give us excuse to get even with those who do us wrong. He is really asking us to give up our self-seeking ways, and to focus upon the needs and desires of other people instead. What he asks of us is unnatural! It takes his saving power to reverse the normal trends of our lives so that we can open ourselves to others in such a real and full way. We can't live by these words on our own. We need Christ's saving power to reorient our lives in love toward our neighbors near and far. Only then will we want for others every bit as much as we want for ourselves.

It is the redemptive relationship with which Christ enables us to love our neighbors as we do ourselves, and thus to relate to them redemptively.

PRAYER: Come into my life, O Christ, and save me from self-seeking. Turn me toward others. Amen.

~ ~ ~ ~ ~ ~

FEBRUARY 26

"OH! SAVE ME, SIR!"

No one has greater love than this, to lay down one's life for one's friends.

—John 15:13

READ: John 15:12-17

There is a typical scene from an old fashioned melodrama which comes to mind when this verse from John is read. It is the scene in which a dashing young man hears the cry, "Oh! Save me, sir!" and jumps in front of an approaching locomotive in order to save a young maiden tied to the tracks. This image obscures the true meaning of this passage, as the idea of physical sacrifice may hinder our fuller understanding of Jesus' thought here. There was a very early time in the church when martyrdom was popular, so much so that Christians had to be restrained from foolishly giving up their lives in sacrifice for Christ.

The sacrifice required of us is the giving up of our natural desire to "lord it over" others, to dominate, or to try and maintain egotistical advantage over others. Rather, we are asked to do all we can in our power to enhance the lives of others, even at cost to ourselves of position or advantage. Jesus asks us to give our coat to warm our neighbor, to limit our own consumption so that others may live more adequately. At another time Jesus pictured this attribute in the Good Samaritan's treatment of the injured traveler. From that story we know that sacrifice extends to the starving of Africa and the homeless of America, and to many others around the world. We are called, as Christians, to hear and heed the cry, "Oh! Save me, sir!"

Sacrifice does not mean submission to the dominance of another person, or blind compliance to another's wishes. It means the mutual offering of love for the up-building of both the giver and the given to.

PRAYER: Show me, O God, how I can share the abundance and advantage I enjoy with others near and far. In Christ. Amen.

~ ~ ~ ~ ~

FEBRUARY 27

THOSE EVERLASTING RULES

For freedom Christ has set us free. Stand firm, therefore,
and do not submit again to a yoke of slavery.
—Galatians 5:1

READ: Romans 6:5-14

Do you remember those childhood clubs? How the first thing

after a club was started was to devise some sort of clubhouse, perhaps in a tree, and the very next order of business was the establishment of rules. You had to have rules; and every member had to follow the rules. Some of the members would be expelled because they hadn't followed the rules. And pretty soon it wasn't fun anymore.

Paul cautioned the Galatians not to get tied up with a new set of rules after Christ had died to free us from the Law. Previously the Jews had a great many rules by which to try to satisfy God, and it was very hard to follow all of the rules. People always felt guilty for not having fully satisfied God's demands upon them. Christ came to free us from such guilt, replacing it with the satisfaction of following him. Now we can joyfully do what we understand he wants of us. But, oddly enough, we still fall back into the trap of setting up a long list of rules for living by which to prove ourselves good, and worthy of God. Various religious groups impose their own lists of "do's and don'ts" upon their members, thus enslaving them under new yokes.

The good news is that Christ frees us from the yoke of slavery and gives us his yoke, which he proclaims is "easy." His yoke is not a new list of rules, but a new attitude toward God and others. Because of Christ we are made able to love God and to love our neighbors. That's what members of his "club" have fun doing!

PRAYER: Free me, O God, from the yoke of slavery to rules and its resulting guilt. Help me to gain a new attitude by which to live in freedom. By your grace lead me to love. In Christ. Amen

~ ~ ~ ~ ~

FEBRUARY 28

PLEASURE CAN BE A PAIN

For you were called to freedom, brothers and sisters;
only do not use your freedom as an opportunity for self-
indulgence, but through love become slaves to one another.
—Galatians 5:13

READ: Romans 6:12-23

Spill a bottle of exquisitely scented perfume and whatever it permeates will give you sensory discomfort for months afterwards. Pleasure can be like that! It can so easily slip into over-indulgence and pain. We have come through an excessive period in our culture when freedom was the shrill shout of an entire generation. However, for many people in our society the exercise of personal freedom has brought intense pain. The abuses of body, mind, spirit and relationships which have come as a result of the drug culture, the sexual revolution, and other expressions of the "self fulfillment-generation" continue to be the source of monumental pain to countless numbers of people today.

Paul cautioned that we should not use freedom for selfish ends; but that love for one another ought to take precedence over such abuse of freedom. Jesus talked about the danger of a whole bunch of demons invading where one demon has been removed, leaving a vacancy, When the Gospel offers us freedom from the Law, it provides us at the same time grace by which we are made willing and happy to give ourselves to God's service and to others in love. When we freely commit ourselves to such Christian values we limit our own freedom in order to pursue those values.

Paul wrote to the Romans that even though he was free to eat meat which had been ceremonially sacrificed to idols, he chose not to, because there were those around him who did not feel they possessed such freedom and would thereby be tempted. Since Paul's eating such meant might be an offense to them, he freely decided against eating sacrificial meat. This is the principle of "voluntary abstinence" by which many Christians have made the decision not to use alcoholic beverages. In order not to offend or to tempt others, abstinence is chosen out of love for neighbor.

PRAYER: Thank you, O God, for personal freedom. Give me the

mind of Christ by which to use my freedom for your will and intention in my life. In Christ. Amen.

~ ~ ~ ~ ~ ~

FEBRUARY 29

ON BUILDING TOWERS

His master said to him, "Well done, good and trustworthy slave, you have been trustworthy in a few things, I will put you in charge of many things; enter into the joy of your master."

—Matthew 25:21

READ: Matthew 25:14-29

Two small children are left alone with a box of blocks. One child builds a tower. The other child shuffles the blocks in the box and around the floor, until with one swing he knocks over the tower built by the other child. Both are using their freedom; but in two very opposite ways: one to build, the other to create confusion. The one who builds is no less free because she carefully abides by the principles of gravity. In fact, she is really more free to create for having followed the rules.

Our God-given freedom is like that. We can use it to build, or to cause chaos and destruction. To build we must observe the principles by which the world and its relationships have been made. Abiding by such laws of life allow us to use our freedom creatively.

The attitudes and concepts God reveals to us in the Bible regarding human relationships need not restrict our freedom; but rather these help us in our effort to employ personal freedom in the building of a better world around us.

Jesus spoke of the servants who were given the freedom to invest their master's resources; and he commended the ones who followed the principles of good stewardship, thus increasing the master's holdings, and their standing in his eyes. So, we also ought to use the resources given to us by the Master.

PRAYER: Thank you, O God, for my freedom. Make me a wise and prudent steward of freedom. In Christ. Amen.

MARCH

MARCH 1

ON COLLECTING FOR THE HEART FUND

But love your enemies, do good, and lend, expecting nothing in return. Your reward will be great, and you will be children of the Most High.

—Luke 6:35

READ: Luke 6:27-36

We assume that everyone is to some extent motivated by self-interest, since it is a necessary ingredient for our own survival and satisfaction. We have inherited the Darwinian idea of the survival of the fittest, which informs us of our normal attention to our own interests. Translated into everyday language that is,

"You'd better look out for yourself, no one else will!" Those who have not had the opportunity to pursue self-interest as successfully as others, become losers at great cost to their own welfare. And so there are many people in our society who do not have access to adequate health care. A growing number of skilled workers are out of work, and an overwhelming number of people are homeless. Self-interest as a national policy helps some, but hinders a growing number of our neighbors,

Self-interest coupled with a belief in unlimited personal freedom needs to be off-set with a commitment to the common good of all. In the early days of the U.S., the Christian view of responsibility to society served as a balance to the concept of personal pursuit of wealth. This compensating value is often missing today and needs to be brought back into our every day view of how we ought to participate in society.

Jesus' words in Luke help us to renew our commitment to society: "Give to everyone who begs from you . . . do to others as you would have them do to you . . . do good and lend, expecting nothing in return. (Luke 6:30,31, 35) As followers of Christ we ought to be alert and sensitive to the needs of others around us. We ought to be on the look-out for ways to serve such needs.

When it is your turn to canvas your neighborhood for the Heart Fund, or for any other such effort, pray for the commitment to the common good, on the part of your neighbors. And for yourself as well.

PRAYER: O God, as a Christian may I see beyond my self-interest, so that I may commit myself to the common good. Through Christ. Amen.

~ ~ ~ ~ ~ ~

MARCH 2

ON HOW THE COOKIE CRUMBLES

We know that all things work together for good for those who love God, who are called according to his purpose.
—Romans 8:28

READ: Romans 8:26-30

"That's how the cookie crumbles!" was a common response a few years ago. It expressed one's lack of control over life's events, and probably the belief that how things turn out is really a matter of chance. This statement may reveal a fatalism in many people. World War II produced a fatalistic reference to the "bullet with your name on it." Something similar is often spoken today: "When it's my time!" These statements point to our confusion over the question of how things happen, and what makes life's events take place. Is it all by chance? Is it all laid out beforehand? Is everything that happens God's doing? How does the cookie crumble, anyway?

The Bible tells us that the answer lies somewhere between pure chance and God doing everything. The word for this is "providence." As Christians we believe that in all of life, God is in ultimate control, and that the final outcome will be according to God's will. However there comes to each of us adversity due to events and circumstances that happen which are not God's will. But in everything, whether God's will or not, the loving, providing God is at work bringing about his intention, always for our benefit! The Heidelberg Catechism says that God "rules in such a way that leaves and grass, rain and drought, fruitful and unfruitful years, food and drink, health and sickness, riches and poverty, and everything else, come not by chance," but under God's ultimate control. From this we "learn that we are to be patient in adversity, grateful in the midst of blessing, and to trust our faithful God and Father for the future, assured that nothing shall separate us from his love."

It is a denial of God to believe that things happen merely by chance. It is a denial of human freedom in a real world to say that everything is directly done to us by God. It is a statement of Christian faith to affirm that in everything God is at work providing for our good and for God's will.

PRAYER: Help me to trust your Providence, O God, no matter what happens in my life. Through Christ. Amen.

~ ~ ~ ~ ~

MARCH 3

ON CONTEMPLATING CONTEMPT

Then Peter began to speak to them, "I truly understand
that God shows no partiality . . . ."

—Acts 10:34

READ: Acts 10:23-36, 44-48

For whom do you have contempt? Who are the undesirables
in your world? In 1937 girls from an elite upperclass prep school
in Marin County, California protested the building of the
Golden Gate Bridge. Their head mistress had objected to the
bridge, feeling that it would permit undesirables from San
Francisco to come north into Marin County. Times have
changed, fortunately. Now 13% of the enrollment in private
prep schools are minority students, no longer considered
undesirable. However, what about other minority persons?
Those who are dealing drugs, engaged in gang violence, and
making the streets unsafe. While we have learned to treat with
respect minority people who have in some sense "measured up."
we still have contempt for those whom we consider undesirable.

This is not the way of the Christian. While one must surely
condemn destructive behavior and acts of violence, those
involved are to be seen as children of God needing help. Peter
learned that lesson early on. Gentiles were held in contempt
by Jews, and so it took some radical changing for Peter to accept
Gentiles into the faith. From Peter's time onward, the Christian
church has sought to accept everyone who comes to Christ,
undesirable or not.

But each of us must ask the question again: "Who are the
people whom I hold in contempt?" Christ calls us to ponder this
question deeply and honestly—to contemplate our own
contempt—and to pray to be healed of our contempt, so that no
longer will we consider any other human being undesirable. As
with Peter this will take some doing.

PRAYER: Help me to admit whatever deep seated contempt I
    hold, and by your grace purge me of it. Through Christ.
    Amen.

～ ～ ～ ～ ～ ～

MARCH 4

WAITING EXPECTANTLY

Now when Jesus returned, the crowd welcomed him,
for they were all waiting for him.

—Luke 8:40

READ: Psalm 40:1-3 and Luke 8:34-40

As Jesus went from place to place crowds followed him, while other crowds awaited his arrival. Luke tells us of his leaving a crowd after performing a healing. He then went around the lake to find an expectant crowd waiting for him. Put yourself in the shoes of those who were waiting. Word comes that Jesus is walking in your direction. You are expectant. Your waiting is a very positive experience because you have the assurance that Jesus will arrive soon. When he comes your expectancy turns to joyous welcome.

In the Christian life there ought to be many times of expectant waiting during which we prepare to welcome Christ into our particular situation. We can expect him to enter our lives frequently, while we wait for his entry eagerly. When he comes to us our welcome will be joyous. When these times come to us will vary, but there are certain events in which we can expect Christ. This is what worship should be. His coming may be manifest in an insight we gain from the reading and exposition of the Bible, when we sense that we are hearing the Word of God. Prayer may very well be the moment when Christ seems even more real to us. In the bread and cup of communion we are told we can expect the presence of Christ. The music of the church and the singing of hymns may be the pathway upon which we meet Jesus. While we wait for him, we may find that he appears to us in our fellowship with others, as well as through the more formal acts of worship.

PRAYER: I wait for you, O Christ. I eagerly expect your visit! Amen

~   ~   ~   ~   ~   ~

MARCH 5

PATIENT WAITING

*You also must be patient. Strengthen your hearts, for
the coming of the Lord is near.*

—James 5:8

READ: Psalm 25:4-5 and James 5:7-11

One of the most thoroughly frustrating things about waiting
is one's lack of control over the situation. There seems to be nothing
one can do. The arrival of an airline flight, the phone call, the
letter in the mail, or the specific item of news for which you wait
will all come to pass as a result of what someone else does, and will
not be affected by ones own action. So you just wait. Where then
does patience come from? When you can commit the situation to
someone else's keeping, thus removing your own desire to control
the matter, then you can wait more patiently. "The testing of your
faith produces endurance." (James 1:3) Faith is one's full
commitment of life, and its multitude of situations, to God. When
you have given God control over your life, patience is one of the
results.

Commitment to Christ rests not only upon the knowledge
and belief that Christ lived, died and rose again, but also upon the
conviction that in some sense Christ will be present when life has
ended. Down deep the Christian is waiting to see Christ, and in
faith is waiting patiently for that. Paul wrote to the Romans: "But
if we hope for what we do not see, we wait for it with patience."
(Romans 8:25)

Against the back drop of waiting for Christ's final resolution of
life's problems, all other periods of waiting take on a different
perspective. We wait patiently for the report of a biopsy, the outcome
of surgery, the result the committee's action, the visit of a loved

one, or for whatever event in one's life is yet to come. Let us wait with minds and hearts committed to God's loving care for us, and with trust in God's directing Word for our lives. Such faith brings patient waiting.

PRAYER: Most loving God, help me to wait patiently as by your grace I commit my life and all the situations of my life to Christ. In whose name I pray. Amen

∼ ∼ ∼ ∼ ∼

MARCH 6

TWO TIMES IN A GARDEN

> For as all die in Adam, so all will be made alive in Christ.
> —I Corinthians 15:22

READ: Genesis 3:1-13 and Matthew 26:36-39

Two times in a garden the awesome question of life and death was determined in the Bible. The first was in the Garden of Eden when Adam tried to live according to his own needs and desires and was confronted by the HOLY ONE who took issue with such a self-serving approach to life. The result of the self-willed action of our first parents was death—expulsion from the Garden—the ultimate separation from God. Much later in the Bible there is another scene set in a garden.

The second time it is the Garden of Gethsemane in which Jesus made his final decision to let God have total control over his life. ". . . yet not what I want, but what you want." (Matthew 26:39) The result of Jesus' complete submission to the will of God was life for us through the Cross and Resurrection. Paul declares that as we unite with Christ in complete submission to God, we inherit life through Christ's resurrection.

The contrast between Adam and Christ is extremely important for us. Adam pretended to be God and sought to satisfy his own hunger, determining on his own what was best for him. He went against God's directive that the eating of the fruit of the tree in the midst of the garden would not be good for him. But Adam took the matter into his own hands, and decided what he wanted to do. What resulted was Adam's alienation from God. It is the conviction of the Bible that all human trouble, and finally death itself, come from this act of willfulness which is common to all of us. But in Christ there is an end to such confusion and death. It is eternal life, which Christ's submission to God brings to us.

PRAYER: O God, let me choose the way of the Garden of Gethsemane. Through Christ. Amen

MARCH 7

A BRIGHTNESS NO EYE CAN TAKE, NOR ANY HANDS MAKE

> Then the Lord said to Moses, "Go down and warn the people not to break through to the Lord to look; otherwise many of them will perish."
> —Exodus 19:21

READ: Exodus 19:16-23 and John 14:6-9

The holiness of God is expressed in the Old Testament conviction that no one can look upon the HOLY ONE and live. As looking directly into the sun does damage to one's eyes, so looking upon God causes our own destruction, so awesome and holy is the Lord God Almighty. Translated into theological terms: God is transcendent. Often we resist this idea of the complete transcendence of God, whose holiness places God totally apart from us. The people in Moses' following resisted the idea too. They wanted to rush right up the mountain to have a look at God. But God said, "No." Later in the Old Testament the prophets contrasted the God of Covenant Faith with the hand-crafted idols of the surrounding religions, referring to our God as a God not made with hands. Thus the only true God.

The temptation in our day to shape one's religion and church into a custom-made experience fitted especially to serve our needs, tastes, and desires is our version of hand-crafted idols, which take the place of the God not made with hands. When we jump from church to church, from pastor to pastor, in search of an approach to a religion which will fit our own prejudices, and not bind us in an uncomfortable way, we are trying to make God in our own image. But the HOLY ONE of the Bible is separate from such human fabrication.

But, you say, what good is a God whom you can't reach? The Christian Faith answers: God has reached into our lives instead. In Jesus Christ God comes to us from the mount and shows us the way, the truth and the life. While it is death and destruction to build one's own God, it is life and eternity to let Jesus Christ bring you to God and build your life anew.

PRAYER: O Christ, bring me to the HOLY ONE, and make me yours. Amen

~ ~ ~ ~ ~

MARCH 8

THE GREAT REVERSAL

And I said, "Woe is me! I am lost, for I am a man of unclean lips; yet my eyes have seen the King, the Lord of hosts!"

—Isaiah 6:5

READ: Isaiah 6:1-7 and Acts 26:12-18

Perhaps one of the reasons we want to trim God down to our size, by fashioning a God after our own opinions and desires, is that down deep we sense that to stand in the presence of the HOLY ONE is to face our own unworthiness and guilt. That is what happened to Isaiah. In the scene as told by Isaiah, God is pictured as weird and exotic, thereby declaring God to be the HOLY ONE, not at all like one of us. Before such a ONE we instinctively kneel. Isaiah, humbled in God's presence, confesses his unworthiness and sin and experiences God's forgiveness. Thus Isaiah's life is turned around—the great reversal. Isaiah then responds to God's call to action.

Similarly, Saul of Tarsus, is turned around when God breaks into his life through Christ, after which he begins a lifetime of following Christ's call to mission. Again, the great reversal comes when a person is brought into the presence of the HOLY ONE.

For each of us, an authentic call to Christian faith and action comes when we are brought into God's presence on God's terms, not ours. We appear before God with all our excuses neutralized and our defenses down, and with no agenda of our own. We let go of our own control of the situation. Then in God's presence we understand our own human condition and confess our sin and unworthiness as Isaiah did. God is quick to forgive when such acknowledgment is true and full. Then, like Isaiah and Paul, we are given God's work to do. This ought to be the dynamics of our experience each week in worship.

PRAYER: Let me see you, O Lord, high and lifted up. Let me hear you, O Christ, coming near to me and calling to me. Amen.

~ ~ ~ ~ ~ ~

MARCH 9

BAREFOOT IN PARADISE

Then God said, "Come no closer! Remove the sandals

from your feet, for the place on which you are standing is
holy ground." God said further, "I am the God of your
father, the God of Abraham, the God of Isaac, the God of
Jacob." And Moses hid his face. For he was afraid to look at
God.

—Exodus 3:5,6

READ: Exodus 3:1-15 and John 16:4-15

We can assume that Moses was a reasonable person. When he
came across a bush that was on fire, but which was not burning
up, he found that to be unreasonable. Thus, it caught his attention.
By the time God cautioned Moses to take off his shoes because he
was standing on holy ground, Moses knew that this was no ordinary
experience. He found himself in the very presence of the HOLY
ONE. No way could he take that in his stride. This would be a
most spectacular occasion, one which would alter the course of
Moses' life, and of human history as well. The God beyond all
human reason had defined himself for Moses: "I am who I am."
God's being does not depend upon any cause, or any human reason.
God just simply IS!

Those who want proofs of God's existence, are asking God to
conform to human reason, to be restricted to the boundaries of
our minds. Moses found that God needs no such reasonable proof.
God IS, and God reveals himself to us when and where and how
God wants to. God came to Moses in a burning bush and turned
the area into holy ground. God comes to us in Jesus Christ, in a
very specific way. When Jesus' time was nearly over, he promised
that God would continue revealing himself and his will to us
through the Holy Spirit, the Counselor, the Sprit of truth, who
would always be available to us.

In a sense we are always on holy ground, upon which the Holy
Spirit is present with every breath we take. The Holy Spirit is the
HOLY ONE in our midst. As a result of Christ's coming and the
gift of Holy Spirit, we can live constantly in God's presence. In
this way we are "barefoot in paradise" all the time as we take off
our sandals, so to speak, as Moses did in God's presence!

PRAYER: Come to me, Oh Holy Spirit, that I may always be in God's presence. In Christ. Amen

~ ~ ~ ~ ~ ~

MARCH 10

WHEN THE MORNING STARS SANG TOGETHER

> For I know that my Redeemer lives, and that at the last
> he will stand upon the earth; and after my skin has been
> thus destroyed, then in my flesh I shall see God.
>
> —Job 19:25-26

READ: Job 38:1-7 and John 20:24-29

To Job the evidence pointed away from God. Job was plagued with almost impossible disease and deprivation. His friends tried to convince him that a God of human reason and proportions had caused Job's problems, and for good reason. Job denied such reasoning and struggled to affirm a faith in a God who is beyond human scope and imagination, a God who loved Job despite his suffering. "I know that my Redeemer lives . . . I shall see God." (Job 19:25)

Ours may not be the patience or the faith of Job. We may well be more like Thomas, who said, "Unless I see the mark of the nails in his hands . . . and put . . . my hand in his side, I will not believe." (John 20:25) The beautiful part of the Resurrection appearance to Thomas is that Jesus gave Thomas opportunity to see and touch. It is God's desire that we have faith, and the story of Thomas assures us that God will do everything possible to grant us the gift of faith. But, like Thomas, we must reach out and perceive God.

Whether we are a Job or a Thomas, it is the HOLY ONE who comes into the midst of our life struggles and seeks to grant us faith. God "custom fits" the approach to each one of us according to our own particular faith development, for it is God who created us "when the morning stars sang together.," (Job 38:7)

PRAYER: Come to me, O God, where I am and grant me faith in the midst of my own particular struggles. Through Christ. Amen.

~ ~ ~ ~ ~ ~

MARCH 11

IN FAVOR OF FORGETTING

A time to plant, and a time to pluck up what is planted . . . a time to tear and a time to sew.

—Ecclesiastes 3:2,7

READ: Philippians 3:12-16 and Luke 9:57-62

Most of us wish we had better memories: for names, for facts, for pieces one has read and now has forgotten. But on the other side, there are things which are better forgotten. It would be more kindly to forget much of the negative gossip which abounds. The old three monkey trinket: "see no evil, hear no evil, speak no evil," needs another voice: "Forget the evil talk!"

More seriously still, there is need for each of us to turn our minds and hearts from the past in order to engage more effectively in life's progress toward the future. Jesus used the simple picture of a person plowing. In order to plow a straight furrow one must look ahead to where one is going, rather than behind at what one has already plowed. He symbolized this point of view in what appear to be harsh words: "Let the dead bury the dead." When we get so caught up in the accomplishments or failures in our own past, we become less able to break out of the spell these cast upon us. Instead, we need to put in proper perspective our own histories. Paul declared to the Christians in Philippi that he was forgetting his past so that he could move forward into a more effective future in service to Christ!

A new life of discipleship can be yours if you let go of glorifying yourself, or agonizing over your own past life; for then you will be more free to let Christ lead you into the future, which he has in mind for you!

PRAYER: Help me, O Lord, to resolve the disappointments in my life, to thank you for my accomplishments, and to look ahead to Christ, and his intention for my future. In Christ. Amen.

~ ~ ~ ~ ~ ~

MARCH 12

ACTING YOUR AGE

A time to seek, and a time to lose . . . a time to keep silence, and a time to speak.

—Ecclesiastes 3:6,7

READ: I Corinthians 13: 8-13 and Proverbs 2:1-8

The story line in Proverbs is that of an older person teaching a young person how to become wise, how to attain the knowledge of God, and understanding—in short: how to become a mature adult in the fullest sense of the word. These days this approach is not at all popular among children in our culture. It seems that children and youth are more tuned in to learning from each other than from older folks. Many resist being told anything by adults. This does not point to a hopeful future! High schoolers were interviewed on the street by a TV reporter who was asking people what they thought of Presidents Day. The teenager giggled and said: "I dunno anything about that government stuff." Our democracy will depend upon her vote and that of her peers in a few years! Perhaps we should be glad that she probably will not vote.

Paul compares childish ways to mature life: "When I was a child I spoke like a child, I thought like a child, I reasoned like a child; when I became an adult, I put an end to childish ways." (I Corinthians 13:11) The basic ingredient of maturity, which is so often lacking in a child is self-esteem. Some people struggle with the problem of a lack of a sense of self-worth all their lives, continuing to depend upon the approval of others for emotional survival. This emotional dependence produces what could be described as childishness, which causes a great deal of inter-personal tension and turmoil in the life of a person who remains immature in this way. The good news of the Christian faith is that in Christ we can gain God's approval, and find self-esteem thereby, when we receive God's acceptance. Out of our childhood ways Christ transforms us into mature adults, and by his grace he gives us faith, hope, and love!

PRAYER: O God, in Jesus Christ help me to be done with childish insecurity. Give me grace to act my age. Amen.

~ ~ ~ ~ ~ ~

MARCH 13

NO TIME TO TARRY

A time to kill, and a time to heal . . . a time to weep, and a time to laugh.

—Ecclesiastes 3:3,4

READ: Revelation 21:3-4 and Genesis 19:12-26

There is a promise throughout the Bible that the present age will come to an end and be replaced by a new—and better—age. It is our hope that in the age to come we will be with God in the fullest sense of the word. It is a sad observation that so much that happens contributes to our separation from God, when it is contrary to what God wants for us. The Old Testament described the cities of Sodom and Gomorrah as the epitome of life apart from God. Lot's wife wanted the sinful life of the present age so much that she could not look ahead to a future with God. She could not give up the present age in order to allow God to bring her to the new age. Her unwillingness to allow God to bring her out of sin and into new life is symbolized by her turning to a pillar of salt.

This is a parable for us. We must be truly done with the sinfulness and violence of the present day in order to be ready for God's new day. Our lives turn into "pillars of salt" when we become so taken in by the self-glorifying temptations of our modern, affluent society, or by the lustful search for passing pleasures at the expense of moral integrity. We become stuck on the level of consciousness of the present life around us, and we cannot therefore be led into a new age of re-union with God.

Revelation describes the new age of God's presence as the absence of mourning, pain, and death. Certainly such an existence is what we long for. To inherit such a future we must leave the Sodoms and Gomorrahs of this world and quit clinging to their false pleasures,

PRAYER: Forgive me, O God, for my reluctance to give up what I know to be wrong in my life. Don't let me turn to a block of salt. In Christ. Amen.'

◿ ◿ ◿ ◿ ◿ ◿

MARCH 14

BAPTISMAL BY-PASS

A time to be born, and a time to die . . . a time for war, and time for peace.

—Ecclesiastes 3:2,8

READ: Romans 6:1-11

There is basically something quite effortless about the Christian faith. Preachers tend to make it a gigantic work to be done, a life change to achieve, a moral victory to be won at great sacrifice. It is true that the Bible points us to a major change in direction which each of us must go through if we are to inherit the future God wants for us. We must grow up, put away former experiences, let go of old commitments, and avoid looking back. These all pose problems for us because it is easier to remain as we are than it is to change ourselves for the better

However, Paul shows us that the new person which God wants us to be, comes from God as a gift of grace, not a hard wrought accomplishment. God brings about the needed change in our lives if we will let God into our lives. In our baptism our old person is buried with Christ, and then we are raised with Christ as new beings. All we have to do is to submit to God's renewing action in our lives.

In the days following heart by-pass surgery loved ones who watch by the bedside of the recovering patient see evidence of new and vigorous life in the countenance and color of the patient experiencing renewed and full blood flow. In a way, such patients, without effort on their part, other than to submit to the skilled work of the heart surgeon, have turned from gray to pink so to speak—new color and new life!

This surgery can be understood as a death-resurrection process during which the blood is drained, the heart stopped, while the new arteries are being put in place. Then the blood is restored to the body, the heart is re-started, and new life is given. This is a picture of what God does for each of us through the death and resurrection of Jesus Christ.

PRAYER: Thank you, O Christ, for your death and resurrection
    for me. Amen

~ ~ ~ ~ ~ ~

MARCH 15

OFF THE MAP

Now the Lord said to Abram, "Go from your country and your kindred and your father's house to the land I will show you."

—Genesis 12:1

READ: Hebrews 11:1-3, 8-10 and Psalm 23

The writer of Hebrews admired what he saw in Abraham—his great faith and trust in God, which made him willing to leave everything that was familiar and comfortable in order to follow God off the map! While others stayed home and knew what to expect, Abraham left his nest not knowing what to expect. His was a journey of faith.

The inward journey each of us is making, is a journey of faith, if is any journey at all. In matters of inner being what develops and unfolds cannot be known at the outset. Matters of critical importance give way to new concerns. What we once idolized becomes obsolete and ignored. News turns in life's road provide completely new vistas; and the shape of our horizon changes. Some of the turns along the way are caused by outward circumstances: job change, death, the impact of actions of others on us, or even major world events like war or financial crisis. But each turn in the road requires our moving onward even though outcomes are unknown and new surroundings are unfamiliar.

Life's inward journey may well involve turns in the pathway which come from changes within us. Some new self-understanding, or changed perceptions of past events, may make our pathway twist in new and unfamiliar directions. Growth of our own understanding of life, of the world, and of others, can make our pathway ascend to new heights, from which the road ahead appears very different. Accident or disease, failing health, or waning capacities can plunge our path into a descent to a deeper level, even through dark tunnels at times; but always moving us along unknown lanes. But as Abraham, we journey in faith, knowing God and trusting God to lead us. That is knowledge enough!

PRAYER: Lead me, Lord, in your pathways. In Christ. Amen.

~ ~ ~ ~ ~ ~

MARCH 16

RUNNING SCARED

> Then Jacob was greatly afraid and distressed; and he
> divided the people that were with him, and the flocks and
> herds and camels, into two companies, thinking, "If Esau
> comes to the one company and destroys it, then the company
> that is left will escape."
>
> —Genesis 32:7-8

READ: Genesis 32:1-12 and Psalm 70:1-5

No one in the long history of the Bible ran more scared than Jacob. Long before this story he had tricked his older brother, Esau, into giving up the family inheritance so that Jacob could receive it from their father, Isaac. Jacob had not come home since that act of deceit. On top of that he had been running away from his in-laws as well, for the house of Laban also perceived Jacob as having tricked them. Twice terrified, Jacob now must face his brother. And he was afraid. So much so, that he made all the strategic preparations for a confrontation by force, knowing that his life was in jeopardy. His was a journey filled with fear.

Much of the time our inward journeys hold fear for us. Not

just fear of the unknown, though such fear is frequent and real, but fear of what will happen to us; fear that we may disintegrate in the process. The first step one takes toward psychotherapy is indeed a very fearful one, and many stages along the way may lead one through scary passageways of self-disclosure toward light and life.

Whatever life has involved for each of us there have been periods in which our judgement has been lacking, or we have been caught in unfortunate binds. Associations with others can easily create enemies. Those with whom we have disagreements can often be very threatening to us. It is not unusual to become anxious about what the future holds. "You never know what a phone call will bring!" This can be an ominous declaration, especially when we are running scared for one reason or another.

But the fact which kept Jacob secure was his assurance that God was leading him and would ultimately fulfill the promises God had made. When we run scared we too can have such an assurance. Not so much that God will remove every obstacle in the way of peace and happiness, but that in the midst of life's distress God's promises of ultimate good for us remain unchallenged. On God's love and power we can depend!

PRAYER: O God, lead me through fear which sometimes distresses me. Keep me ever aware of your power and love. In Christ. Amen.

~ ~ ~ ~ ~ ~

MARCH 17

TIRED OF YOURSELF?

So Ananias went and entered the house. He laid his hands on Saul and said, "Brother Saul, the Lord Jesus, who appeared to you on your way here, has sent me so that you may regain your sight and be filled with the Holy Spirit.
—Acts 9:17

READ: Acts 13:1-5 and Psalm 40:1-11

There are times when life's journey needs to have a complete change of direction. Life can become an endless stewing on a negative and unproductive course. We become frustrated and wonder what it is all supposed to add up to. We can even become weary of ourselves and unhappy about our unhappiness! At such a time one becomes blind to the larger purpose of life and to the vision God has for one's life. At this point one's inward journey needs a jarring change of direction.

Saul experienced such a jolt on the way to Damascus, to which he had been headed for the purpose of persecuting Christians, whom he hated. Because of the jolt God gave Saul that day, his inward journey, as well as his outward pathway changed directions radically. He became a follower of Christ and gave the rest of his life to spreading the new word so that others could become followers of Christ and schooled in his teachings. Tired of the old negative, destructive life cycle which went nowhere, Saul changed his name to Paul, and headed into the world as an evangelist, pastor and teacher of the new faith in Christ.

Are there aspects of your life which need complete renewal, or which need to be turned around and set on a new course? Maybe habits which now have you in their grip need to be let go of, so new efforts and activities have a chance to take hold in your life. Might you have prejudices which have kept you from relating positively to other people to whom God is leading you? Do you need to give up some old and unexamined ways of thinking and doing in order to do a new thing for Christ? Are you tired of yourself? Let God turn you around in your tracks! And you can have a new "me!"

PRAYER: Turn me around, O God, at those points at which I am little good to anyone, including myself. Through Christ. Amen.

~ ~ ~ ~ ~ ~

MARCH 18

PONDER YOUR SQUANDERING

The sacrifice acceptable to God is a broken spirit; a
broken and contrite heart, O God, you will not despise.
—Psalm 51:17

READ: Luke 15:11-24 and Psalm 51:1-2

Perhaps the most poignant journey in the Bible is the return
of the prodigal son to his father, as told by Jesus in the parable of
the Two Sons. The younger son's journey was one of guilt, an inward
journey which every faithful Christian must make over and over
again. You may be tempted to say, "Wait just a minute. I haven't
been involved in any loose and riotous living as that boy had been."
In our post-Victorian society we focus on the lurid footnotes here,
imagining all the immoral things he did while away from home.
However, the message of the parable is that the son squandered
the part of the family fortune which had been given to him. He'd
been a poor steward. That was his sin, for which he pled guilty at
the front gate of the ranch. Now we are featured in the story, aren't
we? We may not live reckless and debauched lives, but we do waste
time, talent and money. We do squander our lives, when we could
have been serving Christ. And when we ponder our squandering
we feel guilty of sin against others and against God.

Like the prodigal, we need to return home. Laden with guilt
we need to seek God's forgiveness for having wasted opportunities
to serve God. This journey is not easy, but Jesus' assurance in his
parable is that when we return honestly facing up to our
squandering, God forgives us joyfully! That is the Gospel!

PRAYER: Forgive me for wasting so many opportunities to do
good and to do your will. Forgive me for my squandering.
Through the mercy of Christ. Amen.

~ ~ ~ ~ ~

MARCH 19

DOING WHAT ONE MUST

They were on the road, going up to Jerusalem, and
Jesus was walking ahead of them; they were amazed, and
those who followed were afraid.

—Mark 10:32

READ: Luke 19:28-40 and Psalm 24:7-10

During the closing weeks of Jesus' earthly ministry, he went to
Jerusalem and thus to his final arrest, trial and execution. Those in
his inner circle had tried to dissuade him because of the mortal
danger ahead in Jerusalem. But, Jesus made the decision to follow
as the Spirit led him, even if it meant going to the pain and death
of Good Friday.

Sometimes our inward journey leads us through periods of
struggle and pain. And sometimes well-meaning friends and loved
ones try to dissuade us. But ultimately decisions about our journey
must be our own. Jesus is a heaven-sent model for each of us in his
forthright acceptance of God's will for him. Thus Jesus leads the
Christian to do what she or he must!

What will that entail on your journey? For some that has meant
getting an education or training at considerable cost to comfort
and pocketbook. For others, doing what one must means
committing to some volunteer task to which God calls one. This
may mean some sacrificial giving to the cause of Christ and his
church. Doing what one must, can mean working on existing
relationships in order to reconcile differences.

As with Jesus, our own courageous pursuit of God's goals for
our lives can take us to our own Jerusalem in which we must face
opposition, ridicule, persecution, or some form of exile. These are

crosses which we are called to bear as faithful followers of Christ. Every faithful inward journey will include some cross-bearing.

PRAYER: Help me to turn to "Jerusalem" and to be faithful in my witness there. As with Christ. Amen.

~ ~ ~ ~ ~ ~

MARCH 20

RIGHTS INSTEAD OF RITES

> But let justice roll down like waters, and righteousness
> like an everflowing stream.
>
> —Amos 5:24

READ: Amos 5:21-24, Matthew 6:1-6, and James 2:14-17

The prophet Amos lived in a time when the rights of the poor and oppressed in his society were being trampled, although it was a time when religious rites were being enthusiastically practiced. Amos was drawn to the contrasts which existed in his society in his day, between rich and poor, between what Israel thought of itself and what it really was, between those who sold at a profit and those who were forced to buy at a loss, and between religious piety and social injustice. He said in effect that God wants rights, not rites.

Years later James reflected this same point of view when he wrote, about the necessity of faith resulting in acting toward the poor in a helpful way. Neither James nor Amos felt that religious rites were enough, but that justice and love must follow.

This is not to say that we ought not to practice our religious life in worship, prayer and devotion; but it is to say that when our reverence for God is authentic, our respect for others around us, near and far, will result in the doing of justice in whatever ways we can, as responsible Christians in society.

PRAYER: O God, let me live in such a way that my respect for others brings justice into their lives. Through Christ. Amen.

~ ~ ~ ~ ~ ~

MARCH 21

IT'S WHAT'S IN THE HEART THAT COUNTS

For you know the generous act of our Lord Jesus Christ,
that though he was rich, yet for your sakes he became poor,
so that by his poverty you might become rich.

—II Corinthians 8:9

READ: Jeremiah 31:31-34 and Matthew 6:19-21

One of the peak portions of the Old Testament is Jeremiah 31, for there the prophet promises that in the final analysis, it's what's in the heart that counts. Pleasing God, and keeping his covenant is a matter of intention. Life's basic values and direction is the core issue here, more than one's good deeds and meticulous rule-obeying. Jesus tells us that you can sum up a person's life by looking at what is in his or her heart—basic values and motivations by which one lives. When your heart is filled with reverence for God and respect for others, then you are rich in the attitudes and motivations which God intends for people. That is to have a heart full of the riches God offers us.

Paul understood Jesus' death on the cross as the act by which God's wealth has been bequeathed to each one of us who belongs to Christ. Paul pictures Jesus as unbelievably rich in the sense of being close to God, but who was willing to give that up in order to be with us and to die for us. And by his self-sacrifice the treasure house of God's wealth is opened and showered upon us. The Christian, then, is one whose heart is filled with the wealth of God's forgiveness and reconciling love. Out of such a heart full of riches we are able to share spiritual wealth with others

PRAYER: I thank you, O God, for the generosity of your love by which from your heart to mine wealth flows through Christ. Amen.

~ ~ ~ ~ ~ ~

MARCH 22

NEITHER CALVES, RAMS, NOR RIVERS OF OIL

Blessed are the merciful, for they will receive mercy.
—Matthew 5:7

READ: Micah 6:6-8 and Matthew 5:17-20

If the many rules and regulations which were derived from the Old Testament Law, were to be written in English, they would fill a volume of over 800 pages. In Jesus' day it took a special group of people to get it all straight. They were the Scribes. Another group, the Pharisees, pledged themselves to follow all the rules. To follow these legalistic requirements, the Pharisees, had to make many personal sacrifices in order to get it right. In fact, the Old testament Law laid down in very specific detail how and what to sacrifice. Micah refers to these directives as he comments upon calves, rams and rivers of oil which were used in the sacrificial practices of devout Jews of his day.

Jesus said that he came to fulfill or to complete this Law, not of abolish it; and yet he, himself, broke many of the detailed rules of the Law, as in the case of his healing on the Sabbath. How could this be? It is in this very healing that we see what Jesus brought to us as an alternative to the complex sacrificial system. For in healing we see the mercy toward one's neighbor, which Jesus lifted up as a basic principle underlying the Law. "Blessed are the merciful . . . ." By giving us the underlying principle of MERCY, Jesus is showing us how to obey God in whatever events and developments come into our lives.

Think what being merciful could mean in your relationships with others. You would try to understand where the other person is coming from. You would develop sympathy for the other person, and modify your reactions with a new sensitivity. You would be more patient, kind and generous. You would be helpful; and you wouldn't be overly critical and judgmental. In short, as a follower of Christ you would be merciful!

PRAYER: O God, help me to be merciful! Through Christ, the channel of your mercy. Amen

~ ~ ~ ~ ~ ~

MARCH 23

AN INSIDE LINE

> Now the Lord came and stood there, calling as before, "Samuel! Samuel!" And Samuel said, "Speak, for your servant is listening."
>
> —I Samuel 3:10

READ: I Samuel 3:1-10

Have you ever said, "Whatever made me think of that?" How often thoughts come into our minds, seemingly at random, and for no reason. Usually these thoughts are trivial and of little consequence—or so we think. How quickly many of these inspirations are brushed aside and forgotten. A seminary professor used to advise his students, "Keep a pad of paper and pencil on your bed stand. There are many good ideas which come to us in the night."

The boy, Samuel, had such a thought in the night. In the months and years ahead he pointed to that nocturnal experience as the beginning of his career as a prophet. The "thought in the night" was none other than the Lord God speaking to him! Samuel believed that God, on that fateful night, had used an "inside line"—so to speak—to communicate with him; indeed to call him into service as a prophet of the Lord.

What about the inside line God is using in our lives? Are we as attentive to the chance thoughts which pop into our minds as we ought to be, evaluating whether or not these may be God's communication to us night or day? While we must not fall into the habit of thinking every notion comes from God, neither can we decide that none come from God. How can we tell which call is from God? Samuel went through a process of testing by consulting with Eli. So we must use the resource of a more experienced listener by which to test what comes to us on our inside line. This is what the Bible can do for us. The more familiar we are with its recorded experiences of spiritual insights which come from God, the more clearly we will be able to evaluate God's communication to us.

PRAYER: O God, help me to know your "voice" when I hear it. Through Christ the Word. Amen.

~ ~ ~ ~ ~ ~

MARCH 24

PASSING THE GAVEL

Elijah passed by him and threw his mantle over him.
He left the oxen, ran after Elijah, and said, "Let me kiss my
father and my mother, and then I will follow you."
—I Kings 19:19-20

READ: I Kings 19:15-21

During university commencement exercises, when a candidate for an advanced degree is presented, an academic hood is placed upon the candidate signifying the degree conferred. Often when a man or woman is ordained to the ministry a stole is placed upon the newly ordained clergy person. In many organizations and clubs, more frequently and with less ceremony the gavel is passed from an outgoing chairperson to the newly elected officer.

Elisha was busily engaged in working the family farm when what could have been dismissed as a casual gesture took place in such a way as to change his life completely. The well known prophet, Elijah, passed by, and "passed the gavel" so to speak, by putting his own coat on Elisha. The young man read the symbol correctly and left the farm to become Elijah's assistant and later his successor. He could have misread the sign. With the air turning chilly he might have concluded that the kindly old prophet wanted the young man to stay warm. But by the grace of God Elisha understood the meaning of the mantel conferred upon him.

On a deeper level the community of faith which composed the words of this event and put them in scripture understood the passing of the mantle to mean that God had chosen Elisha as Elijah's successor. Watch the signs, study the symbols, observe life's events. What might God be doing in your life through such simple actions as having a coat thrown over your shoulders!

PRAYER: Open my eyes that I may see; open my ears that I might hear; open my mind that I might understand your calls to me, O God. In Christ. Amen.

~ ~ ~ ~ ~

MARCH 25

TWO HEADS ARE BETTER THAN ONE

"Come and see a man who told me everything I have done! He cannot be the Messiah, can he?" They left the city and were on their way to him.

—John 4:29-30

READ: John 4:7-30

Discussion groups, brainstorming sessions, dialogues, and think-tanks are modern means of developing ideas and of making progress toward agreed upon goals. Business firms with only one mind at the top making all the decisions are fewer in number these days. Such solo directors have been replaced in many instances by some form of group process. Similarly the call of God comes to us more clearly through the interaction of more than one mind and consciousness. Two heads are better than one, when trying to determine the will of God for our lives. That's why discussion groups in churches are popular and effective. The same principle applies to the practice of seeking a pastor's advice before making life changing decisions.

The woman of Samaria, whom Jesus came upon at the well outside her village, is an example of one for whom discussion seemed to be the means by which her mind and heart were unlocked, allowing God's message and messenger to gain entrance. After much questioning of her neighbors, she concluded that Jesus spoke with authority, and had insights relevant to her, that indeed he must be the Messiah. That is why she wanted others in her village to come and discuss things with him.

Just as it is necessary to test our inner feelings and ideas against the standard of understanding found in the Bible, so it is often helpful to test our ideas with trusted Christian friends, and to allow others to assist us in the development of our own recognition of God's will for our lives. It would be very difficult to grow in faith without the fellowship of other Christians in the church.

PRAYER: Help us, O God, to find friends in the Faith with whom to discuss your word and will for our lives. Through Christ. Amen

~ ~ ~ ~ ~ ~

MARCH 26

A GUILT TRIP CANCELED

"Who do people say that I am?" And they answered him, "John the Baptist," and others, Elijah, and still others, one of the prophets."

—Mark 8:27-28

READ: Mark 1:1-8

Guilt is a common ailment among people. If you haven't felt guilty about your own human failings, you are rare indeed. Sooner or later each one of us makes a mistake, or says something which hurts someone, and we embark on what popularly is called a guilt trip. Some of our guilt is almost as old as we are. Perhaps years ago you did not return something you borrowed, and you kept putting it off until you moved away and lost all contact with the rightful owner; and you have felt guilt ever since.

Every normal person has a need for forgiveness. On a deeper level this guilt comes about as a result of one's basic separation from God, and one's alienation from other people. When Jesus asked his disciples about their understanding of his identity, they reported that many felt that he was John the Baptist. John's message was repentance and forgiveness of sins. The human need for forgiveness would be answered by this one who was called Jesus of Nazareth.

It is true that Jesus' identity, if he means anything at all, will be in terms of his gracious answer to our human needs. Our need for forgiveness finds its relief in Jesus Christ, who came to provide us with the opportunity to obtain God's forgiveness. John the Baptist, while pointing to the truth, was only a partial answer. Jesus came to do more. Not only to redeem us but to grant us grace to live new lives, as well as to provide us with a continuing relationship with God.

PRAYER: Thank you, O God, for the forgiving of my sin, which you offer to me through Jesus Christ, your Son, my Savior and Lord. In Christ. Amen.

~ ~ ~ ~ ~ ~

MARCH 27

POWER TO THE PEOPLE

"Who do people say that I am? And they answered him, "John the Baptist, and others, Elijah, and still others, "One of the prophets."

—Mark 8:27-28

(A second look at this important passage!)

READ: Malachi 4:1-6

What you have just read is the last chapter in the Old Testament. The scriptures of the Hebrew people ended with a yearning for the return of Elijah, who possessed the power of God. He had the power to do miraculous things, like providing a certain widow with an unending supply of food during a drought, and of reviving her son. Elijah had the power of God to put down wrong ideas, which he did when he demonstrated the power of God to supercede the power of Baal. He had the power of God to confront kings who had failed to honor God. Leaders with such power were earnestly hoped for in the years after Elijah. Thus, the Hebrews came to believe that God would send Elijah back at the end of time. When the Jews saw Jesus, some of them saw in him the power of Elijah, and were glad for it.

How we yearn for the kind of power Elijah brought to bear on his times. In our yearning about the world we live in we wonder, "Isn't there someone who can put down crime and drug traffic? Can't someone stop war? We need someone to remove the terrorists of this world. Isn't there some way I can get my life in order?" We feel powerless in these matters, and we want a powerful intervention to set things straight.

Christians believe that Jesus brings the kind of power which Elijah possessed; and that he will set things straight in the world ultimately. So Jesus is in some sense Elijah returning to God's world. But he is much more!

PRAYER: Thank you, O Lord, for the power to changes lives which you brought in Jesus Christ. Amen.

～ ～ ～ ～ ～

MARCH 28

INNER LINK

Who do people say that I am? And they answered him, "John the Baptist, and others, Elijah, and still others, One of the prophets."—Mark 8:27-28 (Looking at this passage again!)

READ: Jeremiah 31:31-34

Students of modern society say that we have changed from an industrial society to an information society. More people are now engaged in the business of distributing information than in the manufacture of goods. Ours is the day of the computer, the internet, the fax machine and the cell phone. And new information technology is coming almost daily! These instruments of modern communication have become the links among people all over the world, binding us to one another in one global village. My wife and I enjoy instant contact with our friends in New Zealand via the internet, by which we cross the international date line in the twinkling of an eye.

In Old Testament times the prophets were the links between God and the people of God providing essential information for the conduct of Israel's life. As such they brought the people in contact with God. Throughout the times of the prophets, not only was information the precious item of their trade, but also relationship. Relationship between God and the people of God, called the Covenant, was the link which the prophets sought to maintain.

We have a basic human need for relationship with our Maker, without which we feel a profound sense of loneliness. "Our hearts are restless, until they find their rest in thee," is a familiar Christian proclamation. When we anticipate who Jesus is, it is comforting to know that he provides that communication link with God, for which we yearn. When some of the Jews said that Jesus was one of the prophets, perhaps it was such a critical communication link which they were finding in him.

Jeremiah went the furthest of any of the prophets in pointing toward an inner link which God would establish with us. "This is the covenant . . . I will write upon their hearts."(Jeremiah 31:33) Jesus came to be that inner link, to write a new covenant with God upon our hearts.

PRAYER: For your new covenant in our hearts I thank you, Lord; and for Jesus who links me to you. In him. Amen.

⌐ ⌐ ⌐ ⌐ ⌐ ⌐

MARCH 29

THE REAL THING

"But who do you say that I am?" Peter answered him, "You are the Messiah."

—Mark 8:29

READ: JOHN 1:19-23, 29-34

It is to John the Baptist's credit that when his hearers asked him if he was one of God's special people, like Elijah, or the prophet, he did not take the ego-bait. Rather, he pointed to Jesus and said,

"There is the Son of God!" It is always a temptation to those who eloquently speak of Christ to slip into the trap of letting people focus their attention on them, instead of upon Jesus.

It is a human need to want to have God in our midst, and to be near God in worship. When God appeared, it was in Jesus of Nazareth. He was not the forerunner, but the real thing. Jesus Christ is God coming to us that we might have forgiveness for our sin, that we might have the power to overcome wrong and injustice. and that we might have an inner relationship with God.

On Palm Sunday Jesus' identity was shouted by the crowds. Even on that day they could not know the fullness of the One who had come to the world, but their proclamation was the beginning of the world's celebration of God's redemption in Christ "All glory, laud, and honor to thee, redeemer, King!"

PRAYER: Even so, come Lord Jesus! Amen

~ ~ ~ ~ ~ ~

MARCH 30

THE ONLY WAY TO GO

"Are you the one who is to come, or are we to wait for another?"

—Matthew 11:3

READ: Matthew 11:2-6

In the fickle ways of human life, leaders come and go with great speed. Yesterdays's candidate was bright and promising. He is today's disappointment, and will be barely remembered tomorrow, when we will be busy looking for the next leader to save us from whatever ails us. That's the way it was in the time of John the Baptist. There had been a succession of promising people who had turned out to be flashes in the pan, leaving the Jews without much hope for change—until, of course, another star rose to temporary popularity. John wondered about his cousin, Jesus. Was he just another instant success at rallying the people to his cause? Would he soon merge into the mosaic of history without much continued identity? And people would be left again to look for some other person to lead them and to save them from chaos?

Young and old in our time have answered John's question with a "Yes, we will look for another." And they have gone on looking for some other, some looking to Eastern religions for new hope; others have been sucked into cults; while others fall into despair, looking nowhere except in their own minds.

Jesus' answer to John is also his answer to us today. Look at the results of my ministry, Jesus is saying. With John we are led to see such results as signs of the authenticity of Jesus. Leper and blind person, deaf ones and lame, all found relief from the devestation of their diseases in Jesus' healing. And an even more dramatic sign—there were the dead who had been raised. Beyond all these outstanding works of mercy, the poor were hearing some very good news about their future. Should we expect some other? No! Jesus Christ can fix what ails you. He's the only way to go.

PRAYER: Help me, O God, to re-capture my enthusiasm for Jesus, as the answer to life's perplexities. In his name, I pray. Amen.

~ ~ ~ ~ ~

MARCH 31

ENOUGH TO GO AROUND

And all ate, and were filled.

—Mark 6:42

READ: Mark 6:34-44

One of the most beautiful ways of explaining the story of Jesus feeding the great crowds with a few morsels of food is to point out that when Jesus shared the little bit which he and his disciples had with the crowd, countless others in the crowd reached under their robes and brought out what they had, and shared it with those around them. In that way everyone ate to their heart's content. Though it really isn't necessary to explain away the miracle of the feeding of the crowd, such an explanation itself becomes a parable which teaches us to see the needs of our brothers and sisters through the loving and sharing consciousness of Jesus. And then to do something ourselves about the needs of others.

Today church related hunger programs are attempting to raise our consciousness to the needs of the starving people throughout the world. Food Banks have become massive programs for collecting and distributing of food to those in need.

It is said that there is enough food to go around. But, who will make it go around? Matthew bears witness to the fact that Jesus will make it go around. The feeding of the crowd is a sign that one way or another the love of God in Jesus Christ is powerful enough to solve the world's food crises—if we will obey him and extend his loving, sharing hand, as his disciples did that day in Palestine.

PRAYER: Open my eyes to see the need for food near and far, O Lord. Open my hands to share what I have with those in need. Open my mind and give me understanding for the solving of the problem of world hunger. Open my will with the courage to align my will with yours. Through Christ who shares bread. Amen

APRIL

APRIL 1

STEPHEN: CALLED AND FAITHFUL

While they were stoning Stephen, he prayed, "Lord Jesus, receive my spirit."

—Acts 7:59

READ: Acts 6:1-7

Stephen will be forever remembered as the first martyr for Christ. His unflinching, faithfulness was constant. It brought him through to the ultimate sacrifice of his life for Christ. A controversy had developed in the early church over the respective positions and functions among the followers of Christ. To settle the conflict and to provide equal treatment for everyone in the group the first deacons were called forth to care for the needs of the entire congregation. Among the first such servants chosen was "Stephen, full of grace and power." (Acts 6:8)

There are a number of significant issues here. The church was experiencing one of its first ethnic tensions between the Greek speaking Jews and the native Jews. The church was entering its first phase of organizational strategy in the development of certain groups for certain tasks. And finally, martyrdom was emerging. It would continue to be a reality within the life of the early Christian church, and in every century since that time, including our own. Missionaries in Latin America, Confessing Christians in Nazi Germany, Anabaptists in 17th century Europe, all have experienced persecution and death among their particular groups for their faith in Christ.

From Stephen we see a model for the faithful life we are called to live. He readily accepted the task of discipleship for which he was chosen; and he resolutely remained faithful, even unto death. Christ needs each of us in the work of his church, and calls us to faithfulness. When we readily accept his call we signify our willingness to pay whatever price will be exacted.

PRAYER: Call me to your work, and make me faithful, O Christ. Amen.

~ ~ ~ ~ ~

APRIL 2

SIMON: POWER WITHOUT FAITH?

> Now when Simon saw that the Spirit was given through the laying on of the apostle's hands, he offered them money, saying, "Give me also this power so that anyone on whom I lay my hands may receive the Holy Spirit."
>
> —Acts 8:18-19

READ: Acts 8:4-24

Simon, the magician, represents a sinful human tendency in religion. Simon was a man who had converted to Christ formally, but was unwilling to give up his basic commitment to himself. He wanted God's power in order to build up his own business interests. If he could latch onto the Holy Spirit for his own ends what magic he could perform for the paying customers! What wealth he could amass!

In our time we have seen blatant examples of modern-day Simons who have performed to great crowds and have taken huge offerings from them after demonstrating their power to heal on stage. There have been church officials over the years who have lived luxuriously as a result of having shown great power of tongue or pen, and thus have elevated themselves above the ordinary people. Again this is an example of using God's power for private gain.

Let us not do as Simon did. Whenever we try to enlist God's power and support for our own worldly gain, or personal prestige, we are falling into the trap of Simon the magician. This can be a very seductive temptation. Excuse is sometimes given that having nice things, like flashy cars, custom tailored suits, and fine homes shows others that God has blessed us and that others should follow our example and give themselves to God, as we have. Peter's answer is appropriate to those who make such excuses. "Your heart is not right before God." (Acts 8:21)

True faith is without the promise of power or wealth. It is a willingness to suffer for Christ. It is not loving Jesus in order to succeed. It is true that life will be better as his follower, but in ways that God intends and supplies, not in the currency we choose.

PRAYER: Grant me faith, not for my own ends, but for yours. In Christ. Amen

~ ~ ~ ~ ~ ~

APRIL 3

FAITH SEEKING UNDERSTANDING

"How can I (understand) unless someone guides me?"
And he invited Phillip to get in and sit beside him.
—Acts 8:31

READ: Acts 8:26-39

The un-named man from Ethiopia described in Acts 8, might have been someone tired of the confusion of a religion with many gods, and of a society of loose morals. Such persons had found their way to the Jewish faith in ancient times, either joining as proselytes or as "God-fearers." Obviously this man was a man of faith who was acting upon such faith by traveling to Jerusalem to worship God. His faith was leading him to seek understanding. Philip helped to provide understanding as he interpreted the scriptures to the Ethiopian.

This is the reverse of our cultural bias. We are such rational and educated folk that we want as much understanding as possible before taking a step of faith. We want to *know* first. "Will it work? Is it true? What can I expect?" These are the kinds of questions we want answered before we take as step of faith in religious matters. Unfortunately, understanding and knowledge does not always lead to faith. In fact, it seems that for many intellectuals, knowledge obstructs faith. The Ethiopian wanted meaning and order in his life, and he was willing to step out in faith to worship God. His was faith seeking understanding.

This should be a comfort to us. We don't have to know all the answers to theological questions, or know all the stories in the Bible. The beginning of our spiritual life is the revealing of God in Jesus Christ. In faith, like the disciples, we follow Jesus, and grow in our knowledge and understanding along the way.

PRAYER: O God, you have given me faith. Help me understand. Through Christ. Amen.

～ ～ ～ ～ ～

APRIL 4

ANANIAS: FROM FEAR TO FAITH

> So Ananias went and entered the house. He laid his
> hands upon Saul and said, "Brother Saul, the Lord Jesus,
> who appeared to you on the way here, has sent me so that
> you may regain your sight and be filled with the Holy Spirit.
> —Acts 9:17

READ: Acts 9:10-19

Whenever you feel called to a fearsome task, think about Ananias. He should be an inspiration to anyone who feels that Christ is commanding them to do some hard thing. He had heard of the ruthless persecutor of Christians, Saul of Tarsus. In modern terms—a bounty hunter. He had even heard through the grapevine that Saul was coming to Damascus with papers authorizing him to take Christians as prisoners for persecution. If there was ever a man to keep clear of, it was Saul. Then to hear that he had arrived in town, and that he must go to him, must have struck fear in Ananias. But, his faith was deep and strong, and he yielded to Christ's call to a fearsome task.

We may not have experienced the extremes of fear that Ananias and his fellow Christians had felt. We live in a culture which is mildly tolerant of Christian convictions—if we don't get too political! But Christians elsewhere in the world have been under persecution for their faith. For us, fear may come when we are called to some work for Christ. Having to teach church school for the first time is a fearsome task. Being asked to make a public announcement in worship may be equally intimidating. Speaking to someone about your faith and Christian experience may also be fearfully difficult for you. Visiting a terminally ill patient is not always easy. But, in whatever task for Christ you find yourself, remember Ananais and his faith. What a victory for him when he could stand face to face with Saul and say: "Brother Saul . . ." and lay his hands upon him. If God gave Ananias such courage, so can God grant it to each of us,

PRAYER: Give me courage to do your work, fearful though it may be at first. Through Christ. Amen

～ ～ ～ ～ ～ ～

APRIL 5

BELIEVING

"You stiff-necked people, uncircumcised in heart and
ears, you are forever opposing the Holy Spirit, just as you
ancestors used to do."

—Acts 7:51

READ: Acts 17:29-34 and John 1:43-51

The attitude with which you listen will determine what you
believe. When you listen to a lecture, or read an article thinking,
"You can't convince me," you won't be convinced. If you are so set
in your mind, you will respond to every new idea with: "That
doesn't make sense, since it does not go along with what I know to
be true." You won't believe what you hear.

Nathaniel almost didn't believe in Jesus, merely because of his
prejudices about Jesus' origin in Nazareth. "Can anything good
come out of Nazareth?" How many times we say something like
that and thereby resist some new truth. There were those in Athens
who dabbled in hearing things new, who remained skeptical when
Paul told them of the resurrection. They listened, but with deaf
ears because of distancing themselves from disturbing ideas.

We are always in danger of complacency of thought, confident
that we know the truth, and that ideas which differ from ours are
probably wrong. But as Christians we believe the truth is a living,
active message from God to which we must humbly listen.
Therefore, we must listen with expectant ears and an open mind,
so that God can lead our thinking along new paths on which God
would have us go.

PRAYER: Open my ears and my mind to hear and believe your
truth, O Christ, the Word made flesh. Amen.

~ ~ ~ ~ ~ ~

APRIL 6

NOT SET IN CONCRETE

O send out your light and your truth; let them lead
me....

—Psalm 43:3

READ: John 8:31-40

The Jews of Jesus' day were imprisoned in some wrong thinking, falsehood. Jesus called them on it, saying to them that they were slaves to sin. They believed that as descendants of Abraham, all they had to do was to live rigidly following the Law as interpreted by the religious establishment. Jesus called this slavery, and proclaimed the good news that the truth would set them free.

We too are slaves to sin when we allow untruth to dominate our thinking. As we look at some of the untruths by which we live, and which thus enslave us, we begin with the untruth: "My life, my future, my destiny are determined by forces outside my control. This enslaving falsehood can make us think that the bad things which happen to us are sent to us by God, or by fate determined a long time ago, by our heredity, or by the relationships and events which came our way. We think our lives are set in concrete, and we try our best to understand why God does to us what he does. We need to bury such a dismal view of life and discover the truth which sets us free.

That truth is that God loves us and does not bring evil and hurtful circumstances upon us. Rather, God accompanies us through the difficult times, strengthening and supporting us. Furthermore, God is involved in the events which befall us in such a way as to seek to reduce the pain and to reverse the damage to us. God wants health and wholeness for each of us, and he is at work in our lives pursuing that goal. That is the truth which sets us free from the falsehood of thinking that things are set in concrete, and will remain just as bad as they are right now.

PRAYER: Thank you, God, for your love which frees me from wearisome despair. Through Christ. Amen.

~ ~ ~ ~ ~

APRIL 7

RETURN FROM THE DEAD

You desire truth in the inward being; therefore teach
me wisdom in my secret heart. Purge me with hyssop, and I
shall be clean; wash me and I shall be whiter than snow.
—Psalm 51:6-7

READ: Romans 6:1-11

Many people are strongly affected by the pervasive feeling that God is against them, that God is an adversary to be reckoned with. Oftentimes rooted in childhood fears of arbitrary parental power, many have developed a view of life which is infused with the idea that: "If you don't watch out, IT will get you." the IT may be God, other people, life itself, luck, or whatever power one senses is out there opposing one's well being. Is it any wonder that such a person wants to stay away from God, the church, the Bible, prayer and religious people. This negative feeling about religion is reflected in the bumper sticker: "If you want religion to run your life, go to Iran." This is clearly a false view of life which needs to be buried with Christ, so that the truth may be raised with him.

One of the most wonderful results of Jesus' return from the dead is the assurance that God is in ultimate control of the world, and that it is God's will and intention to replace hatred and violence with love, to reconcile us to himself in place of the separation from God we normally feel, and to overcome every power which opposes

God's will. This is the victory of the Risen Christ over death. When we are raised with Christ, we can live in the awareness that we belong to God. We can then feel at home in the world over which God presides.

When we feel at home with God in God's world we can become re-united with each other, no longer assuming that others around us are hostile. Good news! Things aren't out to get me afterall!

PRAYER: Help me to accept your love for me, O God, through a new awareness of the Resurrection of Jesus Christ from the dead. In him. Amen.

╌ ╌ ╌ ╌ ╌ ╌

APRIL 8

A NEW ME

For the Lord is good; his steadfast love endures forever,
and his faithfulness to all generations.
—Psalm 100:5

READ: Romans 7:4-11

Tragically many times very damaging falsehoods are forced upon people early in their lives. Various versions of, "You're no good," are sometimes hurled repeatedly at children by their parents or by other influential adults. And, sad to say, the naturally trusting child in such situations grows up believing those negative messages; and in adulthood he or she will live under the false impression, that, "I'm not a good person." A son may grow up to be awkward and inept because his father kept drilling into him, "Why can't you do anything right?" A daughter may grow up to see herself as "dumb" because her parents never gave her credit for having an adequate mind of her own. To some extent everyone has been a victim of negative conditioning of one sort or another. Even if it is something as trivial as, "In our family we can't seem to take good photographs." We need to bury the falsehoods by which we evaluate ourselves, and each of us needs to be given a "new me!"

The good news of the resurrection is that we can bury such false notions about ourselves and allow God to raise us up as new beings, ready to live for him. In his letter to the Romans Paul says: "But now we are . . . . dead to that which held us captive, so that we are slaves not under the old written code but in the new life of the Spirit . . . . in order that we may bear fruit for God." (Romans 7:6 & 4)

The good news of the Resurrection is that now we can be able and useful—indeed good persons—in God's service. Here is the "new me!"

PRAYER: Take away the false ideas I have about myself, and reveal to me your truth about my life as you see me, O God. Through the Risen Christ. Amen.

~ ~ ~ ~ ~ ~

APRIL 9

NOT MY LIFE, BUT CHRIST'S

I have chosen the way of faithfulness; I set your ordinances before me.

—Psalm 119:30

READ: Galatians 2:15-21

There is deep within us the desire to be accepted and loved by others; and if we think about it—by God. But running contrary to that desire is the very normal sense of not being acceptable—guilt for not being a better person. To varying degrees each of us struggles at this point of tension: wanting to be loved, and not feeling that we deserve to be loved by others or by God. We react to this collision of feelings in very different ways. Some become arrogant and bullying. Others become shy and cringing, while all sorts of behaviors between these two extremes are to be found among us all. One way or another this conflict makes us want to do something to earn our way into the love and acceptance of others and of God. Religions have been devised to provide ways of earning divine acceptance. That is what the Jewish Law was designed to do. But following the Law was so difficult that the one who attempted to fulfill the Law's demands was in danger of ending up feeling worse about his/her acceptability.

Paul declared that, "a person is justified not by the works of the law but through faith in Jesus Christ." We must bury the untruth that leads us to believe that by works of the Law we are made acceptable to God. Let us then be raised to the truth: *that it is faith in Christ that puts us right with God and with others.* "It is no longer I who live, but it is Christ who lives in me." (Galatians 2:20) Christ is acceptable to God. Therefore I am acceptable to God. The deep desire to be loved by God is satisfied through Christ. This is the best news of the Resurrection.

PRAYER: O God, I thank you for your love for me, even me! Through Christ in me. Amen.

~ ~ ~ ~ ~

APRIL 10

"IN PASTURES GREEN"*

The Lord is my shepherd, I shall not want. He makes
me to lie down in green pastures;

—Psalm 23:1,2

READ: Psalm 46 and Mark 4:35-41

One of the chief figures in a Wall Street scandal some years

---

*   Titles used for April 10-14 are taken from the metric version of Psalm 23 in the Scottish Psalter of 1650.

ago, who had piled up millions for himself through insider trading, said in a commencement speech for the School of Business Administration of the University of California in 1985 (before his downfall), "Greed is all right . . . I think it is healthy. You can be greedy and still feel good about yourself." How opposite to the Biblical description of the person who is devoted to doing God's will, and who depends upon God for all his/her wants and desires. Yet, the insider trader's affirmation of greed probably met with approval, for it reflects a business bias found in our society.

Beyond depending upon God for the fulfillment of our needs, the Psalmist invites us to consider how God slows us down in times of stress, encouraging us to think more deeply as God makes us to "lie down in green pastures."

When Jesus entered the fishing boat in which the disciples were dangerously storm-tossed, he provided the power to still the storm and to save the boat with its cargo and crew from destruction and loss. Does your life ever seem storm-tossed? Are you ever buffeted by ill winds? Do you ever feel as if one more blast will make your ship go under? It is the faith of people in the Bible that God is the Good Shepherd who protects us from such turmoil by inviting us to slow down, to let go of our constant grasping and to consider the eternal values upon which we depend.

PRAYER: Slow me down, O God; show me your truths; point me to your values; fulfill my wants in your pastures green. In Christ. Amen

~ ~ ~ ~ ~ ~

APRIL 11

"MY SOUL HE DOTH RESTORE"

He leads me beside still waters; he restores my soul.
—Psalm 23:2,3

READ: Luke 9:28-35

The high point in the lives of Peter, James, and John came on what has been named the Mount of Transfiguration. It was during this experience that Jesus was transformed in their consciousness to become the Christ, God's Messiah—the Savior. In this moment of discovery the lives of the three disciples were also transformed and lifted to new heights. And so it was that Peter declared: "Master, it is good for us to be here; let us make three dwellings, one for you, one for Moses, and one for Elijah." (Luke 9:33)

Therapists talk about the "AHA!" experience in therapy when the client makes a significant discovery about him/herself, which often constitutes an important break-through in the progress of that person toward health and strength. In religious life there are times of extremely high emotion, or deeply penetrating insight, which come explosively. These religious experiences are times when the soul is in some sense transformed—restored. We often call these mountain-top experiences. The psalmist locates these events "beside the still waters." Peter, James and John found their consciousness opened and their lives renewed on the Mount of Transfiguration when they had an "AHA!" recognition of Jesus' true identity.

God wants to lead each of us beside the still waters and to meet us there through Christ's presence in order to gives a new discovery of ourselves in relation to Christ. In this way our lives can be transformed, restored, and refreshed.

PRAYER: O Christ, come to me in such a new way that I will be re-shaped and made ready for future days with you. Amen

~ ~ ~ ~ ~ ~

APRIL 12

"THY ROD AND STAFF ME COMFORT STILL"

He leads me in right paths for his name's sake. Even though I walk through the darkest valley, I fear no evil; for you are with me; your rod and your staff—they comfort me,

—Psalm 23: 3-4

READ: John 10:7-15

The picture of Jesus as the Good Shepherd is a familiar one to anyone who has ever been in Sunday School. It has long been a favorite image by which to teach children that God loves them. With his rod and staff he both defends and protects his sheep. So God defends and protects us. Jesus expands on this scene by describing himself as the shepherd lying across the entrance to the sheepfold at night to keep marauding animals away, as well as to keep thieves from coming in to steal the sheep.

Modern life presents each of us with a vast array of choices in an often confusing progression of days. Influence peddlers, promoters, advertisers of all kinds assault us on every side, attempting to shape us according to their own desires and benefit. Paul refers to our precarious trek in these words: ". . . children, tossed to and fro and blown about by every wind of doctrine, by people's trickery, by their craftiness in deceitful scheming." (Ephesians 4:14) Is it any wonder we need a shepherd to keep us from dangerous snares and pitfalls, and to ward off evil influences?

The shepherd's long staff with its crook is a symbol for the way in which Christ gently but firmly guides us through life's maze of uneasy decisions. Like sheep under his care, let him guide and protect you on your way.

PRAYER: Guide me, O Christ, my shepherd, that I may not be hurt, snared, or stolen. Amen

~ ~ ~ ~ ~ ~

APRIL 13

"MY TABLE HAST THOU FURNISHED
MY HEAD THOU DOST WITH OIL ANOINT"

You prepare a table before me in the presence of my enemies; you anoint my head with oil; my cup overflows.

—Psalm 23:5

READ: Luke 14:15-24 and John 21:1-12

Have you ever thought about how many of the Resurrection episodes involved meals which the disciples and the Risen Christ enjoyed together? There is something about a meal together which involves a very close relationship as certainly the Last Supper symbolized. The church pot-luck can be seen as such a meal together after the resurrection. This closeness to Christ and each other is present in our sacrament of the Lord's Supper. Very early our ancestors in the faith felt this about the common meal when they sang the words of the Twenty-third Psalm with its reference to God's table furnished for us. That is where God wants each of us—with him in close relationship as experienced in the meal shared with one another.

Ordinarily there is so much in our modern, rushed, and diverse life which makes God seem far removed from us. Down deep, it is characteristically human to feel the pain of estrangement from God. Many theologians in our day believe that what psychologists call anxiety, guilt and depression stems from our alienation from God, our Creator. The good news of the Gospel is that God does not want to be separate from us, but rather, in Jesus Christ God has taken decisive steps to close the gap between himself and humankind. Christians sense therefore, their welcome to God's table, so to speak. Not only to the household of God, but once there, to be anointed with oil which in New Testament terms points to an act of loving grace.

PRAYER: I thank you, O God, for your welcome to come to your table, to be with you, and to be anointed by you. Through Christ. Amen

~ ~ ~ ~ ~

APRIL 14

"AND IN GOD'S HOUSE FOREVERMORE"

Surely goodness and mercy shall follow me all the days
of my life, and I shall dwell in the house of the Lord my
whole life long.
—Psalm 23:6

READ: Romans 8:28, 31-39

There is a certain quiet confidence in the way in which a Christian faces the future with all its uncertainties. This is not the self-assured confidence of one who holds a bigger stick as a detriment to aggression; but rather the assurance that whatever comes, God is our strength and the source of wisdom upon which we can draw.

Paul spent many lonely days traveling by land and ship from town to town. In those years of ministry he lived through many natural disasters, and endured much persecution and mistreatment from those who opposed the Christian cause. And yet he could write to the church in Rome saying: "We know that all things work together for good for those who love God, who are called according to his purpose, nor anything else in all creation will be able to separate us from the love of God in Christ Jesus our lord." (Romans 8:28, 39)

Our security in the midst of a changing and disturbing world is not rooted in a knowledge of how things will work out. That is precisely what we do not know. Our security comes from recognizing our place in God's family or flock; and in experiencing the love of God for us which the Psalmist compares to the love of a shepherd for his sheep. An uncertain future need not shake our confidence in God the creator and sustainer who changes not.

PRAYER: O God, give us the confidence and security of knowing that we are at home with you. In Christ. Amen.

~ ~ ~ ~ ~ ~

APRIL 15

LIFE AT THE TOP

And have clothed yourselves with the new self, which is being renewed in knowledge according to the image of its creator.

—Colossians 3:10

READ: Colossians 3:1-15

Have you ever stopped in a shop in which you had the distinct feeling that the boss was not in? Somehow the interaction of the employees with one another, and possibly the way in which customers were treated revealed the absence of the manager. On the positive side of this dynamic in human relationships the presence of a respected, if not feared, leader has a way of making those serving underneath rise to new levels of diligence and job performance. The person at the top can lift up the others.

This is what Paul said would happen in the life of the Christian who has been raised with Christ to a new and higher level of life. The Resurrection of Christ to new life would be shared with those who follow him until they, too, would be renewed in an image of Christ's own likeness.

It would be a mistake, however, to conclude that tremendous changes will occur in a follower of Christ without some effort. Paul instructs the Colossians to set their minds on higher things, and consciously to forsake earth-bound things. And anyone who has ever tried such an exercise will testify that such resolve is not easy to fulfill. Put away, he said, "whatever in you is earthly . . . . As God's chosen ones, holy and beloved, clothe yourselves with compassion, kindness, humility, meekness and patience."(Romans 3:5, 12) Such a person will experience life at the top!

PRAYER: Help me, O Christ, to live at the top, where you are, my Risen Lord. Amen

~ ~ ~ ~ ~

APRIL 16

WHERE THERE IS HOPE

> By his great mercy he has given us a new birth into a living hope through the resurrection of Jesus Christ from the dead.
>
> —I Peter 1:3

READ: I Peter 1:3-9

Not a great deal is said about the little word, hope. Yet, without hope life ebbs to a near standstill. The most gruesome fate imaginable is to die of suffocation in a collapsed mine shaft. Whenever such a tragedy is reported on the news one can't help but imagine what it must be like to come to the point of giving up hope in such a situation. When there is no longer any light coming through the jagged rocks, when all sound ceases, and when the air begins to run out, then certainly hope must fade in the hearts of the victims. And then what it must be like, suddenly to hear the rocks being removed, to see light once again, and then to hear the voice of one's rescuer!

That is what Peter speaks of when he tells of the great mercy of God by which Christ was raised from the dead, thereby giving us hope of salvation. As with the trapped miner, there may very well remain some hard times and suffering before the final rescue, but hope makes all the difference. One can endure suffering where there is hope. Without such hope of final release, suffering can bring debilitating despair. Where there is hope there is life. When there is the risen Christ there is hope and there is life.

PRAYER: O God, fix in my mind and heart such an awareness of Christ's resurrection and what that means for me, that my life will be filled with hope for the future. In Christ. Amen.

~ ~ ~ ~ ~ ~

APRIL 17

THE PERFECT CONFIDANT

Through him you have come to trust in God, who raised him from the dead and gave him glory, so that your faith and hope are set in God.

—I Peter 1:21

READ: I Peter 1:17-21

Each of us needs someone in whom we can confide. It has been said somewhat flippantly that the two busiest persons in our society are the psychiatrist and the bar tender, and both for the same reason. For each hears the stories of hurting clients. When one selects a confidant one looks for certain conditions: (1) the person in whom I confide must not judge me, condemning me in any way for what I may reveal about myself.; (2) I must sense a continuing respect and caring from my confidant; (3) I must trust my confidant that nothing I say will be used in any way to harm me; (4) I must be assured that what I reveal will be kept in strict confidence. For some this confidence is found in a family member. For others in a friend; while others seek professional help for such a confidant.

Peter sees that the Christian's relationship to God can be as with a confidant. In God we can have complete confidence. In Jesus Christ, God has bridged the gulf between us and himself, taking care of whatever might have been an obstacle to good trusting, caring, communication. We can pray to God and not be judged. In our prayer life we know of God's continuing care and love for us. In the privacy of prayer we have confidence that whatever we reveal to God, will be accepted, and that God has the power to bring good to us out of our trials and tribulations, foibles and failures.

PRAYER: O God, you hear and understand when I pray. You offer me a "shoulder to cry upon," and a safe place to confess my sin. Through the mercy of Christ. Amen.

~ ~ ~ ~ ~

APRIL 18

SUFFERING: TAKE IT OR LEAVE IT

But if you endure when you do right and suffer for it,
you have God's approval.

—I Peter 2:20

READ: I Peter 2:18-25

People in the Christian tradition have viewed personal suffering from two opposite points of view. There have been those who believe that if you are truly Christian, and have complete faith in Christ, you need not suffer. On the other hand, there have been Christians over the centuries who have seen suffering as a mark of true obedience. Each of these extremes can lead to some pretense. Those who believe that faith precludes suffering, can pretend to be especially blessed by God if no suffering has darkened their door. Or they might deny suffering in order to appear to have faith. A plastic smile face is worn to hide the trouble underneath. The other danger is a martyr complex in which the more you suffer the better a person you claim to be. Such persons may feign trouble and suffering with a sorry face to prove their own goodness.

Peter carefully distinguishes between suffering which can be avoided and suffering which is awarded unjustly. When you have done what you can to avoid trouble, and have lived in such a way as to do right and you still must suffer, such is unjust and patient endurance is admirable. We ought to do all we possibly can to avoid suffering, and to alleviate the conditions which might cause pain in others or in us. We dare not conclude that there is nothing we can do because suffering is God's will. Rather, we ought to acknowledge that God does not want us to suffer; but when we must, God will go through the "valley of the shadow of death" with us.

Looking to Jesus on the cross, who suffered unjustly for us, and knowing of his resurrection, can offer us the faith and courage we need for our times of trouble.

PRAYER: O God, help me to do what I can to remove trouble from my life and from the lives of others; but help me also to endure what I cannot change. In Christ. Amen

~ ~ ~ ~ ~ ~

APRIL 19

NOT A PRINCIPLE, A PERSON

Do not fear what they fear, and do not be intimidated,
but in your hearts sanctify Christ as Lord.

—I Peter 3:14-15

READ: I Peter 3:13-18

We have come through a long period of time when religion
was based upon rational proofs; and how we thought about God
was a principle we reasoned in our minds. We arrived at conclusions
which we were willing to defend in arguments with those of different
philosophies. So, a lot of people hid in a corner, so to speak, and
said, "I don't discuss religion or politics." And they were probably
wise not to. It is pointless to try to determine whether the God of
the Bible is better than the gods of other religions. Instead of such
intellectual exercises, Christians have a person whom they revere:
Jesus.

An awareness and a reverence for Jesus Christ is what we hold
on to. This relation to a real person who remains in our lives because
of the Resurrection, gives us courage to live, supports us in our
times of trial, and gives us a sense of purpose and direction in life.
No matter what others may believe, we look up to Jesus as the
model for our lives and the source of power for our living. The
more we can know about him through constant study of the Bible,
and the closer we can feel to him through prayer and meditation
the more secure will be our faith in God.

In this way reverence for Jesus Christ is expressed through the
worship of his people. The risen Christ is the reason Christians go
to church. That is why every Sunday is Resurrection Day.

PRAYER: Come into my heart, Lord Jesus. Amen.

~ ~ ~ ~ ~ ~

APRIL 20

NOW IS THE ONLY TIME

There is need of only one thing. Mary has chosen the
better part, which will not be taken away from her.

—Luke 10:42

READ: Luke 10:38-42

For some people the anticipation of an event and the
remembering of it are better that the event itself. Have you ever
felt that way. If you spend a great deal of emotional energy looking
forward to events which turn out not to give as much pleasure as
you had hoped for, there is something tragic going on in your life.
If events in your life, which do not provide much pleasure, are
remembered as better than they really were, there is something
unreal happening in your consciousness. While there is a valid
place for anticipation and nostalgia in life, the present moment is the
only one in which we are truly alive. Now is the only time we have.

While Martha was busy getting ready for something yet to come,
Mary was enjoying the fullness of the present moment with Jesus.
Jesus, himself, pointed to Mary's awareness of the moment as "the
better part which will not be taken away from her." (Luke10:42)
Having put away whatever concerns might have intruded, Mary was
free to hear everything Jesus had to say, to carefully observe everything
about him, and to allow his presence to fill her life. That, Martha
could not do. She was "worried and distracted by many things."

How fully do you enjoy each moment? Are your aware of the
beauty around you? Do you observe the less obvious details about
each person you meet? Are you aware each moment of God's

undergirding power and presence? God not only created us, but now sustains us each present moment.

PRAYER: O God, thank you for each moment of life; for every event in which your goodness is found; every relationship which reveals your love. In Christ. Amen

~ ~ ~ ~ ~

APRIL 21

ACT YOUR AGE

Do not work for food that perishes, but for the food that endures for eternal life, which the Son of Man will give you. For it is on him that God the Father has set his seal.

—John 6:27

READ: Colossians 3:1-4 and Psalm 90:1-12

A college religion professor once told his class of his desire to be seen as wise, so that students would seek his counsel. He therefore hoped that his hair would turn gray, to make him look wise. Instead it fell out and he became bald. Some early teenagers in middle school try to dress and appear like high school seniors. Some folk who are past their prime try to dress and act like young adults, or worse yet like teen-agers. On the other hand the person who is content with his or her own particular age, whatever it may be, is a person with a good self-image. It is refreshing to find someone who does not seem to be bothered by his/her age.

The Christian faith refers to this lack of concern for age, as eternity. To focus upon what is eternal is to concentrate on God's intention for the world, rather than upon temporary pleasures and fancies. When the true meaning and significance of our lives rests upon God, who is "from everlasting to everlasting,"

(Psalm 90:2) it won't matter what our number of years may be. What we do in response to God takes on the eternal dimension of his work.

Jesus advises us not to commit our lives to values which come and go, and will soon perish; but rather to give our lives to eternal values which will never disappear. When we follow his advice we find that we are quite satisfied to be twenty-five, or eighty-six, or any other age." Whatever the age, God reveals his intention for us at that moment in time, intention for us to serve God's eternal purposes.

PRAYER: Help me to be content with my particular age, and to spend my life productively for your eternal purpose, O God. In Christ. Amen.

~ ~ ~ ~ ~ ~

APRIL 22

TRUE CONTENTMENT

Keep your lives free from the love of money, and be content with what you have; for he has said, "I will never leave you or forsake you"

—Hebrews 13:5

READ: Philippians 4:8-13

One of the popular misconceptions about domestic cats is that they are content. They are not. Anyone who lives with a cat knows that when they are inside they want to be outside, and when they are outside they scratch at the door to come in. When they are fed tuna, they want kidney, and when you give them kidney they want tuna, and it had better be a name brand. The only time a cat seems to live up to the myth of contentment, is when the cat is asleep. And even then it twitches once in a while.

Some lives are like that of a cat—always discontented. We want more money to move to another place; to have an entirely different set of circumstances including new relationships to replace the old.

Paul wrote from prison, of all places: "I have learned to be content with whatever I have." He declares further that he is ready for anything life may bring through the strength which God gives him. The fact that he wrote this from prison lends credibility to his words.

While it is intriguing to ponder what tomorrow may bring, it is quite realistic to assume that tomorrow will be much like today. Today's circumstances make up my life situation, not some other desired description. God asks us to be faithful in our present conditions. It is our own selves which hopefully will grow and change to meet tomorrow's realities. As God did for Paul, he will provide us with power and wisdom to live faithfully in the present moment and circumstance. This is true contentment.

PRAYER: Most merciful God give me grace to fulfill faithfully my commitment to Christ in the circumstances of my life today. In Christ. Amen.

~ ~ ~ ~ ~ ~

APRIL 23

MAKING THE MOST OF TWO BITS

"To one he gave five talents, to another two, to another one, each according to his ability."

—Matthew 25:15

READ: Matthew 25:14-23

It is difficult for a young person to learn to live with whatever level of capability he or she possesses. It is so easy to point to others who are more talented in one field or another. It is also easy to ignore or down-play ones own abilities. An older and wiser pastor once said to a young student, "Some people have nickel minds, others have quarter minds, and still others have dollar minds. If yours is a two bit mind, make sure that it is the best two bit mind possible." Whatever one's capability, it ought to be used to the fullest.

Whatever our capacity, it is a gift from God and should be used to further God's intentions for the world. The master in the parable noted above, was as pleased with the work of the two talent servant as he was with the five talent worker. It is a tragedy when a person refuses to contribute to society from his own meager resource merely because someone else may have more to offer. If you can sing in the shower, bring your voice to choir. Can you read? A great deal of what you read can develop your understanding of the world, and allow you to take part more constructively, if in no other way, through your responsible voting. God wants you, whatever your talent.

PRAYER: O God, I thank you for my life and its talents. Help me use these talents for your work. In Christ. Amen.

~ ~ ~ ~ ~ ~

APRIL 24

OVER THE SHOULDER

You shall not covet your neighbor's house; you shall not covet your neighbor's wife, or male or female slave, or ox, or donkey, or anything that belongs to your neighbor.
—Exodus 20:17

READ: Proverbs 27:7-10

Have you recently been at a social event like a coffee hour, when the person talking with you was looking over your shoulder to see who else to visit with? This is very offensive, not only because eye contact is broken, but because of the implication that there is someone better to talk to out there. In the selection from Proverbs noted above there are these words: "Better is a neighbor who is nearby than kindred who are far away." (Proverbs 7:10) Celebrate the relationships you already have in your life. Whoever they are, the people in your life circle—friends and relatives—loved ones and strangers—are God's gift to you. The relationships which develop close at hand may well be among the most meaningful and significant dimensions of your life. Nathaniel Hawthorn has a story of a man who traveled the globe in search of love, only to find it in a neighbor back home when he returned.

This concept can be expanded to include one's political and social activity. True, each of us will probably not influence the course of history in any dramatic way. What then can I do for world peace?

Studies in peacemaking these days are showing us that peace begins in the one-on-one relationships each of us has in everyday life. Making peace with those in your own family or work-place is the beginning, for you are making peace in what Robert McAffee Brown calls, "the global village."

PRAYER: "Let there be peace on earth; and let it begin with me." Through Christ. Amen.

~ ~ ~ ~ ~ ~

APRIL 25

RAISED EXPECTATIONS

For everyone who asks receives, and everyone who searches finds, and for everyone who knocks the door will be opened.

—Matthew 7:8

READ: Matthew 7:7-11

One's mood can be very different after Easter, if one follows the Christian themes of the season. Before Easter there was an air of expected doom. Good Friday was still to come. Jesus would still hang on the cross. And there would be sorrow because of it. Two of the statements Jesus made plaintively just before his death express this doleful mood. "If it is possible, let this cup pass from me,"(Matthew 26:39) spoken in the garden at Gethsemane: and, "My God, why have you forsaken me?" (Matthew 27:46) uttered from the cross. The Resurrection answers both of these pleas with a very positive expectation. God did not forsake Jesus. He took the cup from him ultimately. While there was little expectation of relief when Jesus first spoke those words, there is now expectation and assurance of God's good answer to Jesus' yearning.

Because of Easter; because of the Resurrection, we now have our expectations raised. Our pleas do not fall on deaf ears. History is not locked into a downward slide. Things need not turn out badly. The resurrection of Christ has the power to raise our expectations from deadened yearnings to lively anticipations. "For everyone who asks receives."(Matthew 7:8) Because Jesus asked in Gethsemane and at Calvary and God answered in the empty tomb, you and I can expect God's good answer to our deepest longing. Because Jesus was raised, our expectations are raised.

PRAYER: Oh, almighty God, who raised Jesus Christ from the dead, we raise our hearts to you in humble expectation of your gracious gift of life. In Jesus Christ. Amen.

~ ~ ~ ~ ~ ~

APRIL 26

RAISED THOUGHTS

Finally, beloved, whatever is true, whatever is honorable,

whatever is just, Whatever is pure, whatever is pleasing, whatever is commendable, if there is any excellence and if there is anything worthy of praise, think about these things.

—Philippians 4:8

READ: Philippians 4:1-9

Thoughts are catching. Have you ever noticed how a conversation can be markedly changed when another person enters the room? The topic can be gossip, or worse, until a respected person enters; and then the thoughts of the group seem to be lifted to a higher level.

Because of the presence of Christ in our midst, our thoughts can be noticeably changed from mean or dismal, selfish or resentful to thoughts which are more positive and up-building. Because of the resurrection of Jesus from the dead, our thoughts can be raised.

Paul is urging his Christian friends in Philippi to lift their thought to a higher level using specific words to outline such raised thoughts: TRUE, HONORABLE, JUST, PURE, PLEASING, COMMENDABLE. It is significant that these are the very terms which apply to Christ. Think of each of these words and ponder how each describes something important about Jesus. Had Good Friday been the end of the story we would have felt betrayed, and unable to put much confidence in Jesus' qualities of truth, honor, justice, purity, goodness and loveliness. We would have felt that the world crushed such qualities when it put Jesus to death. But because God raised Jesus, vindicating his attributes, our thoughts can be raised. There is now reason to think good thoughts. These characteristics of human life have been affirmed and made worthy of our effort to attain them.

PRAYER: O God, lift my thoughts so that they are good, true, noble, right, pure, lovely, and honorable. Through the Risen Christ. Amen.

~ ~ ~ ~ ~ ~

APRIL 27

RAISED ACTIONS

But love your enemies, do good, and lend, expecting
nothing in return. Your reward will be great, and you will be
children of the Most High; for he is kind to the ungrateful
and the wicked.

—Luke 6:35

READ: Luke 6:27-36

Christian faith and the earlier faith of Israel present a God
who acts. God called Abraham, led the people, spoke through the
prophets, ruled through the kings, sent his Son, brought a new
order in Jesus, raised him after the death on the cross, and spread
reconciling love to the ends of the earth. Notice the active verbs.
Ever since the days of the Bible, Christian people have actively
engaged in God's work in the world. In our time some of the most
significant action in which Christians are engaged is aimed at
bringing peace and justice to human society. For some that entails
traditional missionary activities of evangelism, healing, teaching,
and economic and social assistance. Others are led into hunger
programs around the world, efforts to help victims of AIDS, peace
demonstrations, civil rights efforts, advocacy for the poor and oppressed,
or assistance for handicapped. What will your action verbs be?

Jesus shows us that our activities should extend to our enemies
and that we should be uncalculating without thought of result.
God, he said, would reward in his own way. Peacemaking in our
violent world begins when I forgive my own personal enemy, and
pray for him or her. The cynical among us laugh at such an
approach, and ridicule Christian efforts at peacemaking. But the
actions of Christians are raised to new heights of effectiveness
because Jesus Christ has been raised from the dead and justice and
love have been vindicated. The Resurrection gives us incentive to
raise the level of our actions toward love, justice and peace for all.

PRAYER: Lift my hands, O God, to new levels of action for my risen Lord. Amen.

~ ~ ~ ~ ~ ~

APRIL 28

RAISED HOPES

We have this hope, a sure and steadfast anchor of the soul, a hope that enters the inner shrine behind the curtain, where Jesus, a forerunner on our behalf, has entered having become a high priest forever.

—Hebrews 6:19-20

READ: Hebrews 6:13-20

In Old Testament times the hopes of the people hinged upon the work of the High Priest who made sacrifices on their behalf. The High Priest had the privilege and responsibility of going into the very holiest placed in the Temple, there to meet God and to secure God's blessings for the nation, Israel. But the High Priest, himself, had to go through purification rites in order to be worthy of such action and experience. So the hopes finally rested upon a mortal man, who could certainly have his own failings. Indeed over the centuries the fortunes of Israel rose and fell as the quality and faithfulness of its leaders, both kings and priests wavered.

The writer of Hebrews, assures us that our hope for eternal life, for God's rich blessings, is dependent now upon one whose life and sacrifice are perfect—Jesus Christ. Because of the Resurrection we know that Christ is more than man; he is God's own son. When he enters the presence of God on our behalf our future is secure, our hopes are raised.

PRAYER: I thank you, O Christ, for bringing me such high hope for eternal life, here and now, as well as later on. Amen.

~ ~ ~ ~ ~ ~

APRIL 29

TO TELL THE WHOLE TRUTH

"For this I was born, and for this I came into the world,
to testify to the truth. Everyone who belongs to the truth
listens to my voice."—John 18:37
"I am the way, and the truth, and the life."
—John 14:6

READ: John 14:1-7

Following long standing custom, witnesses appearing in court are asked to swear to "tell the truth, the whole truth, and nothing but the truth." Much of the justice done in the courts depends upon honest compliance with that promise. Recently a man wrongly sentenced to prison was released after serving mistakenly for nine long years. His release and eventual justice were obtained on the basis of someone finally bearing witness to the truth, bringing forward thereby the one who had actually committed the crime.

Jesus said of himself that he was the one who was born to bear witness to the truth. On the basis of his witness the rest of us are given release from sin. We are set free from the cells of injustice in which we live. On Jesus' testimony to the truth, we now know what God wants of us and what God's love is all about. In fact until Jesus' birth, it was impossible for people to know God as fully as we can now know God. It is as if Jesus uncovered the face of God and brought God into our daily lives as a living reality.

How can Jesus do this? Strangely, it is because he himself not only tells the truth but to use his words, he is the truth. Thus, if you want to know the truth of God, study Jesus. Dwell on his words as the gospel writers record them. Walk with him on his journey from town to town. Go with him as he cares for human need and as he proclaims the Kingdom of God. Come to know the whole truth in Christ.

PRAYER: O Christ, show me the truth about myself, about your world, and above all the truth of God's love for me. Amen.

~ ~ ~ ~ ~ ~

APRIL 30

A MATTER OF BREATH AND LIFE

Then the Lord God formed man from the dust of the ground, and breathed into his nostrils the breath of life; and the man became a living being.

—Genesis 2:7

He was in the beginning with God. All things came into being through him, and without him not one thing came into being. What has come into being in him was life, and the life was the light of all people.

—John 1:2-4

READ: Genesis 2:4-9 and John 1:1-5

Amid the current controversy over teaching creationism in the schools, little is said of the fact that Genesis 1 and 2 contain two differing stories of creation. While they differ in order and detail, they agree theologically. God is affirmed as the ultimate source of all that is. Furthermore, a third story of creation is to be found in the New Testament in the first chapter of John. John doesn't seem to conflict with science because he doesn't try to answer any scientific questions about the process of creation. What he does give us is the Christian theological belief that human life depends upon God for its ultimate origin and that from the very beginning the Word of God brought life into this world. John affirms that the Word made flesh is Christ.

Thus it is most significant that Jesus defined himself as life. Isn't it deeply right that the One who made us and breathed life into us should be the One to show us how to live—the One who gives us new life now! "I came that they may have life and have it more abundantly." (John 10:10)

PRAYER: O God, I thank you for every breath of life, and for the abundant life you breathe into me through Christ, the Word. In Him. Amen.

MAY

MAY 1

DON'T ROCK THE BOAT!

Conduct yourselves honorably among the Gentiles, so that, though, they malign you as evildoers, they may see your honorable deeds and glorify God when he comes to judge.

—I Peter 2:12

READ: I Peter 2:9-17 and 4:12-18

"Don't rock the boat," has come to express an overly cautious lack of courage. However, there is a deeper sense in which Christians in a society guided by other values need to heed such advice. In I Peter Christians in a hostile environment are cautioned to conduct themselves honorably so that the non-Christians might look upon the Christian faith more favorably. Some years ago in an interview with Terry Waite, who had been taken hostage while trying to gain release of other hostages in Iran, Barbara Walters asked him why he did not escape at a critical point when he could have used violence to free himself. Waite explained that he had previously tried to persuade the hostage takers to use their minds and hearts instead of violence to solve political problems, and that if he had used violence in his own case, it would have rendered his message a hypocritical lie. Waite had served as a catalyst by which a few hostages had been set free. His determination to preserve the credibility of his witness prevented his escape. He might have remembered Jesus' words: "But if salt has lost its taste, how can its saltiness be restored? It is no longer good for anything . . ." (Matthew 5:13)

In ways we may not realize, we are being watched. If we are identified as Christians by others in the world around us, how we respond to life situations will be seen as a Christian response. It is our responsibility to reflect the message of Christ and not some other. Peter advises that proper conduct may very well bring a favorable view of God. Again Jesus comments, "that they may see your good works and glorify your Father who is in heaven." (Matthew 5:16)

PRAYER: Help me, O God, to give glory to you through my life and conduct. In Christ. Amen.

⁓ ⁓ ⁓ ⁓ ⁓ ⁓

MAY 2

SEARCH AND RESCUE

Finally, brothers and sisters, pray for us, so that the
word of the Lord may be spread rapidly and be glorified
everywhere, just as it is among you, and that we may be
rescued from wicked and evil people for not all have faith.
—II Thessalonians 3:2

READ: II Thessalonians 3:1-15 and Genesis 8:1-5, 12-19

We search. God rescues. The Bible, almost from start to finish, is the story of God's rescue, God's salvation. God setting us free, and redeeming us. When Paul considered his relationship to those without faith he used the term "rescue." He asked his fellow Christians in Thessalonica to pray for his rescue. He saw the Christian people of faith in sharp contrast to those who did not have faith, calling them the wicked and evil ones. God's rescuing work began when he rescued Noah and his family from the destruction of the world around them. God rescued the people of Israel through Moses and released them from Egyptian captivity. Christians affirm that the greatest rescue of all was the raising of Jesus from evil's death-grip.

From what aspects of the world around us do we need rescuing? We need rescuing from over-attention to material goods and the love of wealth; from greed, envy and strife; from self-destructive attempts to solve life's problems through one addiction or another. We need to be rescued from interpersonal rivalries, resentments, and from temptation to give in to the lusts of the flesh. We are in need of rescue from many of the destructive excesses and tragic violence in today's secular society.

Like New Testament Christians, we affirm with thanksgiving that God has rescued us and brought us into a colony of safety in a dangerous world.

PRAYER: O God, rescue me from the forces "out there" which would destroy me. Through Christ. Amen.

~ ~ ~ ~ ~ ~

MAY 3

ON NOT GOING NATIVE

> For this is the will of God, your sanctification . . . that each of you know how to control your own body in holiness and honor, not with lustful passion, like the Gentiles who do not know God.
>
> —I Thessalonians 4:3-5

READ: I Thessalonians 4:1-12

What the Old Testament calls idolatry, we might call "going native," meaning that one adopts the thought and behavior, values and customs of the surrounding neighborhood. Paul was concerned about this temptation among the Christians in Thessalonica. He urged them to live a life of purity according to God's will rather than a life of lust and licence as do others who do not know God.

In New Testament times the Christian groups in each city were surrounded by people who believed and acted very differently from the standards set for Christians. The Christians needed constantly to monitor their own actions lest they "go native," and fall into commonly practiced immorality of every kind.

In our time we see much behavior and many life styles which do not meet Christian standards by any stretch of the imagination. Mass media reinforces the thought and behavior of the majority population by constantly giving us the results of polls showing what the norms of behavior and thought are. So, we are told that one out of four teen agers is sexually active, and therefore any teaching of sexual abstinence before marriage is naive and misses the mark. So we are subtly encouraged to settle for the average. Such analysis may be used to shape public policy, but if the Christian today is to avoid "going native" on this matter, then our basis for deciding what to do and what to teach, must come from a source other than the consensus of the general population. In other words, our source is God and God's will for us. Allowing God's Spirit to sanctify us, will of necessity make us different from others in thought and behavior.

PRAYER: Help me to know your will, O God, and give me courage to follow it in every area of my thinking and my living. Through Christ. Amen.

~ ~ ~ ~ ~ ~

MAY 4

WHISTLING IN THE DARK

So then, brothers and sisters, stand firm and hold fast
to the traditions that you were taught by us, either by word
of mouth or by letter.

—II Thessalonians 2:15

READ: II Thessalonians 2:13-17

For a group to remain distinct and intact, and not to merge into the surrounding scenery, certain rituals and traditions must be kept. In this way members of the group are given a special identity which is reinforced as the history and stories of the group are constantly re-told and remembered. Christmas and Easter are two times when churches do this especially well. But Paul is encouraging the church in Thessalonica to hold to its traditions and to practice its rituals all the time, not just on special days.

A little like whistling in the dark, remembering our traditions helps to maintain in us the values these stories embody. While passing through a dark world, we celebrate the light of Christ, and our Christian traditions turn the darkness into light.

In a pluralistic society in which not everyone shares our Christian traditions, it is essential that in each of our homes and families, we remember the words and images of our tradition in celebration and conversation. "Tell me the old, old story!"

PRAYER: Help me to hold fast to the wonderful story of your redeeming love for all the world, O God. In Christ. Amen,

~ ~ ~ ~ ~ ~

MAY 5

JESUS THE PREACHER

Jesus answered, "Let us go to the neighboring towns that I may proclaim the message there also; for that is what I came out to do."

—Mark 1:38

READ: Luke 4:16-20

The word, "preacher" doesn't have very good "vibes" these days. Too often it implies "preachy" or being "preached at." In Jesus' time the use of the word is more readily understood as "to proclaim," as a king's herald would do when he brings a message from the king. It is a word of authority with no hesitation or apology. Jesus brought a proclamation or announcement from God to humankind. Jesus regarded himself as having come with truth which all the world needed to hear.

We are surrounded and submerged by proclamations of all sorts. The media shouts its ads to us day and night, and news casts report the messages of people in high places daily. Add to that the fact that we have grown so accustomed to Jesus that what he proclaims does not seem newsworthy to us. Consequently we need to pay special attention to the story of Jesus and to the message which he *preached.*

We need to know what kind of life God intends for us in his kingdom. Jesus preaches that. We need to know that God reaches into the life of the world to rescue people from their own folly. Jesus preaches that. We need to know the good news that God wants peace and justice, and wholeness for each of us. Jesus preaches that. We need to know that God wants us to change direction in our lives so that we live for God and in harmony and helpfulness with each other. Jesus preaches that.

PRAYER: Oh God, I thank you, that you sent Jesus the preacher, to proclaim your good news. In Christ. Amen.

~ ~ ~ ~ ~ ~

MAY 6

JESUS THE TEACHER

When Jesus saw the crowds, he went up the mountain; and after he sat down, his disciples came to him. Then he began to speak, and taught them . . . .
—Matthew 5:1-2

READ: Matthew 5:1-11

Jesus taught in quite a number of different "classrooms." These included synagogues, the Temple, at the seaside and in cities and villages. The very well-known and popular sermon, which is noted for today was on a mountain. Sometimes he taught his disciples as he walked along the roadways. They referred to him as "Rabbi," which meant master-teacher.

Jesus not only taught in words, but in deeds as well, modeling for his listeners the life he taught. He invites us to live by his words and influence by his life as well. He showed us how to love others by loving those whom he met along the way. He did so in very concrete ways, often healing them of whatever distressed them. He taught honesty and integrity in the way he addressed and spoke to the Pharisees.

The most well known of Jesus' teachings are put together by Matthew in what we have come to call the Sermon on the Mount. Within that teaching is the most succinct and memorable portion known as the Beatitudes. In that lesson, Jesus told us what makes for happiness. "Happy are the merciful . . . happy are the humble . . . happy are those who want to do what God requires . . . happy are the pure in heart . . . happy are those who work for peace," is the way one modern version of Matthew puts it.

Jesus' teaching goes on from generation to generation as people continue to study the words and deeds of Jesus, the teacher, and as they try to apply his teaching to their everyday living. In a time when we are pulled in all directions, and when we feel the need for guidance, Jesus can teach us the way to live.

PRAYER: Thank you, O God, for Jesus, the master teacher of our lives. In his name. Amen.

~ ~ ~ ~ ~ ~

MAY 7

JESUS THE PHYSICIAN

When Jesus heard this, he said to them, "Those who
are well have no need of a physician, but those who are sick;
I have come to call not the righteous but sinners."

—Mark 2:17

READ: Mark 2:13-17

When we think of healing, we immediately think of the physical body. In many Yellow Pages the listings of physicians far outnumber those of churches. While health-care costs soar, church offerings shrink. So much emphasis is given to diet and exercise and to many different health issues, while our culture seems to relegate the "cure of souls" to a quaint past time for those who like such things as religion

Is it any wonder then that the healing which we remember Jesus performing are those instances when he healed bodies? We tend to forget the incidents when Jesus healed people of the universal human disease of sin. Levi, the tax collector was healed of his sin of greed. The Samaritan woman was healed of her sin when she met Jesus at the well. The woman taken in adultery found forgiveness and new life when Jesus healed her. In much of the physical healing Jesus linked such healing to his forgiving of sin.

Jesus brought peace into the lives of people. He said. "Peace I leave with you. My peace I give to you." (John 14:27) In our frenzied lives, we need peace and forgiveness which Jesus the physician of souls brings to us.

PRAYER: Take from my mind the strain and stress, give me peace and forgiveness, that my soul may be cured, O Christ. Amen.

~ ~ ~ ~ ~ ~

MAY 8

JESUS THE SHEPHERD

"For the Son of Man came to seek out and to save the lost."—Luke 19:10 "I Am the good shepherd. The good shepherd lays down his life for the sheep."

—John 10:11

READ: Luke 15:3-7

Jesus often uses the imagery of the shepherd to describe himself and the work he is doing. An important element in the task of the shepherd is to seek the lost ones. He is our shepherd who seeks us when we are lost.

These days a great amount of attention is given to finding oneself. Some parents of young adults have sadly confided to their friends that their son has moved home to try and "find himself." In some cases this quest for one's own identity goes on for many years. In a related effort many people are seeking meaning for their lives and their place in the scheme of things. On the deepest level these searches are for God. Isn't it a comfort to know that while we are seeking God, God is seeking us! Many times our search for self can obstruct God's search for us. So engrossed in self-fulfilment efforts are we that, we hardly sit still long enough to allow God to enter our lives.

Jesus sought out those whom he needed for his inner circle. The stories in the New Testament which tell us of Jesus calling his disciples are models of how he seeks each one of us to be his follower. When we are lost in a confusion of experiences which toss us to and fro, Jesus comes as our shepherd, to remove us from the thicket in which we are tangled, and to show us the way.

PRAYER: Seek me, O Christ, save me from being lost in confusion, doubt and despair. Show me your way for my life. Amen.

~ ~ ~ ~ ~ ~

MAY 9

JESUS THE SON OF MAN

Then he took the twelve aside and said to them, "See, we are going up to Jerusalem, and everything that is written about the Son of Man by the prophets will be accomplished."

—Luke 18:31

READ: Matthew 26:57-66

"Son of Man" is the name Jesus often uses to describe himself. Yet it is difficult to understand its full implication. It is the self-description which cost him his life. "Jesus said to him . . . 'From now on you will see the Son of Man seated at the right hand of Power and coming on the clouds of heaven.' Then the High Priest said . . . 'He has blasphemed . . . he deserves death.'" (Matthew 26:64-66)

"Son of Man" was startling to the Jews because they understood the term to mean the one who would establish a victorious Kingdom of God which would last forever. But Jesus gave the term a deeper meaning when he said, "For the he (Son of Man) will be handed over to the Gentiles; and he will be mocked and insulted and spat upon. After they have flogged him, they will kill him, and on the third day he will rise again." (Luke 18:32)

Jesus knew that he was what the prophets had spoken of, whom we call the Suffering Servant, and that his suffering would be for our ultimate salvation In the term, "Son of Man," we see reflected the cross and the resurrection, the coming of the Kingdom of God, and our redemption. What a term it is!

PRAYER: May the Son of Man claim me as one of his own, O God. Through Christ. Amen.

~ ~ ~ ~ ~ ~

MAY 10

THE MOST IMPORTANT IDEA

After his suffering he presented himself alive to them
by many convincing proofs, appearing to them during forty
days and speaking about the kingdom of God.

—Acts 1:3

READ: Acts 1:1-4 and Matthew 28:16-20

If you had only a few minutes to speak with your family before
leaving on a very long trip, what would you tell them? No matter
what is on such an agenda, you can be sure that each item would
be of great importance. If only one thing could be shared, it would
be the most important of all. In reading the stories of Jesus' very
last moments with his disciples we can be assured that the very
most important subjects were covered. There was no time for trivia
or small talk. The account of the last moments with Jesus as given
in Acts says that the one thing Jesus talked about with his disciples
was the kingdom of God. Jesus' idea of the kingdom of God must
therefore be a most important idea. If we are Jesus' followers, we
should understand the idea of the kingdom of God.

Many Bible scholars believe that the kingdom of God sums
up Jesus' entire life. He came to proclaim it. His life, death and
resurrection define in a significant way the kingdom of God, insofar
as he is lifted up as the king in the cross and resurrection. When he
talked with his disciples at the end of his time with them he was
affirming that in him the kingdom of God had come. The new
kingdom had come, and his disciples were a part of it.

It follows that you and I, as followers of Christ, are subjects of
the King. We dwell in his kingdom. This new identity for each of
us should re-shape our entire lives. Bring to this idea what you
remember from childhood stories of good monarchs, and their
loyal subjects. As subjects of Christ, the King, we worship him, we
follow his orders, we trust our lives and our destinies to him, and
we do all we can to defend him and his kingdom.

As you live in the midst of today's world at work, at home, and in your community, you serve Christ as king. Think what that means each day!

PRAYER: O Christ, my King, I worship and obey you. Amen.

~ ~ ~ ~ ~

MAY 11

THE MOST IMPORTANT JOB

"But you will receive power when the Holy Spirit has
come upon you; and you will be my witnesses in Jerusalem,
in all Judea and Samaria, and to the ends of the earth."
—Acts 1:8

READ: Acts 1:6-8 and Mark 16:14-20

When one leaves on an extended trip there are usually important tasks which must be done by those who are left behind, like feeding the cat, paying bills, and cutting the grass. A teacher must leave lesson plans for the substitute. The vice president needs to briefed about the meeting to be conducted.

When Jesus departed from his "assistants" he commissioned them to do the most important work in his kingdom. The disciples were directed to bear witness to the life, death and resurrection of Jesus, and to make his kingdom known to the whole world. Tradition has it that each disciple went to a different region of the world to witness to Jesus: Thomas to India, Andrew to Asia Minor, Peter to Rome, John to Ephesus, Philip to Asia. We know also that later missionaries of the gospel covered the globe witnessing to Christ and salvation.

What does this mean for us today? How are we to do the most important job as followers of Christ? It seems apparent that every day we can witness to Christ by being hopeful of God's victory over evil, by working for justice, mercy and peace, by encouraging the downcast and the lonely, by caring for the environment, and by sharing God's love with those who suffer. And we can support the worldwide mission of our church through our prayers and our giving.

PRAYER: Help me to witness to you, O Christ, wherever I am, Amen.

~ ~ ~ ~ ~

MAY 12

THE MOST IMPORTANT ASSURANCE

"Men of Galilee, why do you stand looking up toward heaven? This Jesus who has been taken from you into heaven, will come in the same way you saw him go into heaven."
—Acts 1:11

READ: Acts 1:9-11 and John 21:20-24

In preparing for his departure Jesus told the parable of the talents, in which a landowner, before leaving on a trip, entrusts his business to three servants. He returns for the accounting of each servant. In modern language a summary of the message of this story might be: "Don't just stand there, get busy. When I get back I want to see results!"

Jesus' promise of his return is the most important assurance to the disciples because it holds them accountable for their lives and productivity after Jesus' departure. Ever upon their minds is the anticipation of that time in the future when they will want to report their activities and their faithfulness to Jesus. When they will say: "Here, Lord, is an accounting of how I tried to do what you wanted me to do."

Because you and I are assured of Jesus' return, we are motivated to get to work. We know that it is his approval that we seek, his evaluation which counts, and his desires which must be uppermost in our decision-making.

This is not so strange an idea of the second coming as we usually have about Jesus' return. In many jobs there is an annual review. That makes for better workers. Isn't that a way of describing how Christ relates to each of us with loving concern for how we are doing with his work?

PRAYER: help me, O Christ, to have a good review, Amen.

~ ~ ~ ~ ~

MAY 13

THE MOST IMPORTANT RESPONSE

> All these were constantly devoting themselves to prayer,
> together with certain women, including Mary the mother
> of Jesus, as well as his brothers.
>
> —Acts 1:14

READ: Acts 1:12-14 and Luke 24:50-53

What would you do if you were presented with the most important message of Christ—the Kingdom of God, and you were asked to share this idea with the world, and you were told that Jesus would return to see how you were doing? That is the send-off the disciples experienced. What was their response?

(1) They stuck together; (2) They prayed. An awesome responsibility is more easily done when done with others and in continuing communication with the one assigning the task.

The most important response of Christians is to pray together in a group, worshiping God as a community of faith and obedience. You cannot be a Christian alone. It is not a solo performance or a private delight. It is a group experience, a corporate activity, a group identity. Jesus calls us into the church to be his people, as he called the disciples into his band of close-knit followers. The only disciple who went out on his own separating himself from the group was Judas, who betrayed Jesus. The other eleven remained together as a group, and faithful to Jesus.

Trouble begins when an individual sets out to formulate religious beliefs and requirements on his or her own, without continual submission of such ideas and practices to the wisdom and discipline of the church. Even our private prayer and devotion should be understood as an extension of the whole church at prayer.

PRAYER: Help us to be your people, O God, and to carry out your work together. In Christ. Amen.

~ ~ ~ ~ ~ ~

MAY 14

THE MOST IMPORTANT QUALIFICATION

> So one of the men who have accompanied us during all the time that the Lord Jesus went in and out among us, beginning with the baptism of John until the day when he was taken up from us—one of these must become a witness with us to his resurrection.
>
> —Acts 1:21-22

READ: Acts 1:15-22

The first major decision the group of followers of Jesus faced was that of replacing Judas. The significance for us in this account of the early church's problem is that in the selection process, the most important qualification for church leadership is clearly set forth. Those who are to represent Christ in the work of the church must be people who know Christ well, having shared in his story from beginning to end.

Here is the mandate for a thorough and effective educational program in the church. We need to teach each generation of disciples the story of Christ so well that they can be judged to have been "with Jesus from his baptism to his ascension."

When a child or a young person has been given the opportunity to know and experience Jesus Christ so deeply that he or she responds to the call of Christ, then that person is fit to be a loyal subject in the Kingdom of God. This task of educating in the faith we must do in our homes as well as in our churches. In so doing good and faithful leadership for Christ's church will be made available.

PRAYER: Help me to share the faith with children and youth, as well as with adults. In Christ. Amen.

~ ~ ~ ~ ~ ~

MAY 15

NO LONGER ALONE

Meanwhile the church throughout Judea, Galilee, and Samaria had peace and was built up. Living in the fear of the Lord and in the comfort of the Holy Spirit, it increased in numbers

—Acts 9:31

READ: Acts 9:26-31

When you must face a tough situation it is particularly difficult if you have to go through the ordeal alone. What a relief it is in such a situation when a friend or loved one volunteers to accompany you as you face the difficult confrontation or experience. It is such a comfort, we would say. It is this use of the word "comfort" that the New Testament applies to the action and the presence of the Holy Spirit in our lives. The King James version had the phrase, "Walking . . . in the comfort of the Holy Ghost." Acts 9:31 (King James Bible)

We live in a time and in a society in which many people are very much alone. Young people often tell us that they have no one to talk to, no one who will really listen to them. The popularity of advice columns in newspapers, and call-in programs on radio and TV expose the loneliness of thousands of listeners and viewers. Frequently the most significant assistance given by a counselor is to "sit where the person is" and to listen to the yearnings and questions of that person's innermost life. In a highly competitive society each of us needs an advocate, someone to befriend and defend us. This function of the Holy Spirit is one of the most needed ministries in our time—someone to stand by, and thereby to strengthen us. *Walking in the comfort of the Holy Spirit.*

The early Christians felt very much alone in a world which opposed their faith. Acts declares that it was the Holy Spirit who comforted such believers. Certainly each Christian needs such befriending so that we need no longer face life alone.

PRAYER: Stand by me, O Holy Spirit and give me comfort. In Christ. Amen

~ ~ ~ ~ ~ ~

MAY 16

THE OLD ELECTRIC LIGHT BULB

Then the Spirit said to Philip, "Go over to this chariot and join it."

—Acts 8:29

READ: Acts 8:26-40

Do you remember the old electric light bulb used in cartoons and comic strips to indicate a sudden idea, a flash of insight? The electric light bulb could be a modern symbol for the Holy Spirit. If one were to put the story of Philip in Acts 8 in a cartoon strip, there would be a frame in which Philip would be shown with a light bulb over his head and the words: "Go over to that carriage, and stay there," That was a moment of significant insight for Philip, even though at that point he was unaware of its far-reaching implications. The result was the conversion of an Ethiopian man to Christ. Notice that Philip was not led every step of the way like a puppet. As soon as he obeyed the initial command of God, it seems to be Philip's resources which enabled him to speak effectively with the stranger. Not that God was not involved in what followed, but that Philip himself was taking action in obedience to God's original request.

Each of us needs to become alert to the messages of the Holy Spirit. The moment of truth, the flash of insight, the inner urging, all of which come to all of us, need to be taken seriously, as we discern the voice of God in our thinking process. Not every idea comes from God. Each thought needs to be carefully evaluated. The standard of judgment ought to be our knowledge of how God works. The Bible is the most helpful source of information about how God works and what God does. Philip discerned that the inner urging he experienced was the Spirit speaking to him. Hopefully we too will be able to reach such discernment.

PRAYER: Help me to discern the working of the Holy Spirit in my life, O God. In Christ. Amen.

〰 〰 〰 〰 〰 〰

MAY 17

CUSTOM FIT FAITH

Amazed and astonished, they asked, "Are not all those who are speaking Galileans? And how is it that we hear, each of us, in our native language?"

—Acts 2:7-8

READ: Acts 2:1-13

People vary widely in their religious consciousness, in their capacity for spiritual experience. Not every kind of religious experience is expected to happen to everyone. Each of us is a different person, though with certain similarities. From time to time someone who has had a particularly rewarding spiritual experience will want the rest of us to have the same. When we do not seem to have the same experience we are sometimes judged inferior. And yet each of us may have had his or her own individual experience which has been equally as important, and life shaping.

It is the Holy Spirit who custom fits the faith to each of us. That is one of the messages of the Pentecost story in Acts 2. The early disciples were filled with the Holy Spirit and He gave them the capacity to communicate the Christian message to a wide variety of people in a way that seemed to fit each one. Each one in the crowd that day heard the message in his or her own language.

The Holy Spirit brings the love of Christ to you and me where we are on our journey of life. He custom fits the message of Christ to each of us. If we have been hurt in a certain way, He brings insight at that point. To each need He brings fulfilment.

PRAYER: O Holy Spirit, come to me where I am and speak to me in my own language. In Christ. Amen.

~ ~ ~ ~ ~ ~

MAY 18

I JUST KNOW IT TO BE SO

And when he comes he will prove the world wrong
about sin and righteousness and judgment.

—John 16:8

READ: John 16:1-11

We live in a time when every idea seems to be up for grabs as to what is true and what is not true, what is right and what is wrong. People will say, "But who's to say what is right and what is wrong?" or "What you believe is a matter of private opinion. A thing is wrong only if you think it's wrong." This is a very spongy pathway to walk on. Nothing is solid. Nothing is true. We are bombarded with advertising messages all the time, until we are jaded and don't know what the "truth in advertising" really is. What to me is wrong may be right to you. Do we believe this? Are there not some things which I just know to be so?

As Christians we know what is acceptable to God and what is not. We know that Jesus is the Christ, our Savior and Lord. When challenged we say, "I just know it to be so." This hidden knowledge is the work of the Holy Spirit in our minds, convincing us of the truth and convicting us of the sin in our lives.

John tells us that Jesus told his disciples that he needed to leave them so that the Holy Spirit, the Helper, will come to our aid. The Holy Spirit tells each of us what the truth is. If we really believe Jesus' promise, we will know that the Holy Spirit will convict and convince the world, not just Christians of the righteousness and truth of God.

Our task is to follow the truth as we believe the Holy Spirit tells it. And to bear witness to his telling, so that more and more may believe and follow what God intends.

PRAYER: O Holy Spirit, tell me the truth about myself and the world, and of God's will. In Christ. Amen.

~ ~ ~ ~ ~

MAY 19

THEM BONES SHALL RISE AGAIN

When he said this he breathed on them and said to

them, "Receive the Holy Spirit. If you forgive the sins of
any, they are forgiven them; if you retain the sins of any,
they are retained."

—John 20:22-23

READ: John 20:19-23 and Ezekiel 37:7-10

"Them bones, them bones, shall rise again," from the old
spiritual which follows Exekiel 37 with its message that God will
restore life to the failing Israel. Similarly the story in John 20 shows
how God intends to offer new life to people who have failed his
intentions for their lives. John 20 is another "Pentecost" story of
the sending of the Holy Spirit into the gathering of Christ's
followers. Here Jesus gives the Holy Spirit to his inner circle of
disciples by breathing upon them. To the original readers this was
a very meaningful and familiar way of referring to the Holy Spirit,
who was understood as a wind, or breath. While one cannot see
the wind one feels its force nevertheless. Breath, though unseen, is
the essential life-giving element upon which we depend. Jesus was
giving such life to his disciples, the force of which would turn the
world upside down.

It is difficult for us to accept the implication that in this
giving of the Holy Spirit Jesus was giving to his followers the
authority to forgive sins or to withhold forgiveness. In its less
faithful periods the church has assumed this literally and abused
the mandate. But, look at it this way. Christ gives to his people
such a sensitive, caring capacity that they are made able to
bring God's healing and forgiving love to those who need God's
grace. Because forgiveness costs God the cross, God's grace is
precious to us. We must take care lest we cheapen it by offering
it dishonestly. Our task is to offer God's love to others as we
are directed by the Holy Spirit.

PRAYER: Help me, O Holy Spirit, to be a channel of your love
and grace to others. In Christ. Amen.

~ ~ ~ ~ ~ ~

MAY 20

ASK ONE WHO IS ONE

". . . for he his is an instrument whom I have chosen to
bring my name before Gentiles and kings and before the
people of Israel; I myself will show him how much he must
suffer for the sake of my name."

—Acts 9:15-16

READ: Acts 22:6-11

There is a formula which runs through the Bible, by which
one can summarize how God deals with us, what God wants us to
do. This formula appears over and over again as the key to
understanding what is going on in the Scriptures. Examining the
formula is like reading the directions for some new piece of
equipment. There is, however, a simpler way to learn the directions
for a new gadget. Ask someone who has a similar item.

Since the formula in the Bible has to do with people who
belong to God, the key to understanding what God wants to do in
your life is to "ask one who is one." One of God's own people! The
one to ask is Paul, He gives us a complete formula three times in
the book of Acts. The passage suggested above is one of his formulas
or directions.

The formula Paul uses has four steps: CALL, RESCUE,
SEPARATION, INHERITANCE. In all three descriptions of his
conversion to Christian faith Paul identities these four factors. God
called him by name: "Saul, Saul . . ." to follow God's commands
in a very specific way. God rescued Paul from his former ways of
thinking and acting. No longer would Paul spend his energies
persecuting Christians. God separated Paul from his former
situation. No longer would he be associated with the strong
Pharisaic Jews who were dead set upon removing Christianity from
the earth. Finally God gave Paul an inheritance involving both an
affirmation of his own roots as well as a life and mission he was to

assume in all his days to come. CALL, RESCUE, SEPARATION, INHERITANCE are the factors of our Christian lives as well.

PRAYER: Help me, O God, like Paul to become your own. In Christ. Amen.

~ ~ ~ ~ ~

MAY 21

WOE IS ME

"Now that this has touched your lips, your guilt has departed and your sin is blotted out."

—Isaiah 6:7

READ: Isaiah 6:1-8

One of the most exotic descriptions of the formula by which God deals with his people is found in the sixth chapter of Isaiah. Here Isaiah uses ancient Middle Eastern imagery to tell how God called him to become a prophet. One aspect of this event in his life is really quite familiar to us. When God calls us there is an immediate reaction of introspection. In the presence of God we feel unworthy and it is a very human response to say. "Woe is me! I am a sinful person living in a sinful world." For Isaiah, God's forgiveness came immediately. Isaiah is rescued from the unworthy life of the past and is made ready for a new life of service to God in the future.

In a strict sense, the forgiveness God offers to those whom God calls is forgiveness for one's past sins. In a wider sense what God does for us is to rescue us from danger and self-destruction, which so easily comes in a sinful world. So often our own fears and resentments can cause us trouble. We are apt to say things which are misunderstood, or we forget important considerations. We get into unfortunate relationships or unproductive activities. In so many ways we find ourselves caught in a negative spiral which bogs us down. This is what God rescues us from when God calls us to live according to Divine intentions for us. God is alert to the potential for danger and self-destruction in the choices we make, and has a way of guiding us away from the edge of disaster if we are alert to his counsel! The Psalmist knew this when he wrote, "Your rod and your staff—they comfort me." (Psalm 23:4) The more we become familiar with how God works in human life, the better able we are to hear and heed his rescue warnings. Another good reason for knowing the Bible!

PRAYER: O Divine Guide, Help me to know when I am going astray, and guide me to a more solid footing for my pathways. In Christ. Amen.

～ ～ ～ ～ ～ ～

MAY 22

A MATTER OF LETTING GO

When they had brought their boats to shore, they left everything and followed him.

—Luke 5:11

READ: Luke 5:1-11

We assume that in the years following the call of Christ, Peter and Andrew probably fished as a matter of economic survival. However, fishing was a priority which they let go in favor of discipleship. As a practical necessity fishing was secondary to their primary life commitment to the mission of Christ.

One can only do so much. You can be at only one place at a time. There can only be one top priority in one's life. These are ways of saying that when we accept Christ's call to follow him, certain other of life's commitments must be let go, and others must be relegated to a secondary position.

Becoming a consciously committed Christian means taking on a new set of values and letting other values diminish. Christ calls us to live for the greater good of humanity rather than for personal satisfaction and gain. Christian faith makes us stewards of the earth rather than voracious un-caring users of its resources. We are therefore concerned about the wise use of natural resources and the careful treatment of the environment in order to preserve it. Christian commitment keeps us from viewing the news of world affairs from a narrow nationalistic vantage point. We develop concern for the needs of people all over the earth, even in so-called enemy countries, or nations which harbor terrorists.

Our commitment to Christ separates us from the many "lesser gods" of life which tend to serve ones pride rather than the larger purposes of the only true God.

PRAYER: Separate me from all that keeps me from full commitment to you, O Christ. Amen.

~ ~ ~ ~ ~

MAY 23

KNOWING WHO I AM

> Samuel took a vial of oil and poured it on his head, and kissed him; he, said, "The Lord has anointed you ruler over his people Israel."
>
> —I Samuel 10:1

READ: I Samuel 9:17-10:1

Knowing who you are in the fullest sense of the word is not as obvious as it may seem. Knowing who I am means accepting my own family heritage, which has played a significant part in making me who I am.

What each of us has inherited from the past is a mixture of good and ill. Knowing who I am means coming to grips with the negative events which have impacted my life. I must take responsibility for how I have dealt with past influences and I must no longer "scape-goat" in an attempt to absolve myself of wrong choices. By God's grace I can begin to see how God has been at work in my life in a redemptive way.

My inheritance also involves the place I must occupy in the future. Hopefully the person "finding himself" will perceive his or her own place in life, and then will be able to move ahead. When Saul was anointed, he was given a special inheritance—to be Israel's first king. When I am called and rescued by God, the purpose of that call is to do the work God has for me to do. As a Christian knowing who I am means recognizing and accepting the life and mission God calls me to.

PRAYER: Almighty God, who has called me by name, you save me from my sin and help me to let go of selfish ways, grant me now the inheritance you have for my life. Through Christ. Amen.

MAY 24

PRUNING TO KEEP FROM GOING WILD

"I am the true vine, and my Father is the vinegrower.
He removes every branch in me that bears no fruit. Every
branch that bears fruit he prunes to make it bear more fruit."
—John 15:1-2

READ: Zephaniah 3:1-13

A few years ago people enjoyed exchanging popular proverbs like, "Whatever can go wrong, will go wrong," or "Situation normal: all fouled up." These phrases grew out of frustrations normally experienced by service people in the military during World War II. Summing these up, one might arrive at an elemental truth: "Left on their own, things tend to get worse." In other words, it does take effort to make life better.

Journalists have often sounded the horn on injustice and wrong in society, and have helped to reverse downward trends so that things could be improved. "60 Minutes" and other television news magazine shows often uncover unethical and shady practices in government or in the private sector.

You can think of Zephaniah as a journalist of his day, exposing the evils of his society and calling for the reversal of downward trends. Writing in 630 B.C.E., he was one of the prophets seeking to reform Judah. However, there is another dimension to the message of Zephaniah. He proclaimed that injustice and self-seeking dishonesty were contrary to God's will, and that God would bring destruction upon a people bent upon such evil. The prophets almost always added an affirmation that God would eventually bring blessings upon an obedient people.

We need always to hear what God has to say about our decisions and our life-style. We need our consciences to be alerted to God's intention for us.

PRAYER: O Divine Ruler, speak to me your word of truth about my life and the life of the world. In Christ. Amen.

~ ~ ~ ~ ~ ~

MAY 25

YOU GET WHAT YOU PAY FOR

Do not be deceived: God is not mocked, for you reap whatever you sow. If you sow to your own flesh, you will reap corruption from the flesh; but if you sow to the Spirit, you will reap eternal life from the Spirit.

—Galatians 6:7-8

READ: Nahum 1:1-10

One of the major mail-order houses used to assign "Good," "Better," or "Best," to the products pictured in its catalogue. Over the years many people learned not to order the "Good," which really meant "least expensive," because it was of lesser quality. We keep telling ourselves, "You get what you pay for." And then we look at the prices and settle for less.

On a more serious note, Nahum acknowledged the same truth around 615 B.C.E. when he told his people in Judah that the Assyrians would get what they had paid for. They had conquered Israel in an earlier decade and were now threatening God's people in Judah. But, the Assyrians were now getting their just reward. They were being destroyed by the Babylonians. In the midst of this "pay-back" God's chosen people would gain God's protecting love as a result of their faithfulness to God.

We look at this formula for destruction or blessing today and are apt to conclude that we certainly have a more advanced view of God. But don't be too quick to rule out the possibility that "you reap what you sow," which is what Paul wrote to the Galatian Christians six hundred and fifty years after Zephaniah.

In a family in which a child is not actively loved, that child will develop serious problems which could result in anti-social behavior. In a society in which some people are unjustly deprived of material benefits, the seeds of revolution are sown. On the other hand, peace is reaped when justice is sown.

PRAYER: Help me, most just God to sow seeds of goodness. In Christ. Amen

~ ~ ~ ~ ~ ~

MAY 26

BY THE SWORD DEFEATED

Do not repay anyone evil for evil . . . . Beloved never avenge yourselves, but leave room for the wrath of God, for it is written, "Vengeance is mine, I will repay, says the Lord."
—Romans 12: 17a, 19

READ: Obadiah 1-4, 15-16

On June 28, 1914 Archduke Francis Ferdinand of Austria-Hungary was assassinated by Gavrilo Princip, a Serbian nationalist. With that, World War I began, and four years later 8,538,315 military personnel from all countries involved had been killed. How could such vengeance be unleashed over one death? How long will rock throwing and car bombing go on in retaliation and vengeance in the Middle East? How long will ordinary people fear the suicide bombing of a terrorist bent on forcing his or her own will.

In 586 B.C.E., when Judah fell prey to the invading armies of Babylon the Edomites, Judah's bitter enemy flocked to the ruins to loot for the spoils of the defeat of its rival. In revenge against Edom, Obadiah prophesied the immanent destruction of Edom. However, it would not be Judah who would bring down the Edomites in revenge. It would be God who would bring justice through the devastation of Edom.

Antiquated as the accounts of those old wars between people in the Old Testament seem to us now, there is a lesson in Obadiah's message, bitter though it was. Violence begets vengeance and vengeance begets more violence. It is God, to whom we must look for justice, payment for war crimes, not to some super-power who will swoop down upon the cruel aggressors or terrorists of the world. "Vengeance is mine, I will repay, saith the Lord."

Paul concludes this thought: "No, if your enemies are hungry, feed them; if they are thirsty give them something to drink; for by doing this you will heap burning coals on their heads." Do not be overcome by evil, but overcome evil with good." (Romans 12:20-21)

What does this mean for us today in international affairs? In conflicts within the community? In our personal relationships?

PRAYER: Teach us, Lord, your ways, lest we die by the sword. In Christ our peace. Amen

~ ~ ~ ~ ~ ~

MAY 27

INSIDE THE TEMPLE

> But the hour is coming, and is now here, when the true
> worshipers will worship the Father in spirit and truth, for
> the Father seeks such as these to worship him. God is a spirit,
> and those who worship him must worship in spirit and
> truth.
>
> —John 4:23-24

READ: Haggai 1:1-8 and Psalm 137:1-6

While the Israelites were in captivity in Babylon, they were
unhappily separated from their homeland, and from their God, as
well, for it was believed that the Temple in Jerusalem was the only
true place for the full worship of God. Psalm 137 tells of the torment
the exiles experienced when their captors asked them to worship
their God in a foreign land, away from Jerusalem and the Temple.
Not many years later they were allowed to go home. There they
found the Temple in ruins. Economic and social conditions made
it most difficult for the returned exiles to rebuild the Temple.
Haggai's prophecy was to encourage them to build the Temple so
that true worship could be offered to God once again.

In many ways our problem of worship is quite opposite that of
the restored community of Jews in Haggai's time. We have enough
to eat, and we believe that God can be worshiped anywhere. Yet
our worship is sparse. Perhaps Haggai's word to us is to turn to
God and to truly worship him with our entire consciousness. John
has given us the insight that true worship is turning our inner self
toward God, who is a spirit. We truly worship when we allow the
Spirit to permeate our thoughts and feelings, thus to turn our
thoughts and attention to God alone, and to what God wants for
us and for our world. The Temple which each of us must re-build
is in our innermost self, where God would have us commune with
him.

PRAYER: Spirit of God, come into my heart. Lead me to true worship. Through Christ, the Way. Amen

～ ～ ～ ～ ～ ～

MAY 28

WHAT ABOUT THE GOLF COURSE?

> Once you were not a people, but now you are God's people, once you had not received mercy, but now you have received mercy.
>
> —I Peter 2:10

READ: Matthew 18:19-20 and Psalm 67

It could be argued that the term "individual Christian" is a contradiction and that it is impossible to be a Christian alone, without other Christians. There is no such thing as a "saint." only "saints." Jesus promised that where two or three are gathered together in his name we would be present. But he did not promise his presence to one lone individual, no matter how pious he or she might be. Peter refers to us in the plural form—God's *people*. The Christian faith is a corporate affair. Jesus calls a group to himself to do his work and to live his kind of life. From the very beginning of the Christian era the Faith has been carried and expressed by a group—the church. In earlier, times Christian hermits, following a call to solitude, did so as part of the mystical body of Christ, his church.

There is in our time a serious and wide-spread violation of this principle of corporate faith. The "Electronic Church," as the mass media evangelists have come to be called, seems to be in the business of creating and maintaining individual Christians "out there" in radio-land and among TV viewers. Such believers very well may remain isolated from other Christians, bound only to the mass-media preacher through correspondence and contributions.

A more authentic form of Christianity was found in that little band of disciples after Jesus' ascension who met together and prayed together daily. The Faith has been true and strong ever since, wherever Christians meet together and pray together. This is true despite the fact that we so often like to pose the question: "Can you be a Christian and worship God on the golf course?" Or, "What about the native on a desert island?" Perhaps such exceptions prove the rule!

PRAYER: Creator God, I thank you for the family of faith into which you have called me. Keep us close to one another, and may our prayers be deep and real. Through Christ. Amen

~ ~ ~ ~ ~ ~

MAY 29

A PORTABLE FAITH

And they cast lots for them, and the lot fell on Matthias,
and he was added to the eleven apostles.
—Acts 1:26

READ: Luke 24:45-53

In many ways Israel's finest hour was when it was on the move. In the days of Moses when the children of Israel were passing through the wilderness on their way to the promised land, everything had to be movable. The holy place was a movable tabernacle. In order to carry it with all its parts and furnishings a special group of men were selected to take over that important responsibility. Without adequate organization and deployment of certain persons to specific tasks the band of travelers would never have made it. They had to be organized to carry the faith forward.

In the days after the resurrection there were organizational procedures which needed to be developed. The replacement of

Judas by Matthias required such a procedure. To carry out Jesus' mandate to spread the news of God's love to all the world, the early church needed to organize to move the faith forward.

Such is the case of the church in every age. A very complex organization has been needed during the past 100 years by denominations in the U.S. to carry the message to all parts of the world. Boards had to be formed, personnel selected, funds generated, and strategy conceived in order to go forth into the world.

We too need to plan for our action if our discipleship is to be effective.

This may well mean selecting situations in which each of us is suited to act, and to develop ways of making such action effective. No one disciple needs to do everything, but every Christian ought to do something to carry the Faith forward.

PRAYER: O God, organize us to carry your Word to those around us and to the ends of the earth. Through Christ. Amen

~ ~ ~ ~ ~

MAY 30

ONE GOD

There is . . . one Spirit . . . one Lord . . . and Father of
us all, who is above all and through all and in all.
—Ephesians 4:4-6

READ: Ephesians 4:1-6 and Deuteronomy 6:4-9

Scientists say that the natural tendency is for things to fly apart, to disintegrate. Just as the planets are thought to have been originally part of the sun, having separated from it since the beginning, so all matter seems to want to divide and separate. Using this as a model it seems true also among people. There is a natural tendency to pull apart from each other to segregate one clan from another. As a baby grows it must separate more and more from its mother, until finally as a young person he or she must establish an entirely separate identity. This, though natural, has its excesses. Crime and violence, terrorism and war are some of the excesses to which this disintegrating movement can and does extend.

On the other hand the basic dynamic of God is toward unity and integrity. The very creation of the universe was a putting together, the establishing of complex interrelationships and interdependencies. In the concept of the trinity, Christians have symbolized God's unity: Father, Son, and Holy Spirit—one God.

Long before the coming of Jesus, the Israelites were aware of this radical unity of God. They celebrated God's unique oneness in what is called the "Shema." This is found in Deuteronomy, "Hear. O Israel: The Lord our God is one Lord." (Deuteronomy 6:4 KJV)

The God of all the universe is One. God created it out of formless void—nothingness—making a unity which God called good. Because of sinful human divisions human civilization seems bent on returning to the formless void. God is at work keeping that from happening. Can we do less than to join God in this uniting effort?

PRAYER: O God, heal our divisions, and make us one with each other and with you. Through Christ who came to reconcile. Amen.

~ ~ ~ ~ ~ ~

MAY 31

ONE FAITH

Now faith is the assurance of things hoped for, the conviction not things not seen.

—Hebrews 11:1

READ: Ephesians 4:4-6 and James 1:2-8

We have come to use the word, "faith," to refer to one's particular religious tradition. "What faith are you?" we ask. The expected answer is something like, "I'm a Presbyterian." (Or some other name.) But this is a violation of the oneness of faith as envisioned in the New Testament. Faith is that complete dependence upon God and trust in the Divine, which the Christian possesses. Because God is one, such faith in God is one, regardless of who expresses the faith.

Faith, by definition, must be single-minded and whole-hearted. One can't have any reservation about God's power. We must seek God's strength with no doubt about God's faithfulness. Not knowing, but trusting nevertheless, is scary business, especially when the stakes are high. But the more we live by such faith, the more the needed strength to endure life's trials and temptations grows within us by God's grace.

PRAYER: Create in me, O Lord, such trust in Your providing love, that I will grow in my capacity to endure life's trials. Cause me to sense my oneness with people of Christian faith everywhere. Through Christ. Amen

JUNE

JUNE 1

BURN A PINCH OF INCENSE . . . OR BURN!

> And to the angel of the church in Smyrna write: These
> are the words of the first and the last, who was dead and
> came to life.
>
> —Revelation 2:8

READ: Revelation 2:8-11

Not long after the close of the New Testament, the great bishop
of Smyrna was forced to choose between burning some incense as
an act of the worship of Caesar, or burning at the stake for his
Christian faith. He chose the stake saying, "Eighty-six years I served
Christ, and he has never done me wrong. How can I blaspheme
my King who saved me?" Christians in the New Testament times
in Smyrna faced similar extremes. The church there held firm in
faithfulness to Christ. John, in Revelation, commends and
encourages them by reminding them that Christ died and came to
life, and then by promising them the "crown of life" for their
strength of conviction.

Persecution comes in many forms to Christians who stand firm
in their faith to Christ. This pressure can come in connection with
difficult choices in work or in relationships. In one's stewardship
of resources, or one's use of time, and in ethical choices one faces.
In all of these life situations one may be called to suffer for one's
honesty and integrity. Persecution can come in the form of ridicule
or shunning because of the Christian principles for which one

stands. For some Christians in other parts of the world, persecution has resulted in imprisonment for faith positions taken. Christian missionaries and workers have been killed in the line of duty to Christ.

In whatever way we may be called upon to suffer for our faith in Christ, we are promised the strength of Christ who has gone through death to resurrection for us. Thereby we are promised the ultimate victory over evil, which God assures his people in every century.

PRAYER: O God, empower me to stand firm in my faith, that I may share in Christ's victory one day. With Christ. Amen.

~ ~ ~ ~ ~

JUNE 2

EYES OF FIRE AND FEET OF BRONZE

These are the words of the Son of God, who has eyes
like a flame of fire, and whose feet are like burnished
bronze . . . hold fast to what you have until I come.
—Revelation 2:18,25

READ: Revelation 2:18-29

In ancient Thyatira it was likely that its citizens frequently worshiped, trembling, before the bronze image of the god, Apollo, whom they feared would bring them punishment. But in their midst were Christians who worshiped the one and only God, whose Son is Christ. Revelation affirms this faith by showing that Christ is the Son of God, who "with eyes of fire and feet of bronze" (Revelation 2:18) is able to search the heart and know one's faithfulness. Again, to give assurance and to bolster faithfulness, Revelation, the letter written to the seven churches under persecution includes encouragement to the Christians in the small town of Thyatira. A town so important for its many craft guilds, including that of the bronze smiths.

But there is also a warning here. While the Christians in Thyatira had been strong in their faith, there was nevertheless the ever present temptation to give in to the immoral ways of small town life around them. Christ, the searcher of the inmost heart, will not tolerate duplicity. If one intended to stand firm, the seductions of the pagan culture in which they lived had to be resisted.

So with us. In every age and in every society Christians are called upon to choose life styles and values consistent with God's will, and to reject the attractive claims of other more prevalent values. Each of us must come to terms with what such seductive values and life styles may be, choosing for ourselves what we believe to be Christ's way instead. Holding on to Christ's way can bring subtle forms of persecution such as ridicule or shunning.

In this struggle of faith, Revelation encourages us to hold on to the faith we have in Christ against all odds.

PRAYER: Help me to discern your will for me, O God, and to determine what values and behaviors are contrary to what you want in my life. In Christ. Amen.

~ ~ ~ ~ ~ ~

JUNE 3

AS IN FORGETFUL SLEEP

I know your works; you have a name of being alive, but you are dead. Wake up and strengthen what remains and is on the point of death . . . Remember then what you received and heard; obey it and repent.

—Revelation 3:1-3

READ: Revelation 3:1-6

Apparently the Christians in Sardis had gone soft. Their faith appeared dead, and they had forgotten the wonderful blessings of Christ. But Revelation warns of impending danger and the need to wake up, to remember, and to repent. How very contemporary this message is! This describes American middle class "cushy" luxury to which most of us have become so accustomed. We do not ordinarily feel much danger in a society which allows us to believe whatever we choose, so long as we are law abiding, pay our taxes, and don't "rock the boat."

However, we are aware of those who have had to endure hardship for their faith, and have been called upon to renew and maintain their Christian commitment sometimes in other cultures, sometimes in ours.

There are moments when circumstances pressing upon us call to remember Christ and his blessings. A devastating illness perhaps; the stresses and strains of relationships; times of isolation and self-doubt; the death of a loved one; the loss of a job; the disappointments which come into every life. All these have a way of reminding us that we do not live alone very well, and that we need God's continual support, guidance, and protection. We need the risen Christ who bids us to allow him to lead us through life's valleys of the shadow.

PRAYER: Remind me, O God, of your love for me, especially in the risen Christ, in whose name I pray. Amen.

~ ~ ~ ~ ~

JUNE 4

FALLEN OUT OF LOVE

But this I have against you, that you have abandoned

the love you had at first. Remember then from what you
have fallen.

—Revelation 2:4-5

READ: Revelation 2:1-7

The Christians in Ephesus had fallen out of love. Forty years
or so after they had been won to Christ's love, they had lost the
intensity of their love and commitment to their Lord. Revelation
predicted that this would pose a danger for them in the future. In
times of persecution on account of their faith it would be especially
urgent to maintain a deep and abiding love for Christ.

Many a happily married couple have been able to endure trials
and hardships because of the warmth and intensity of the love
they shared for one another. Sometime circumstances in a marriage
make it advisable to "go on a second honeymoon," to renew the
intensity of love the couple shares. Similarly John of Revelation
knows that a love for Christ which remains strong will enable
Christians to go through trials and troubles victoriously.

It is a common mistake in our culture to see *love* as a noun,
but not as a verb. We think that love is something that happens to
us, a condition bestowed upon us by another person or by God.
This, of course, is partly true, but there is more to love than such
a passive interpretation suggests. Love is an active work and effort
on our part. It takes energy to love and to maintain love's intensity
over time. Revelation feels that the Ephesian Christians need to
re-activate their effort and energy of love. "Repent, and do the
works you did at first!" A second honeymoon is needed!

For the Christians the energy of love is expressed through
corporate worship, thought, prayer, and meditation during which
one concentrates attention upon God and his goodness to us, upon
the story of Jesus and his ministry, death and resurrection, and
upon the faithful lives of Christians in the church since New
Testament times. Love's effort is spent in prayer, seeking God's
insight upon our times and our lives. Love is the active energy of
the Christian life.

PRAYER: O God, empower me to love you actively. Through the love of Christ. Amen

~ ~ ~ ~ ~ ~

JUNE 5

NONE OF MY BUSINESS

Then the Lord said to Cain, "Where is your brother Abel?" He said, "I do not know. Am I my brother's keeper?"
—Genesis 4:9

But, resolve instead never to put a stumbling or hindrance in the way of another.
—Romans 14:13

READ: Genesis 4:1-9 and Romans 14:13-23

"Am I my brother's keeper?" has become a household slogan, and we vaguely know it to be in the Bible. Since it is in the Bible, we think that it is quite all right to use it as an excuse to let everyone fend for himself or herself. A few years ago the U.S. Supreme Court took the position that information about legal abortion could not be given out to clients by federally funded health care workers. One of the justices said, "It is not the government's business to give such information to indigent women." Are we, our sister's keeper? "No," they said. We lift up personal freedom, American ingenuity, equal opportunity, and self-reliance as the reason for answering Cain's question with a resounding NO!

And yet that is not what the Bible teaches. Remember the rest of the story. Cain was banished for his murder of Abel. The rest of the message is found throughout the Bible. We are taught to care for our brothers and sisters near and far.

Paul follows this tradition when he advises the church at Rome not to use Christian freedom in a way that would hurt others. As Christians we have responsibility for the welfare of our neighbors wherever they are. Jesus went so far as to say that when you care for others, you are offering care and love to him.

The next time you are tempted to believe as Cain did—that the good of others is not your concern—read more of the story and find that God wants us to go out into the world in love, caring for the needs of others to whom God sends us.

PRAYER: Help me, O God, to be my sister's and brother's helper. Through Christ. Amen.

~ ~ ~ ~ ~ ~

JUNE 6

DON'T ASK ME

> But Moses said to God, "Who am I that I should go to Pharaoh, and bring the Israelites out of Egypt . . . . Oh my Lord, I have never been eloquent . . . . O my Lord, please send someone else."
>
> —Exodus 3:11, 4:10, 13

> His master said to him, "Well done, good and trustworthy slave; you have been trustworthy in a few things, I will put you in charge of many things; enter into the joy of your master."
>
> —Matthew 25:23

READ: Exodus 3:1-11 4:10-13 and Matthew 25: 14-30

Moses was asked by God to go to the king of Egypt and to plead for his people. That was a scary prospect for Moses and he came up with the excuse that he was not expert at public speaking.

Many people are intimidated by experts, winners, and specialists. How could you know all that the experts know, excel like a winner, and do all the things the specialist can do? So, we withdraw and say, "Don't ask me." With Moses we say, "Please send someone else." Afraid of failing, too timid to speak, and overly cautious, we let others take the lead and run the world.

In the parable of the talents Jesus tells us of the cautious servant who was afraid of failure, and so did not do anything with his opportunities. On the other hand he praised the worker who was given a small amount, and yet made the very most of his minimal resource. This is what God wants of each of us. To use whatever capabilities and opportunities we have for the good of God's kingdom. You don't have to be a great theologian to help your neighbor through the sorrow of personal loss. Nor do you have to be a great public speaker to offer a helpful suggestion at the PTA meeting. You might even be able to offer prayer at a church meeting or at a friend's hospital bedside. Don't defer to the experts. Make the most of your opportunities to serve Christ. The result will be for us what it was for the servant to whom the master said, "Come in and share my happiness."

PRAYER: Help me, O God, to use what I have for the good of your Kingdom. Give me a readiness to respond to your requests. Through Christ. Amen.

~ ~ ~ ~ ~ ~

JUNE 7

WHY ME?

Gideon answered him, "But sir, if the Lord is with us,
why then has all this happened to us? . . . . But now the
Lord has cast us off and given us into the hand of Midian."
—Judges 6:13

"Am I not allowed to do what I choose with what
belongs to me? Or are you envious because I am generous?"
—Matthew 20:15

READ: Judges 6:1-13 and Matthew 20:1-16

A few years ago Harold Kushner's book, *Why Do Bad Things
Happen to Good People?* was very popular in the religious book
market. The title itself was enough to make it sell, for that question
is universal. "Why Me?" It was Gideon's question when he wanted
to know why God had allowed the Midianites to overrun Israel.

There is an underlying sense of fairness in us from early
childhood. Small children in a family inevitably raise issues of
fairness in connection with treatment of siblings in the family as
they see it. They quickly echo Gideon's complaint. *It's not fair!*

Kushner wisely did not entitle his book, *Why Does God Do
Bad Things to Good People?* Bad things happen, often at random,
and are not to be seen as acts of God, or as punishment. Rather, as
Matthew teaches in the parable of the laborers in the vineyard,
God freely offers his love to all, regardless of their comparative
records or accomplishments.

If we get stuck on the childish premise of getting what we
deserve, none of us would get much! The
Christian understanding of life is that we get from God what
Christ deserves. The sacrifice of Christ on our behalf should keep
us from the petty bookkeeping that tempts us to echo Gideon's
complaint.

No! Bad things come to everyone as a result of the natural
order, and the freedom God has given to each of us. We are not
puppets manipulated by God. As children who are free to live, we
face life's hazards, but always with God's grace and love to help us
through the bad times as well as the good.

PRAYER: Thank you, God, for your love freely given to all. In
Christ. Amen.

~ ~ ~ ~ ~ ~

JUNE 8

DIVINE BACKUP

"And I will ask the Father, and he will give you another
Advocate, to be with you forever."

—John 14:16

READ: John 14:12-18 and Romans 8:9-17

After a few short years with his disciples Jesus was about to
leave them. Yet, it was upon their inexperienced shoulders that
Jesus would place the very difficult and hazardous task of carrying
on his work in a hostile world, a world which would soon crucify
Jesus. How alone and terrified these disciples would be. How
hesitant and vulnerable. Jesus' answer to their predicament was to
grant them the Holy Spirit as a COMFORTER.

The original Greek for "comforter" meant "one who would be
alongside." Other English versions use the terms: "Advocate,"
"Counselor," or "One who will stand by." Jesus promised a Divine
Backup. The task of the disciples was to go forth into the world
with the message of God's love for humankind as played out in the
story of Jesus' life, death, and resurrection. A task of the Holy
Spirit would be to back up Christ's messengers.

Oftentimes you and I feel quite alone in our efforts to be
obedient to God's will in our lives. We know that we ought to
stand up for the Christian position on a touchy matter, but we are
afraid of the repercussions. If we make a Christian statement, we
might be considered too religious for the real world. We might be
embarrassed if we abstain from some activity on moral grounds. If
someone really wants to know what the Christian opinion is, we
might be too shy or reluctant to speak. In any event we would feel
very much alone. The Holy Spirit comes to us at such times and

backs us up, stands by in giving us comfort and counsel. He is our advocate.

PRAYER: O Holy Spirit, stand by me. In Christ. Amen.

~ ~ ~ ~ ~

JUNE 9

TELLING THE TRUTH

> "This is the Spirit of truth, whom the world cannot receive, because it neither sees him nor knows him. You know him, because he abides with you, and he will be in you."
>
> —John 14:17

READ: John 16:12-15 and I Corinthians 2:9-13

The first disciples of Jesus were uneducated, and probably not very articulate, at least so far as public speaking might be concerned. And yet Jesus was giving them the task of bringing *the* truth into the Greek-Roman civilization with its centuries of classical culture. There were many philosophies and religions among the people to whom the disciples would be sent. Even within their own Jewish community there were varying points of view on religious matters. The Pharisees and the Sadducees argued regularly over theological issues. Others disagreed on points of religious law. Into this mix the plain folk whom Jesus had chosen were sent to speak the truth about God and the world. How were they to know the truth, let alone speak it? Jesus' answer to their ineptitude was the gift of the Holy Spirit—the Spirit of truth. He would reveal the truth to his own people. Sometimes we call this function of the Holy Spirit that of the INTERPRETER. Paul wrote to the Corinthian church, "And we speak of these things in words not taught by human wisdom but taught by the Spirit, interpreting spiritual things to those who are spiritual." (I Corinthian 2:13)

In today's complex world with rapid changes and dramatic shifts in history, we are often hard put to understand what is going on. In the shifting course of one's life one may be troubled about the meaning of events in which one is personally involved. The Holy Spirit comes as the Interpreter, helping us to see more clearly what is going on and how God is at work in the events of life.

PRAYER: Thank you, O Holy Spirit, for telling me the truth about life. Through Christ, the Word made flesh. Amen.

~ ~ ~ ~ ~ ~

JUNE 10

LIKE AN ADRENALIN SURGE

When they had prayed, the place in which they were
gathered together was shaken ; and they were all filled with
the Holy Spirit and spoke the word of God with boldness.
—Acts 4:31

READ: Acts 2:1-6 4:3135

Had the New Testament writers known human physiology as we do today, they might have used the idea of adrenalin to symbolize the surge of power which the Holy Spirit gives to us for the accomplishment of Christ's mission. Perhaps a modern word for being impacted by this power surge would be ZAP. Otherwise, how could plain folk become powerful witnesses to the action of God in Christ on behalf of the whole world? From the day of Pentecost onward Christ's people have gone all over the world with the message of God's love in Christ. Their work has been energized by the spiritual adrenalin provided by God's Spirit. The spread of the gospel from the very beginning can be explained no other way. It would be a mere 325 years before Christianity would become the official religion of the Roman Empire. "They were filled with the Holy Spirit and spoke the word of God with boldness."(Acts 4:31)

Such is the power offered to us through the Holy Spirit. Such is the boldness made possible in our lives when we are filled with the Holy Spirit. We may not have the same missionary task the early disciples had, but for whatever Christian work we are called to, the same power is available to us as Christians. Our task for Christ may be child raising, or teaching, or leadership in the church. It may be to live in a neighborhood or in a community as ambassadors for Christ. It may be to be a Christian citizen, active in politics at some level, or to function in the world of business. The promise is power to do Christ's work in whatever setting he calls us.

PRAYER: Grant me power—an adrenalin surge—to do your will, O God. In Christ. Amen.

~ ~ ~ ~ ~ ~

JUNE 11

THE COMMUNION OF THE HOLY SPIRIT

The grace of the Lord Jesus Christ, the love of God,
and the communion of the Holy Spirit be with all of you.
—II Corinthians 13:13

READ: Ephesians 4:1-6

COMMUNION of the Holy Spirit! Communion is the binding of one to another, or the bond holding an entire group together. In holy communion each worshiper is made one with Christ and all are made one with each other. It is in the communion of spirit whereby two or more persons become for, all intents and purposes, one.

After Jesus' departure his disciples must have felt a painful loneliness. But soon afterward the worship of that earliest Christian group of followers must have taken on an especially important function, for in worship that little group must have experienced a new and deep unity, as they shared memories of Jesus, as their understanding of Christ grew and as they discussed the purposes and goals of their mission.

It is the gift of union—*communion*—which forms the church as the body of Christ and sends it forth into the world to do his work. In fact this communion of the people of Christ has always been essential to the very existence of the church. The Holy Spirit, given to the church on Pentecost, is the binding force holding together the church as Christ's body.

For us today the interaction with other Christians is essential to our full discipleship. This interaction peaks in Holy communion.

PRAYER: Let me be always part of your church, O Christ, and may it be filled with the Holy Spirit. Amen.

~ ~ ~ ~ ~

JUNE 12

"CREATIO EX NIHILO"

> In the beginning when God created the heavens and the earth, the earth was a formless void and darkness covered the face of the deep, while a wind from God swept over the face of the waters. Then God said, "Let there be light"; and there was light.
>
> —Genesis 1:1-3

READ: Psalm 104:1-24

There is a short ancient Latin phrase which speaks volumes about the Christian belief in God. It is *creatio ex nihilo.* Translated it says in English: "*Creation out of nothing.*" To affirm that God created the universe out of a formless void is to believe that all of life is dependent upon God, and that it is God who causes every moment to exist. Christians accompany this belief in creation with the belief that God not only created the universe, but that God is its Sustainer. Thus we believe that God is involved in every event. It is an affirmation of God's ownership of all that is. Our attention to such a belief has been diverted too many times with discussions and arguments about how God made the world and how such thinking conflicts with the evidence of science. It should make no difference to us to know how God created the universe. But it should make a great deal of difference to us to believe that God created from nothing all that is, and that God is involved in everything that happens. It should make a deep difference to us to know that God has a loving, redemptive will for every event and for every relationship.

God cares very much about each of our lives, and wants the very best for each of us—health, wholeness, good relationships, happiness and peace. But there are forces which oppose God's will which often seem to have the upper hand—temporarily! But, because of the resurrection we know that ultimately God's will shall be accomplished. Meanwhile we live under the caring love of God, who guides us through life's trouble spots as well as through its joyful times. Like a loving earthly parent, God goes with us through whatever events befall us, and in the developing relationships which make up so much of life.

God the Creator and Sustainer is with each of us every step of the way. God has been with us from the beginning.

PRAYER: From the very beginning to the very end, you are Creator and Sustainer. In Christ, the Word. Amen.

~ ~ ~ ~ ~ ~

JUNE 13

WHAT YOU PLANT IS WHAT YOU GET

Do not be deceived; God is not mocked, for you reap
whatever you sow. If you sow to your own flesh, you will

reap corruption from the flesh; but if you sow to the Spirit,
you will reap eternal life from the Spirit.

—Galatians 6:7-8

READ: Jeremiah 31:27-30 and Lamentations 5:1-7

We live in an age when personal freedom is highly valued. But
we live in a world which is ordered. One's action sets off a chain of
events, and as a result of a single decision the course of one's own
history can be altered. Paul said it more simply: "What you plant
is what you get." In our time we are painfully aware of the truth of
this equation. Some of the rivers of America have become polluted
beyond recovery.

The ozone layer is already more thin in places than we would
like to have it be. Some bird and animal species have already
disappeared from the earth. Heart disease strikes, surgery is
indicated, your doctor tells you that your cholesterol level is
dangerously high, and you remember all the fried eggs, sausage,
and pancake breakfasts you enjoyed in your life. You are what you
eat, they say. Your life is what you and those who have gone before
you decided to do in the past.

The lesson here is that God calls us to live responsibly in an
ordered world in which, what we decide makes a difference to our
future and to that of other people and generations. Personal freedom
must be balanced by other values which intersect with one's road
to free expression. Consideration of what one understands to be
God's perspective on our lives, must help us make right decisions
and thereby help to shape the future for us and those who come
after us.

PRAYER: Help me, O God, to live responsibly, knowing that you
want the best possible world for everyone everywhere, now
and in the future. Through Christ. Amen.

~ ~ ~ ~ ~

JUNE 14

IT'S NOT JUST THE WAY IT IS

Jesus answered, "Neither this man nor his parents
sinned; he was born blind so that God's works might be
revealed in him.

—John 9:3

READ: Ezekiel 18:1-9 and John 9:1-3

The tendency in Old Testament thought is to make very rigid rules by which things happen and to hold God to such formulas which the scribes and pharisees developed. So, when Israel and Judah found themselves facing Assyrian rule and captivity the proverb was often repeated: "The parents ate sour grapes, but the children got the sour taste." (Ezekiel 18:2) While this proverb speaks some degree of truth, there is more to be said. Ezekiel counters with the affirmation: "It is only the person who sins that shall die." (Ezekiel 184) Each of us must take responsibility for his or her own acts and be willing to pay the price. You can't just blame it on your parents.

Jesus goes much further with this idea when he teaches his disciples that God is the one who is ultimately in charge of every situation. It is too brittle a view to look at a troubled person and to blame his or her particular circumstances of heredity or environment for the unfortunate conditions which have developed. In Jesus' answer to the disciples who wanted to know who had sinned to cause a man's blindness, he focused upon God's action to heal the blindness rather than upon the placing of blame for it.

When trouble comes, instead of throwing up your hands and concluding, "That's just the way it is," or trying to find someone else to blame, see the difficult times as opportunities for God to work with you for the resolution of life's problems.

PRAYER: O God, come to me in my rough times, and help
straighten my pathway. Through Christ. Amen.

~ ~ ~ ~ ~ ~

JUNE 15

NOT A MATTER OF COAT TAILS

This means that it is not the children of the flesh who
are the children of God, but the children of the promise are
counted as descendants.

—Romans 9:8

READ: Genesis 17:1-9

Critics who discount inherited religion as second-hand are right
when they make the claim that each one of us must respond to
Christ's call to faith, that you can't ride in on your grandfather's
coat tails. However, God's promise to Abraham had another side
to it. Abraham's agreement with God to keep the covenant with
God was to extend to his children and to future generations. "I
will establish my covenant between me and you, and your offspring
after you throughout their generations." (Genesis 17:7)

God's promises are not automatically transferred from one
generation to the next. Each new generation must hear the call of
God, learn of the faith, and respond to Christ on its own. It is not
enough that your parents were Christian. You must, on your own
accord respond to Christ's call.

Throughout the Old Testament the covenant between God
and his people was renewed successively under one leader after
another. Finally in the New Testament Jesus declared that in his
blood a New Covenant was formed One of the significant struggles
in the New Testament involved the breaking out of a strictly Jewish
enclave to form a group to include Gentiles, who had not first
become Jews. This struggle reached a milestone when Peter spoke
to the church: "I truly understand that God shows no partiality,
but in every nation anyone who fears him and does what is right is
acceptable to him." (Acts 10:34-35)

Each of us, no matter what our religious heritage, is invited to respond to Christ's call to be his person and to live accordingly. Our true inheritance is God's promise to each of us.

PRAYER: Thank you, Lord, for your call in Christ and your promise to be my God. By your grace I want to be yours. In Christ. Amen.

~ ~ ~ ~ ~ ~

JUNE 16

YOU ARE YOUR PARENTS' CHILD

> They answered him, "Abraham is our father." Jesus said to them, "If you were Abraham's children, you would be doing what Abraham did . . ."
>
> —John 8:39

READ: Ezra 9:10-12 and John 8:25-39

Visiting one's place of origin can be a very significant experience after having lived elsewhere for a long time. When one does not live near one's parents, and when visits are infrequent, such reunions can take on a deep meaning. These experiences of re-visiting personal roots are, however, not always pleasant. They sometimes raise unresolved issues and can even re-fire ancient conflicts.

However, when one recognizes one's own family beginnings, and deals with the memories in a creative and honest way, one can come to accept one's heritage as having contributed mightily to one's present identity. It may take many years to recognize some of the deeply rooted attitudes in your own family which have given shape to your life. This development adds appreciation for your family and for your own past.

When the Hebrews returned to Jerusalem, their homeland, after captivity in Babylon, Ezra, the priest, reminded them of their heritage as Israelites. To keep their heritage pure he advised them not to intermarry with outsiders. In this way he felt that the inheritance could be passed on to future generations.

Jesus reminded some of his detractors of their heritage as children of Abraham and what that ought to mean in their lives. Both Ezra and Jesus saw that spiritual upbringing was a strong and necessary factor in present faithfulness.

Unfortunately, we live in a time when much of the strong religious heritage of the past has been discounted in favor of a free choice approach to life and religion. There is a significant place for one's continued commitment to spiritual and moral principles from one's Christian heritage.

PRAYER: Help me to re-affirm the good things about my Christian heritage. In Christ. Amen

~ ~ ~ ~ ~ ~

JUNE 17

REMEMBERING

> I will call to mind the deeds of the Lord; I will remember your wonders of old. I will meditate on all your work, and muse on your mighty deeds.
>
> —Psalm 77:11-12

READ: Psalm 77:1-12

In the novel, *Watership Down*, the author, Richard Adams, makes the important point that the rabbits who "people" this story love to tell stories to one another—significant remembering of their own past tradition. One commentator on this novel observes that such remembering not only defines who they are but gives them survival skills for the dangerous world in which rabbits live. What's true of rabbits in this novel is true of people in real life.

The stories about your childhood have helped to shape you as a person. In electronic parlance we call those "tapes." You feel, think, and act in certain ways because of the subtle influence of the tapes from your childhood which play over and over again in your subconscious mind. You may say of yourself that you are clumsy, because members of your family used to tell stories about how inept you were as a child, how you would fall so often, and how you seemed to turn everything into chaos. Cute stories? Maybe not. If by remembering them you continue to think less of your capacities, and in a hidden way seek to fulfill those early expectations.

One very powerful thing we can do to help resolve our problems is to remember certain stories of how God has helped us in the past. By remembering such stories we become better able to tap the reservoir of God's power for today's struggles.

The Psalmist reveals a deep personal need for God in order to survive the ordeal of living through life's problems. The answer to our urgent need for help in times of trouble comes in the form of remembering stories of how God has helped us in the past. Read the rest of Psalm 77 and then read all of Psalm 78 which is telling how God's power is remembered. In this way God becomes a "very present help in time of trouble." (Psalm 46:1)

PRAYER: O God, let me hear again and remember the stories of your power in the lives of your people and in my life. Through Christ. Amen.

~ ~ ~ ~ ~ ~

JUNE 18

HOPING

We have this hope, a sure and steadfast anchor of the
soul, a hope that enters the inner shrine behind the curtain,
where Jesus, a forerunner on our behalf, has entered . . . .
—Hebrews 6:19-20

READ: Colossians 1:3-6, 24-29

Some of life's losses will not be recovered and will remain. The resolution of some of our problem situations will be very difficult at best—impossible in some cases. What is one to do with such trouble? When one is utterly frustrated by the turn of events in one's life, what is there left to do? For the Christian the ultimate response is that of *hope*. Christian hope is a deep and abiding assurance of God's ultimate goodness on our behalf. Such hope is grounded in the ultimate triumph of God over all that opposes God's will. This assurance is sealed with the truth of the resurrection. This hope is for our own final well-being, no matter what the temporary set-backs are now.

In *On Death and Dying*, Elisabeth Kubler-Ross follows her description of the five stages of response to death and loss with a chapter on hope. In her study of terminally ill patients she observes that everyone seems to go through the five stages of: Denial, Anger, Bargaining, Depression, and Acceptance. While these stages will remain for varying periods of time and come and go, there runs through all the stages a sense of hope, she has observed. Even when the doctors and others know there is no chance for recovery, we still have the tendency to hope. So often when a family member disappears there is much media attention and a massive public search effort, which lasts only so long. After the public gives up, family members most often still express a hope, bordering on assurance, that their loved one is alive and will be found. Tragically this hope is often dashed when the body is found.

The Christian faith offers us a basis for ultimate hope by placing us within an eternal frame of reference within which health of body and mind, reunion with loved ones, and the resolution of conflicts are assured us—if not in this life, in the life to come. The victory of Christ risen from the dead is our guarantee.

PRAYER: O God, let me keep hoping. Grant me the assurance Christ has won for me. In Him. Amen.

~ ~ ~ ~ ~ ~

JUNE 19

AN IMPOSSIBLE DREAM

After his suffering he presented himself alive to them
by many convincing proofs, appearing to them during forty
days, and speaking about the kingdom of God.

—Acts 1:3

READ: Acts 1:1-5

In a study of Baby Boomers, it is observed that many in this generation would like to know God better but do not like to go to church. If the Bible has any clue to spiritual fulfillment, theirs is an impossible dream. From beginning to end the religious experience of the people in Old and New Testaments is a group experience. In the Old Testament God's work and relationship is with the nation Israel, and with individuals only insofar as they address or lead the corporate group. In the New Testament Jesus is rarely, if ever, seen with a single individual—always with a group. It is to "two or three" he promised his presence.

Immediately after the crucifixion of Jesus, his followers banded together. To them as a group Jesus appeared repeatedly. Certainly their fellowship with one another was greatly deepened by his resurrection appearances. Earlier he had instructed his group of followers to celebrate his life, death and resurrection as they ate together. From that instruction comes our Communion, which can only be celebrated corporately with an assembled congregation, even if that means a group of family members gathered around the bed of a loved one. From the common life of Jesus' followers who met in Jerusalem immediately after his resurrection there developed the church. Immediately after his death comes the fellowship of the church which has been enjoyed by Christ's people ever since.

Thus, it is not necessary to defend church-going as a desirable option for those who want to know God. From the point of view of the Bible and of the Christian faith, regular and meaningful involvement with others in the church is the only way to know God fully.

PRAYER: Bind me together with others in the Faith, O God., that we may know you. In Christ, Amen.

~ ~ ~ ~ ~ ~

JUNE 20

THERE'S STRENGTH IN NUMBERS

So when they had come together . . . . Jesus replied,
". . . you will receive power when the Holy Spirit has come upon you; and you will be my witnesses . . . ."
—Acts 1:6,8

READ: Luke 24:45-53

Over the last few decades there has been a growing number of support groups organized around a whole array of problem areas. Grief groups gather to talk through the loss of loved ones. People who have been through open heart surgery gather to support one another, and to offer help to patients anticipating such surgery. Alcoholic Anonymous is perhaps the oldest of these support groups. And from it many other twelve step groups have been spawned. Over and over again people in these specialized groups testify to the help that such groups have given them.

There is strength in numbers when it comes to enduring difficult experiences. Such strength comes in the form of shared experiences and feelings, instructions, and assistance from fellow members of the group in times of critical need. Members of A.A. are ready to go to the rescue of a fellow member who may be slipping.

The church can be seen as a support group. It is the setting in which Christians receive power, instruction, and assistance for their living as obedient followers of Christ. The Holy Spirit is given to us as we are gathered together as Christ's body.

At first the support group of the early disciples helped them to adjust to the loss of Jesus as they had known him. The early church turned to the active support of Christians who were answering the call of Christ to bear witness to him throughout the world. The church today supports us as we grow in our faith and develop in our obedience to Christ.

PRAYER: O God, fill us with your Spirit when we gather as one body in Christ. In Him. Amen.

~ ~ ~ ~ ~ ~

JUNE 21

LET ALL THE PEOPLE PRAY

All these were constantly devoting themselves to prayer, together with certain women . . . .

—Acts 1:14

READ: Acts 1:12-14 and Hebrews 12:1-2

Immediately after Jesus' departure from the midst of his disciples, they were impelled to be together and to pray. Perhaps they remembered that Jesus told them earlier, "For where two or three are gathered in my name, I am there among them." (Matthew 18:20)

There is something universally human about the need to mourn together or to come together as a group to share memories. Funerals or burial rites are always group events—rarely individual experiences. A more adequate expression of our memory of a loved one is made possible by sharing such thoughts with others.

The worship and teaching of the church is first of all a group event. The Confession of 1967 of the Presbyterian Church U.S.A. puts it this way, "Jesus Christ has given the church preaching and teaching, praise and prayer . . . . The church responds to the message of reconciliation in praise and prayer." This view of the corporate nature of worship and prayer was put forth in the description of individual prayer as "an extension of the church at prayer." Whenever we pray "we are surrounded by so great a cloud of witnesses," (Hebrews 12:1) responding to the God who has brought us together in Christ.

PRAYER: Together with others of faith, even now I add my praise to you, O God. In Christ who brings us together into his body, the church. Amen.

~ ~ ~ ~ ~

JUNE 22

THE JOY OF UNEXPECTED LOVE

"But woe to you Pharisees! For you tithe mint and rue and herbs of all kinds, and neglect justice and the love of God; it is these you ought to have practiced, without neglecting the others."

—Luke 11:42

READ: Luke 11:42-44

Jesus warned that the Pharisees were so caught up in the details of following every legal regulation to the finest point, that they had little left with which to channel God's love and justice into the world around them. While trying to live a perfect life, they neglected the needs of others.

It is possible to become so compulsively obligated to rules of social etiquette, or to the mandates of one's own religion that the larger concerns for persons become lost in the barrage of legalistic obligations. Jesus said, "If you do good to those who do good to you, what credit is that to you?" (Luke 6:33) Rather, we must let the good we do be initiated out of love and a sense of justice, rather than as an obligation to pay someone back or to fulfill the requirements of polite society. How much more fun it is to give an unexpected gift than it is to send a gift to repay for a gift received, making sure that it costs enough, but not too much.

Christ frees us from the obligations of the law, and gives us the freedom to do justice, and to offer love in all that we do.

PRAYER: Thank you, O Christ, for the freedom you give me. Let me love others and help to bring justice into my world. Amen.

~ ~ ~ ~ ~ ~

JUNE 23

PRESENTING A NEW MODEL

"If you know these things you are blessed if you do them."

—John 13:17

READ: John 13:5-17

Modeling is a way of unconsciously teaching and learning. A parent models for the child what the parent is as an adult, and in time the child may unconsciously imitate the parent's life—for better or worse. Sometimes modeling is intentionally done to help another person. A therapist may model a certain response which he/she feels would be appropriate for the client to copy in facing a particular problem. An employer may show by example what the worker should do.

Jesus modeled for his disciples at the Last Supper. He washed their feet, and taught them in this way by example what their behavior ought to be. "I have set for you an example, that you also should do as I have done to you . . . ." (John 13:15) On one level, which is quite superficial, we might conclude that we ought to become foot-washers. Some sects have done just that. But the lesson Jesus is teaching in this event is that we ought to treat one another as equals, and as companions to be served.

Perhaps the most basic commandment for human relations for Christians could be stated in this way: 'Treat others as your equals." When Jesus washed the disciple's feet he was showing them that he regarded them as equals and as friends with whom he wanted to share his love. By asking them to follow the same practice, he was inviting them to treat each other as equals to be served and loved. When the Christian church has been at its finest over the centuries its members have followed this model. In those countries where this has been practiced, democracy has been born and developed. The pay-off is the happiness of those who serve and those who are served.

PRAYER: Thank you, O God, for the joy of following the model which Jesus shared with us, to love one another as equals. In his name. Amen.

⌐ ⌐ ⌐ ⌐ ⌐

JUNE 24

FROM WHENCE THE WINDS OF CHANGE?

"The wind blows where it chooses, and you hear the sound of it, but you do not know where it comes from, or where it goes. So it is with everyone who is born of the Spirit."

—John 3:8

READ: Titus 3:3-8

Many modern middle-class, educated Americans seem to be victims of a pagan fatalism which leaves them hopeless in the face of life's perplexities. A legacy of the social scientists, this fatalism blinds us with the idea that life is the sum total of our genes and the conditions which have shaped us since birth, and in the womb! Nothing more—nothing less. It would appear that you can't help what you are, you can't decide your own destiny, not even your next big decision. These, it is said, are all determined for you by earlier factors over which you have had no control.

Squarely in the face of such pessimism the Christian faith affirms the possibility of creative and radical change in one's life. You don't have to remain chained to your past, imprisoned in the dungeon of conditions laid down for you. The Holy Spirit goes wherever He wants to, and brings renewal to whomever He will. That's good news.

The Christian need never sink into the depression of concluding that there is no hope. There is always the potential of the power of God entering the human situation and changing it radically—for the better. About the time you have lost hope for the life situation of someone in your life, the Christian affirmation counters with, "The Holy Spirit brings new life when you least expect it. So, pray for it."

Returning to the analogy of the wind, note that it blows all the time somewhere. The Holy Spirit is always at work bringing new life and renewal to His children. May that very dynamic be happening in your life, and in the lives of your loved ones this very moment.

PRAYER: Yes, Lord, I pray that you renew us daily with the power of your Holy Spirit, which is at work in the world. In Christ. Amen.

~ ~ ~ ~ ~ ~

JUNE 25

A REAL CONVERSATION STOPPER

> But avoid stupid controversies, genealogies, dissensions,
> and quarrels about the law, for they are unprofitable and
> worthless.
>
> —Titus 3:9

READ: Titus 3:9-11 and Ephesians 4:14-15

"I never discuss religion or politics." So goes a popular conversation stopper. One may very well suspect that at least in some cases this reveals that religion is of little interest or concern. When such is the case, a discussion of religion would be of little value—a pooling of disinterested ignorance. However, there are many situations in which the interest and commitments in the religious sector are so strong that discussions very easily become arguments, and the temperature of the conversation rises.

The letter of Titus warns against stupid controversies, because they lead nowhere and gain nothing. When firmly held positions are flung back and forth, or neat phrases are proudly presented, there is little hope for the growth of thought of any of the participants. But it would be a shame never to discuss the things of God, never to share experiences of faith.

If our religious experience has been important to us we will want to tell others about it. If faith is real, it begs to be shared with others like any other pleasurable experience or story. But sharing is different from arguing. It is good to offer ones own religious insights and awareness to another person in an honest and humble manner. Perhaps what we have to share will expand the life of the other person significantly. If so, it wuld be a shame to withhold our experience, merely because we don't discuss religion.

PRAYER: O God, help me to share my faith with others in a way

that will enhance the lives of others, and help me to accept
their sharing with me, that I might grow because of their faith.
In Christ. Amen.

~ ~ ~ ~ ~ ~

JUNE 26

HARMONY INTENDED

For we are what he has made us, created in Christ Jesus
for good works, which God prepared beforehand to be our
way of life.

—Ephesians 2:10

READ: Genesis 2:4b-9

The story of creation in the second chapter of Genesis we do
not read as frequently as we do the story in Genesis 1. Instead of
reading Genesis 2 as a series of events in the distant past read it as
the story of God's vision for us and our world.

God's vision is that of a perfect garden in which there is harmony
and order and peace. God imagined a garden home for humankind
which is strikingly beautiful. It is balanced and life supporting.
The primeval bioshpere! In this garden whatever mars its beauty
or disturbs its order and balance is against God's will for the world.

With this vision as our charter we can affirm that God does
not want ill-health of any kind. God does not desire confusion and
disorder in our lives. In short, whatever influence causes our life
situation to be less than a Garden of Eden experience, is contrary
to God's best intention for us and for all humankind. Whatever we
do to promote health and safety, whatever effort on our part creates
beauty, and what we do to bring about reconciliation and harmony,
are not only blessed by God, but represent the fulfillment of God's
will, at least in part.

It is a comfort to recognize, while we are experiencing ill-health and confusion of any kind, that God wants health and order in our lives. Our efforts to attain health, order and beauty will be vitalized and strengthened by God.

PRAYER: Almighty God, who brings beauty and intends wholeness for each of us, by your power help me to promote harmony and create beauty all my days. In Christ. Amen

~ ~ ~ ~ ~ ~

JUNE 27

BREAD INTENDED FOR ALL

And God is able to provide you with every blessing in abundance, so that by always having enough of everything, you may share abundantly in every good work. As it is written, "He scatters abroad, he gives to the poor; his righteousness endures forever."

—II Corinthians 9:8-9

READ: Genesis 2:9-15

God intends for the garden into which we have been placed to supply all our needs and the needs of all others. There should be no one wanting for food and sustenance. And yet, we live in a world in which two thirds of the population goes to bed hungry each night. It is a world in which many live with malnutrition and die of starvation. God does not intend for this to be the human predicament. The other side of this affirmation is that God does not intend for us to have more than enough to eat at the expense of a sufficient diet for others. If God does not want such unequal distribution we must do all we can to re-distribute life's essentials throughout the world.

Such effort to alleviate human hunger is not optional, but it is a requirement if we are to consider ourselves truly obedient to God's will.

From the very beginning of the church, Christians have helped one another with economic needs. An early model for this act of generosity was the collection for the Jerusalem church which Paul asked from Christians in Corinth and Macedonia, as mentioned in II Corinthians 9. The history of the church is filled with such examples: the monasteries during the Dark Ages cared for the poor, offerings for world relief have been taken over the years, and most recently such organized efforts as, Community Food Banks, Bread for the World and the World Hunger fund, in which many churches participate.

Whenever you eat your fill of good food, consider prayerfully the ways you can share with others in dire need throughout the world. Such sharing is truly an authentic Christian act, by which we help to fulfill God's intention for the "Garden!"

PRAYER: I pray, most merciful God, for the poor of the earth. Open my heart and hands to them, through Christ, who became poor for our sakes, that we might become rich. Amen

~ ~ ~ ~ ~ ~

JUNE 28

GOOD INTENTIONS

Let love be genuine; hate what is evil, hold fast to what is good.

—Romans 12:9

READ: Genesis 2:8, 16-17 and I Corinthians 12:1-2

"It doesn't matter what you do, as long as you are sincere."

"It's wrong, if you think it's wrong." "Anything is OK, if it doesn't hurt people." "A guilty conscience is nothing more than a result of old fashioned moralistic Sunday School training." These are some of the commonly heard statements which reflelct the moral relativism of our time. It has become out of date to talk of good and evil, and yet God's vision for humanity includes the concept of good and evil, as real elements in the real world. We live in a time when what used to be considered wrong behavior is now called "inappropriate behavior."

In the story of Adam God is seen as envisioning a humanity which would customarily choose to do good and regularly refuse to do evil. Indeed the teachings of the law and the preaching of the prophets in the Old Testament assume a universal moral order for humanity and urge men and women to abide by God's commandments. The teaching of Jesus and the writings of the earliest church take for granted that there is good to be done and evil to be shunned.

At a time in our culture when self expression is emphasized and valued, and sin and evil have been relegated to a theological museum containing former concepts now considered quaint, people are flocking to counselors and therapists of all kinds. Many people who seek such counsel are filled with guilt and anxiety. The further one strays from God's vision of perfect humanity, the deeper the guilt, anxiety and anger will be lodged in one's life, and the more seriously one will need help. It still stands in God's vision for the Garden, that we are asked not to eat of the fruit of the tree in its center. God is still God, whether one acknowledges that fact or not, and we are not to live as if we have taken God's place for ourselves, thus forsaking God's moral order.

PRAYER: O God, giver of all law, call us back to an awareness of the right, the good, and the beautiful. Empower me to live in that way. Through Christ. Amen.

JUNE 29

INTENDED TO KNOW

> We have not ceased praying for you and asking that you
> may be filled with the knowledge of God's will in all spiritual
> wisdom and understanding, so that you may lead lives worthy
> of the Lord, fully pleasing to him, as you bear fruit in every
> good work and as you grow in the knowledge of God.
>
> —Colossians 1:9-10

READ: Genesis 2:19-20 and I Corinthian 13

God intends for us to know about the creation. The pursuit of knowledge is a task appointed by God. Wherever truth is being sought and found, God's intention is being fulfilled to that extent. The work of the scientist in the laboratory and in the field, the mathematician at the computer screen, the historian pouring over ancient documents, the social researcher interviewing people are all engaged in the discovery of truth. They are doing the work which God calls humankind to do.

Some say that a little knowledge is a bad thing. It is also true that knowledge without wisdom and love can be destructive. What shall we do with what we know? Advances in human biology, especially in gene research pose some particularly penetrating problems in the realm of ethics. The most recent and newsworthy development has to do with human cloning, and the moral issues associated with that possibility. Let us pray that we use God-given knowledge in every area of research and development for God-intended purposes.

PRAYER: O God, Author of truth, we thank you for the capability
of discovering truth, and for our ability to put our knowledge
to work for the good of humankind. Give us wisdom and love
as we apply what we know to human problems. Through
Christ. Amen.

~ ~ ~ ~ ~ ~

JUNE 30

INTENDED TO BE ONE

From the beginning of creation, 'God made them male and female.' 'For this reason a man shall leave his father and his mother and be joined to his wife, and the two shall become one flesh.' So they are no longer two but one flesh.

—Mark 10:6-8

READ: Genesis 2:18-25 And Mark 10:1-9

Our forebears in faith were aware of God's intention for union of man and woman in a permanent partnership. The specific details of family law and custom have varied from culture to culture over the centuries since creation, but no society has been able to exist without some regularized marriage law.

When one explores God's intention further, it is clear that God wants us to enter into meaningful relationships with each other, the deepest of which is marriage. God does not intend for us to live in isolation. The ideal society which God wants would provide us with many opportunities for interpersonal dialogue and group interaction on a variety of levels. The fellowship of the church ought to be a model of what God intends for an ideal human fellowship. Love for one another ought to be evident within the social interactions of the church, and such love should enable each of us to extend our concern and care beyond the church to friends, and neighbors, associates and strangers.

Adam and Eve before, "*the fall,*" symbolize God's intention for humanity in both marriage and society at large.

PRAYER: We pray, O God, your blessing upon our lives in family relationships, in marriage, in our friendships, and in the fellowship of the church. Through Christ. Amen.

JULY

JULY 1

TROUBLE IN THE ORCHARD

> So when the woman saw that the tree was good for
> food, and that it was a delight to the eyes, and that the tree
> was desired to make one wise, she took of its fruit and ate;
> and she also gave some to her husband, who was with her,
> and he ate. Then the eyes of both were opened, and they
> knew that they were naked . . . .
>
> —Genesis 3:6-7

READ: Genesis 3:3-7, 13-19 and Revelation 21:1-4

The human condition is quite adequately described in just a few of these early-day verses of Scripture; pain and suffering, interpersonal trouble, hard work, hunger, pests of one kind or another, even unpleasant things like snakes, and finally—death. The ancient story of Adam and Eve certainly has it right about us—about what it is like to be human. But, we do not learn much more than we already know about our circumstances. What the story really reveals to us is an understanding of why we have so much trouble in life.

In plain and simple terms the story of Adam and Eve explains the human condition in terms of sin, and declares sin to be our normal tendency to want to be our own god, thus removing the one true God from our lives. Have you ever noticed that the people who are most difficult, are the ones who know everything, and assume that you do not? They know what's best for you and spare nothing to let you know that. Depending upon how you are put together one of two things will happen as a result. Either you will get angry and separate yourself from such a person, or you will cave in to him or her and become—in some sense—a slave to that person. Such a one is the adult child who can't make a decision because Mother always knows best, or the son who barely speaks to his father for fear of being told what the score is.

Conflicts, large and small, grow out of the all too normal situation of one person "lording it over" another. When two people, each wanting to be god, come together trouble ensues, because by definition only one can be god.

The good news of the Bible is that when we submit ourselves to the one and only true God, we become brothers and sisters to one another and content under God's rulership, and we'll get along with each other. Thus the promise of Revelation will be fulfilled, in part even now! "(God) will wipe every tear from their eyes . . . mourning and crying and pain will be no more."

PRAYER: O Lord, only You are God. Let me be your child, yours only. In Christ. Amen.

~ ~ ~ ~ ~ ~

JULY 2

STAIRWAY TO HEAVEN

Then they said, "Come, let us build ourselves a city and a tower with its top in the heavens and let us make a name for ourselves . . ." And the Lord said, "Look, they are one people, and they have all one language; and this is only the beginning of what they will do . . . Come let us go down and confuse their language there, so that they will not understand one another's speech."

—Genesis 11:4,6,7

READ: Genesis 11:1-9 and Galatians 3:23-29

On the face of it, it sounds strange for God to destroy the unity which people had developed, when we know that so much human misery comes as a result of our disunity. The point of the story is found in verse 4: "Come . . . let us make a name for ourselves." Unity built for such a selfish reason is unity apart from God. It derives from human willfulness, instead of service to God. Genesis gives us in this story of the Tower of Babel another example of sin—humanity trying to supplant God. That vain effort, the story declares, won't work. Such was the imposed unity of Nazi Germany, or of Communist dictatorship, the unity enforced with violence in Iraq before Hussein was toppled. This kind of unity stands in stark contrast to the unity developed in a democracy. These forced, God-supplanting "unities" fell.

This ancient parable of the Tower of Babel explains the reason for misunderstanding between individuals and among nations by saying that when a civilization attempts a "stairway to heaven" without obedience and devotion to God, its attempts at greatness will be in vain, and will end in confusion and disaster, symbolized by the tearing down of the Berlin Wall.

Unity is possible only when each person or group turns to God. Such is the oneness which God gives.

Paul wrote to the Galatians: "For in Christ Jesus you are all children of God through faith . . . all of you are one in Christ Jesus."—Galatians 3:26,28

PRAYER: Ruler of earth and Heaven, Let us be one in Christ with all our brothers and sisters everywhere. In Christ. Amen.

~ ~ ~ ~ ~ ~

JULY 3

HOW COME YOU'RE SO GOOD?

We love because he (God) first loved us.
—I John 4:19

READ: I John 4:13-21 and John 15:12-17

We have often heard it said that disaster brings out the best in us. People help one another by providing needed food, clothing, blankets, beds, and first aid when homes are destroyed by fire, tornado or flood. Some risk their lives to rescue injured people trapped under the rubble caused by an earthquake. Why? Ordinarily we seem to pay little heed to the problems of others. Sometimes we take extra measures to avoid other people's troubles. But in the case of disaster, we tend to rally around those in need. Why?

A number of students of the human mind and of social dynamics answer the question in terms of such principles as human survival instincts, the need to relieve one's own sadness over the event, or to enhance one's own state of mind following a disaster. The very fact that such helpfulness perplexes us says something about our lack of self understanding. Perhaps our view of the human condition is so jaded that we can't understand folks loving each other. The message of the Bible is that our ability to love stems from God and his love for us. The story of God's dealing with humanity is a narrative of love and justice. God's covenant with Israel was a covenant in which God would continue to love people, asking humanity to love in response. The reconciling love of God in Christ gives each of us the capacity to love God and to love each other, as we were designed to do when we were created in the IMAGE OF GOD! Let's do it.

PRAYER: Help me to love my neighbors in good times as well as in times of disaster, as you love me, O God In Christ. Amen.

~ ~ ~ ~ ~ ~

JULY 4

AND OF NATURE'S GOD ENTITLE THEM

> Then Jesus said, . . . "If you continue in my word, you are truly my disciples; and you will know the truth, and the truth will make you free!"
>
> —John 8:31-32

READ: Psalm 119:1-6 and John 18:37-38

Fourth of July—Independence Day! Let's think abut that. In the Declaration of Independence, the first appeal to the Divine is to "nature's God," presumably the Law-giver, the Author of truth. Every civilization, especially a democratic one, depends upon honoring the truth and respecting the law by a majority of its citizens. Without honest speaking of truth, a society soon falls into anarchy, the ordered hold of the law upon the citizenry is thereby diminished. The power of government to rule effectively is eroded to the extent that falsehoods replace truth in the affairs of the nation. False testimony in the court-room, books which white-wash or lie about events and official government double-speak are terrifying examples of the cancerous effect of untruths and cover-ups upon the ability of the courts to carry out justice and the government to rule its people justly. Credibility is a precious virtue without which a nation can fall into decay and ruin.

The Christian's contribution to the freedom and democracy of his/her own country is, in the first place, a high regard for truth and integrity. We serve a Master who "came into the world to testify to the truth." (John 18:37) As followers of Christ in this society our first responsibility is to speak the truth and to have courage to bear witness to the truth wherever we see it. This calls us to name untruth whenever and wherever we find it. What more significant contribution to our country can there be, than to help establish truth, honesty and order throughout the land. It is the patriotic duty of the Christian to bear witness to the truth. Thus we serve not only our nation, but God, the Author of truth, as well.

PRAYER: O God, Author of truth, help me to be a carrier of the truth wherever I go. In Christ. Amen.

~ ~ ~ ~ ~

JULY 5

ENDOWED BY THEIR CREATOR
WITH CERTAIN INALIENABLE RIGHTS

I shall walk at liberty, for I have sought your precepts. I will speak of your decrees before kings . . . .
—Psalm 119:45-46

READ: Psalm 119:41-48 and Galatians 5:1-15

The major portion of the Declaration of Independence lists the abuses of rights by the English Crown, after having affirmed that the Creator is the source of our inalienable rights. Apparently the founders of our nation knew that freedom, human rights, and liberty have their origin in God. The Bible is clear about this. The text printed above declares that my freedom comes from following God's teaching. Paul wrote to the Galatians concerning freedom, declaring that God calls us to freedom in Christ.

The civil rights movement, at its best, taught us that the abuse of rights of any of our citizens has a way of limiting the freedom of all of us in society. When we allow the liberty of others to be taken away through poverty, or racism, our own freedom is in jeopardy.

It follows then that whatever we do to help others in society to live in freedom, makes a significant contribution to the good of our entire nation. The Christian, who knows the commands of God, and has been set free in Christ from the bondage of sin, should have the desire and the capacity to work for liberty in the everyday events and relationships of life. We must stand up against unjust treatment of minorities. We must help to provide the basic human needs to all our fellow citizens. We must do what we can to free the falsely accused, and the unjustly imprisoned. In whatever way we can, we must help insure the inalienable rights of all our neighbors near and far. To do that as a Christian is to be a patriotic American.

PRAYER: Help me identify oppression of all kinds and to work to free others from it. In Christ, who has set me free. Amen.

〜 〜 〜 〜 〜

JULY 6

APPEALING TO THE SUPREME JUDGE OF THE WORLD FOR THE RECTITUDE OF OUR INTENTIONS

> He has told you, o mortal, what is good; and what does the Lord require of you but to do justice, and to love kindness, and to walk humbly with your God?
> —Micah 6:8

READ: Psalm 82:3, Micah 6:6-8, and Philippians 4:4-9

The colonists in drawing up the Declaration of Independence were going very far out on a limb, and they knew that the consequence would be a life and death struggle with the British power. Perhaps at times unsure of themselves, they appealed to God who they prayed would judge their intentions right. Such dependence upon the Absolute Judge has steadily declined, until today when many believe that there is no absolute right or wrong—

only what we are conditioned to think is right or wrong. Or worse yet, letting whether it feels good determine the rectitude of an act. Is it too old fashioned to suggest that many of our social problems in America today result from our failure to appeal to the Supreme Judge of the world for the rectitude (the rightness) of our intentions and actions?

The Christian contributes positively to the good of society when he or she appeals to God for guidance and for evaluation of the affairs of state. We have a responsibility to seek from the Supreme Judge a reading on the policies and actions of our nation, and to participate in the national debates which develop on many issues of national importance. We may not be able to express our opinions in a "thus saith the Lord" mode, for such authority may not hold meaning for the general public, but if we believe something is God's will then our support for such a policy is a patriotic duty as well as our Christian mandate.

PRAYER: Help me to know your will for my country, and give me the courage to work for the accomplishment of your will, O God. Through Christ. Amen

~ ~ ~ ~ ~ ~

JULY 7

WITH FIRM RELIANCE ON THE PROTECTION OF DIVINE PROVIDENCE

> Abraham said, "God himself will provide the lamb for a burnt offering, my son." So the two of them walked on together.
> —Genesis 22:8

READ: I Chronicles 29:1-13

The final sentence of the Declaration of Independence expresses a profound dependence upon God for the common good. With the signing of this statement the colonists embarked upon a new venture in the wilderness of this new land. It would be a dangerous journey over uncharted space. The outcome at that point was unknown. But the one thing they did know was that the "protection of Divine Providence" would be essential in so precarious a position as theirs. The signers of this document knew the story of Abraham, who in faith was willing to sacrifice his son, Isaac, but also in faith could affirm to the boy, "God himself will provide . . . ." (Genesis 22:8) They knew the story of David and the dedication of the Temple when the king affirmed his faith in Divine Providence, "In your hand are power and might; and it is in your hand to make great and to give strength to all." (I Chronicles 29:12)

Faith in the protection of Divine Providence is as needed today as it was in 1776, if the common good is to be served in our land. The Christian can make a helpful contribution to the good of all by living out such a faith in Providence, as did Abraham of old, David, Paul and all the other leaders of God's people.

When one prays for God's protection and provision for all one's fellow Americans, one cannot help but do something about it. We rise from our knees and begin working on the problems of hunger, homelessness, health care, and crime, because we know that God's providence, in part, is made manifest through the efforts of his people. To be thus involved in the common good is to be both Christian and patriotic.

PRAYER: I pray for your protection and your providing hand, O God. Help me to do my part for the common good. In Christ. Amen.

～ ～ ～ ～ ～ ～

JULY 8

IN THE BEGINNING, THE TRUTH-SAYER

For this I was appointed a herald and an apostle (I am

telling the truth, I am not lying) a teacher of the Gentiles in
faith and truth.

—I Timothy 2:7

READ: I Timothy 2:1-7 and Jeremiah 13:12-14

We know nothing of how God looks. It is the tradition of
Scripture not to permit any visual representations of God. But
what we do know is a great deal about what God says. It is the very
nature of God to speak. God is the "truth-sayer."

It is human nature to speak. One of the most important
activities parents carry on with their infants is to talk to them. The
importance of this function continues as the years go by into
childhood and adolescence.

And when they are grown into adulthood conversation with
them becomes a most pleasurable occupation.

We are born to communicate, and without some form of
communication, whether it be speech, sign language, writing, or
non-verbal gestures we are deprived of our full humanness. It is
our nature to communicate with one another. This is one of the
capacities with which we have been endowed as those who have
been created in the IMAGE OF GOD. The God who speaks has
created us to speak.

The prophets in the Old Testament were primarily speakers.
They radically influenced the history of their country on the basis
of their words, words which spoke the truth which came from
God. One could say that the theme of the Bible is found in the
prophet's reoccurring phrase, "Thus saith the Lord."

To be most true to our own creation our communication must
be the truth, for God speaks only the truth. Lying, duplicity,
artificiality, guile, and nonsense are corruptions of our creation.
Let us as God's faithful ones speak only the truth to one another.

PRAYER: O God, you have spoken the truth to me. Let me be a
speaker of the truth in all my communication. Through Christ,
the Truth made flesh. Amen

~ ~ ~ ~ ~ ~

JULY 9

NOT "IT WILL" . . . "I WILL"

Then God said, "Let us make humankind in our image,
according to our likeness; and let them have dominion over
the fish of the sea, and over the birds of the air, and over the
cattle, and over all the wild animals of the earth, and over
every creeping thing that creeps upon the earth."

—Genesis 1:26

READ: Philippians 2:12-18, 4:8-9

When God created human beings he gave them a power which
he had not given to the rest of creation—the capacity to WILL.
"Dominion (power) of the fish of the sea . . . . (etc)" Created in
the IMAGE OF GOD, we are allowed to have power over our own
destiny, as God has power over the ultimate destiny of all that is.
When social scientists ask the question: "Why do people do what
they do?" they operate on the "it will happen" principle. That is to
believe that what happens is determined by the circumstances of
the situation over which we have little, if any, significant control.
People act as they do because they have been programmed by
heredity and environment to act that way. Currently there is
heightened study of our genes in order to isolate those genes which
produce certain reactions. A gene has been found which predisposes
a person to like sweets. The assumption here is that we love, or
hate, build or tear down unintentionally as prescribed by our
genetic make-up. A few decades ago the determining factors were
thought to be in our conditioning. How we were brought up.
How our parents treated us. What the impact of the society or
neighborhood was upon us. These were the factors thought to
determine whether we loved or hated, smiled or frowned. It will
happen because of what has occurred in our lives. More recently

much more attention is being paid to our genetic make-up. How we act is thought to be largely determined by who our forebears were and what genes they possessed.

Christian self-understanding is not *it will*, but *I will*. Created in the image of God, you and I have the capacity to will, to decide, to determine, at least to some extent, what our future shall be. We are not victims of our own circumstances of birth or up-bringing. We cans take matters in our own hands and decide what we will do with what has been given or done to us. According to our own creation we not only have dominion over the fish of the sea, but power over our own life,

Paul writes to the Philippians to encourage them to make good use of their power in choosing the good. Let us *will the good* in our lives.

PRAYER: Thank you, God, for power to decide. Let me *will the good*, that is your will, in my life. In Christ. Amen.

~ ~ ~ ~ ~

JULY 10

IT TAKES TWO

How very good and pleasant it is when kindred live together in unity!

—Psalm 133:1

God gives the desolate a home to live in.

—Psalm 68:6

READ: John 15:11-17

Basic to our human nature is the need to relate to other people. It takes two (at least) to make a life. Without such relationship life is desolate. It is essential to our well-being to have friends, to relate to others in an open, free and accepting way. Each of us needs someone with whom we can be totally at ease, with whom to share life with each other on an equal basis, as "kindred living together in unity." (Psalm 133:1) Fortunately for many people such friendship and sharing occurs within the family or marriage. Most people require friendships beyond family as well—fishing buddies, bridge partners, back-yard neighbors, or friends at work.

The Christian is called by Christ to relate to other Christians in a loving and accepting way. The fellowship of the church ought to provide us with opportunities for the fulfillment of this basic value of human friendship. If our own church experience is lacking in this capacity for friendship we need to do our part to help bring about such fellowship of love and common sharing within our church.

PRAYER: Thank you, O God, for my family and friends. Give me the will and the wisdom to maintain and cultivate such friendships within my church. In Christ. Amen.

～ ～ ～ ～ ～ ～

JULY 11

BETTER THAN SHOPPING

The Lord God took the man and put him in the garden of Eden to till it and keep it.

—Genesis 2:15

In all toil there is profit, but mere talk leads only to poverty.

—Proverbs 14:23

READ: GENESIS 1:26-30 and Luke 19:11-27

By the time July is half over parents of small children, and some whose children are not so young, have heard from them a thousand times, "What can I do?" The need to do something—anything—is apparently bred into us. You can't just sit, doing nothing. At the very least you must be thinking, or meditating or something! There is a basic need to be actively engaged whether that be in productive work of some kind—manual or mental, or in a recreational activity, alone or with others.

One need only to observe the unemployed to realize the dehumanizing effects of idleness. The specter of hordes of young men, many of whom are black, standing around on the streets and alleys of American cities poses a serious problem for our society.

Jesus' parable of the talents very strongly directs us to active engagement which in some sense of the word is productive. He points to the devastating results of idleness as exemplified in the servant who buried his talent. Put in this light the Christian sees work and other significant activity as a matter of stewardship—using what God has given us for God's purposes. This, Genesis declares, is why we are in the Garden. "To till it and to keep it."

One observer of Amish society has contrasted the Amish joy in work with the joy many modern Americans have in shopping. We hate work and like to shop. The Amish love to work and are not much for shopping.

PRAYER: Help me, O God, to engage actively in life around me, gaining joy from my work as a servant of Christ. In whose name I pray. Amen

~ ~ ~ ~ ~

JULY 12

HE'S BEEN THERE, BUT NOT DONE THAT

For we do not have a high priest who is unable to sympathize with our weaknesses, but we have one who in every respect has been tested, as we are, yet without sin.
—Hebrews 4:15

READ: Hebrews 4:14-16 and Jude 24-25

"Been there—done that." "It takes one to know one." "He's one of us." "He's been there." When such statements as these are made about a person that person gains credibility and authority because of the key ingredient of IDENTIFICATION. This is what the writer of Hebrews affirms about Jesus. He has stood where we stand, and walked in our shoes. He has felt the same inner weaknesses that plague us. In fact whatever temptation you have felt, Jesus has felt as well. Ponder that! Think about what tempts you. Jesus felt that too. Really—he has felt it just as strongly as we have—whatever the temptation: to lie, to cheat, to give in to lust, to "Lord" it over others, to run, to hide—you name it. If you have felt it, so has Jesus. That is what Hebrews testifies.

What a comfort to know that Jesus has been where I am. Been there! It is a very big step toward maturity when a child or young person discovers that his or her parents are indeed human, and have been tempted in ways that the child has faced. But it is also a very big let-down to discover that one's parents have not only been tempted in some way, but have at times succumbed—and have fallen.

The neat thing about Jesus is that he never gave in to temptation, but remained strong—his own person, the person God created him to be. Not only do we have one who has been there, but one who has been able to remove himself from danger of falling. Not done that! Thus Jude reminds us that this is the one who can keep us from falling. The one who has been there, but has not done that!

PRAYER: O Christ, I thank you that you have been in my shoes, the spot I'm in, and that you can keep me from falling. Amen.

~ ~ ~ ~ ~

JULY 13

TEMPTED TO BE BEAUTIFUL PEOPLE

"If you are the Son of God, command this stone to become a loaf of bread."

—Luke 4:3

READ: Luke 4:1-4, Luke 12:22-31 and Deuteronomy 8:1-3

At the outset of Jesus' ministry and most likely along the way as well, he was tempted to live for his own pleasure and satisfaction. This idea follows from the Hebrews affirmation that Jesus was "In every respect tested (tempted) as we are." (Hebrews 4:15) Turning stones into bread would have been to twist life's opportunities into self satisfaction. He was, after all, very hungry at the time.

This temptation is especially American, because so much of our energy and productivity is spent on furnishing a life style for ourselves, to make us the "beautiful people." How we drool at the life styles of the rich and famous. They have been our roll models from childhood, and the subjects of countless articles, pictures, and advertisements in print and electronic media.

Jesus was tempted to turn his energies inward and to live like the rich and the famous—but he didn't. He knew that such a beautiful life isn't what gives one meaning and substance. He quoted the portions of Deuteronomy which said that one lives by everything which proceeds from the mouth of the Lord. Serving and obeying God is what gives life zest and meaning—not just piling up luxury upon luxury.

This doesn't deny the value of food and clothing, and other good things. Elsewhere Luke declares that God will take care of our physical needs—not to worry.

PRAYER: Keep me, O God, from going after the gold. Let me

know that beauty is internal and that you are the one to make me beautiful. In Christ. Amen.

~ ~ ~ ~ ~ ~

JULY 14

LUST FOR POWER

Then the devil led him up and showed him in an
instant all the kingdoms of the world. And the devil said to
him, "To you I will give their glory and all this authority; for
it has been given to me and I give it to anyone I please."
—Luke 4:5-6

READ: Luke 4:5-8 and Mark 10:35-45

The second of Jesus' temptations is the most difficult to understand. What really does this mean? The key is in the word, "authority," or power as it is often translated. Jesus was tempted to exert power over others, to claim undue authority over them. This essentially is what James and John asked Jesus to give them. They wanted positions of power. Ultimate power over others is the power of life and death—complete ownership, as in the power a master has over a slave. Rape is an ugly example of such lust for power run rampant. Murder is the exertion of complete power over another human being. Rape and murder are ways of worshiping the devil. But what are the more subtle ways by which we enter into such worship?

Whenever one exercises control over another without his/her consent one determines the destiny of the other, and that is illegitimate power and authority. This can often be very destructive. The parent who controls the child is in danger of either crippling the child emotionally, or of inciting rebellion in future years. The person who controls his/her spouse limits the life satisfaction of the spouse unduly—a little like taking a life. Whenever we control others we limit their freedom, thus enslaving them to that extent. To exert power over others, to exalt oneself as the monarch, is to worship the devil, a worship which Jesus refused.

Jesus' answer to James and John was to say that the greatest is the one who serves, not the one who controls others in order to be served by them.

PRAYER: O God, let freedom be granted to those around me, by my willingness not to control but to serve. In Christ who served. Amen

~ ~ ~ ~ ~ ~

JULY 15

PLEASING AND APPEASING

> Then the devil took him to Jerusalem, and placed him on the pinnacle of the temple, saying to him "If you are the Son of God, throw yourself down from here, for it is written, 'He will command his angels concerning you, to protect you.'"
>
> —Luke 4:9-10

READ: Luke 4:9-13 and Mark 14:10-11

Jesus' final temptation was to be a crowd pleaser. He was tempted to do things which would make others think highly of him. This seems to be one of the motivations behind Judas' betrayal. Notice that when Judas went to the chief priests, it pleased them that he was a defector.

Jesus was tempted to betray his identity as God's own person by putting himself in a position of appeasing the other side, so to speak. To be pleasing to the crowds. But he didn't!

On the other hand, like Judas, we like to please others, to appease their desires at the expense of our own convictions and personal integrity. Whenever we bury our convictions in order to gain the approval of others, we deny Christ as Peter did by saying that he did not know Jesus on the night of Jesus' arrest. When we give approval to opinions or prejudices expressed to us which we know are contrary to Christian values, we defect to the other side in order to be pleasing to them, like Judas did. When we allow others to trample over us and to stymie our own self-expression we are appeasing, in compliance with the wishes of others and in denial of our own God-given identity. To be pleasing and appeasing is to jump off the temple in an attempt to gain approval. God's approval, on the other hand, should be sufficient for us, as it was for Jesus.

PRAYER: Help me to stand by my convictions, O God, and not to give myself over to others for their approval instead of yours. In Christ. Amen.

~ ~ ~ ~ ~ ~

JULY 16

ENJOY

So whether you eat or drink, or whatever you do, do
everything for the glory of God.
—I Corinthians 10:31

READ: Psalm 73:24-26 And Matthew 5:14-16

In a poignant scene in the last act of Thornton Wilder's play, *Our Town,* Emily, the young woman who has just died, is given a chance to come back to earth for a day. She re-visits her family briefly, after which she sadly concludes that people do not fully realize the wonderful life and daily experiences which they take for granted. There are so many good things which people barely notice, she observed.

In a culture in which work and production have assumed great importance, most of us have been taught to put off pleasures until the work is done. Later on the real purposes of life will be realized, but now is the time to prepare for the future, we say. And so, we are always looking forward to the weekend, to a vacation, or to retirement, thereby missing the pleasure of the present moment.

Christian tradition has long affirmed that the purpose of life is to glorify God and to enjoy God forever. When we lead our daily lives as close to God's intention for us as we can, we bring glory to God, and as a result we enjoy life more fully. When we grow in our understanding of what God wants in our lives, and when we develop the capacity for realizing his intentions, we glorify God and find that we enjoy each day of our lives. In this way we would be giving a positive answer to Emily's searching question: "Do any human beings ever realize life while they live it?"

PRAYER: Show me, O Lord, your way and intention for my life, and help me to enjoy fulfilling what you want in my life. In Christ. Amen.

~ ~ ~ ~ ~ ~

JULY 17

LIKE A SIGNAL FROM ANOTHER GALAXY

These things God has revealed to us through the Spirit;
for the Spirit searches everything, even the depths of God.
—I Corinthians 2:10

READ: Psalm 19 and Romans 1:19-23

Highly sophisticated electronic receivers have been positioned in various locations. These function around the clock intended to pick up any possible signals from other planets in the universe. Data fed into a million personal computers is being analyzed constantly to find the unusual signal which will come from elsewhere in the cosmos. Many modern astronomers believe that intelligent life in the galaxy may be sending us messages. Those who doubt this would be convinced if such a signal were to be received by one of the sensitive instruments around the world. Until such a discovery is made it is a matter of conjecture as to whether we are the only intelligent life in the universe.

Humankind has always wondered about the existence of the DIVINE. Christians believe that in answer to our conjecture into the divine, God has indeed made himself known—like a signal from another galaxy.

In a hidden way our search for intelligent life from another place is a search for salvation. Often we think a visitation from another planet might bring some hope for peace on earth. When Neil Armstrong first stepped onto the surface of the moon, there were those who felt that world peace had thereby come closer. Such a hope has since faded.

In truth the signal from God to us contains the hope of peace and salvation. That signal came with words to the shepherds outside Bethlehem, "Glory to God in the highest heaven, and on earth peace among those whom he favors." (Luke 2:14) While things of nature and evidence within humanity reveal the works of God, it is the Word of God as found in the Bible revealing Christ to humankind, which is the only sufficient revelation of God and salvation to us. Christ is the signal that there is indeed eternal life available to humankind.

PRAYER: Tune our instruments, O God, to pick up your signal. Through Christ. Amen.

~ ~ ~ ~ ~ ~

JULY 18

DECODING THE MESSAGE

With my whole heart I seek you; do not let me stray from your commandments. I treasure your word in my heart . . . .

—Psalm 119:10,11

READ: Psalm 119:1-11 and II Timothy 3:14-17

If astronomers ever receive a signal from what they conclude is intelligent life elsewhere in the universe, it appears that the biggest task will remain: that of decoding the message. How on earth will we be able to understand a message sent from beyond earth, from other kinds of creatures from another part of the universe? It won't be in English, to say the least.

When God's signal reached our ancestors in the faith, it wasn't in English, nor in Hebrew or Greek either. It was God's Word in action, the signal from which was discernable in the inner being of people who then put it in their own words to tell one another what they perceived. Eventually they wrote their experience of God's action in their language. The accumulation of the written recordings of their perception of God's signals became the Scriptures of the Old and New Testaments. In a sense they decoded God's message and re-worded it in their own language. In subsequent centuries we have continued this process of re-wording the message into our current languages.

Our task is to read the Bible with such a deep yearning for God's signal (God's Word) that we are able to hear God's message coming to us as fully as to the original "astronomers" of the faith. With the Psalmist we must yearn, "With my whole heart I seek you . . . . I treasure your word in my heart."

PRAYER: By your Spirit, O God, speak to me in such a way that I understand your Word in my language. Through Christ, the Word made flesh. Amen.

~ ~ ~ ~ ~ ~

JULY 19

NO EYE HAS SEEN, NOR EAR HEARD

After he was raised from the dead, his disciples remembered that he had said this; and they believed the scripture and the word that Jesus had spoken.

—John 2:22

READ: Psalm 119:33-40, I Corinthians 2:6-9

"How do you know the Bible is true?" asked the young sceptic. "You just do!" replied the young Christian. Although the answer didn't satisfy the questioner, it is a pretty good answer. The more penetrating question is, "How do you know the Bible is God's Word?" One way of answering this is on a practical level. The Bible proves itself by its own consistency, beauty, and its power to change lives. Some years ago the American Bible Society told the amazing story of a group of Christians found on an isolated island in the Pacific to whom no missionary had ever been sent. Their faith had come, instead, as a result of a shipment of Bibles in the native tongue of their region, which had washed ashore some years earlier.

The ultimate validation of the truth and divine source of the Scriptures comes from the Holy Spirit speaking to the heart of the reader. This, without a doubt, is what happened in the lives of those native people who discovered not only a box of books, but the Word of God. It is our privilege to have access to the Bible daily, and to possess the promise of the Holy Spirit to be the Interpreter.

PRAYER: Send your Spirit into my heart, O Lord, that I may know the truth of your Word for my life. Through Christ, the Word. Amen

JULY 20

A LANTERN TO OUR FOOTSTEPS

> But the aim of such instruction (divine training) is love that comes from a pure heart, a good conscience and sincere faith
>
> —I Timothy 1:5

READ: Psalm 1 and John 16:13-15

Jesus was once asked to summarize the Law. For the Law stood out like the Bible stands out for us. Jesus' answer was: LOVE. Love God and love your neighbor. Paul wrote to Timothy to advise him to hold onto a sincere and authentic faith, to act in such a way as to maintain a good conscience, and to be motivated by a pure heart—one without deceit or duplicity. These characteristics, he said, would produce love.

The most clear definition of God anywhere in the Bible is the statement in John that God is love. Throughout the Bible, particularly in the New Testament, the teaching is to love one another as God has loved us in Christ. Let's go for it!

PRAYER: May I have a pure heart and a good conscience, O God, that I may love you fully and my neighbor dearly. In Christ. Amen.

~ ~ ~ ~ ~ ~

JULY 21

JOINING WITH ALL OF NATURE

~ ~ ~ ~ ~ ~

Let the heavens be glad, and let the earth rejoice; let the
sea roar, and all that fills it; let the field exult, and everything
in it. Then shall all the trees of the forest sing for joy.
—Psalm 96:11-12

READ: Psalm 95:1-7 and Psalm 148:1-12

July has its bright and beautiful days with clear blue skies and
golden sunlight. And at night in July the vaulted skies are starlit.
July is the month for taking outdoor scenery pictures. It is natural
to have an urge to try to capture the stunning natural vistas on
film. Some folks set up their easels, get out their paints and try to
put the scene down on canvas. This same desire makes some people
want to know all the names of flowers, trees, and birds, as well as
rocks, insects and rivers. As human beings we are part of nature
and there is something deep within us which wants to experience
the rest of God's creation in a profound way. Some biologists believe
that we carry in our human memory material stored there millions
of years ago in our animal past.

The Bible does not try to separate us from nature as sometimes
we modern Christians have tried to do. Rather, as the Psalmist
proclaims, that together with nature we praise God for God's
goodness. After decades of exploiting nature for personal gain, let
us re-gain a reverence for nature by joining her in songs of praise to
our common creator.

PRAYER: With all of nature I join in praising you our Creator and our God. Through Christ through whom the world came into being. Amen.

~ ~ ~ ~ ~ ~

JULY 22

CRYING FOR HELP

Give ear, O Lord, to my prayer; listen to my cry of supplication. In the day of my trouble I call on you, for you will answer me.

—Psalm 86:6-7

READ: Psalm 64:1-6, Psalm 86:1-2 and Psalm 140:1-6

Many of the Psalms begin with a cry for help. There are many times in our lives when these very cries for help echo our cries as well. The feelings expressed in such Psalms strike universal human chords. Born out of deep struggle, the Psalms call to God for help.

When we are confronted with a serious crisis over which we have little or no control, and when we come to the end of our resources to deal with the problem we must turn to someone for help. This often a difficult step to take. But even more difficult is the situation for which there is no one available to help. We have no one to turn to in some dire circumstances, such as a disease pronounced terminal, or a hopelessly broken relationship, a total financial reverse, a fear with an edge of panic which is getting out of hand, or a task too difficult to accomplish. The common factor in these crises is the sense that we have lost control over our lives. Like a tiny boat which has lost its mooring and is now at the mercy of the storm, our lives are dashed this way and that, and we don't know what to do. In such moments of abject need, turn to God and cry for help. The cries of the Psalmist for help can be your means of expression.

PRAYER: "I call to you, Lord; help me now. Listen to me when I call to you." Through Christ. Amen.

~ ~ ~ ~ ~ ~

JULY 23

CONFESSING THE MESS

> Lord, hear my voice! Let your ears be attentive to the voice of my supplications. If you, O Lord, should mark iniquities, Lord, who could stand? But there is forgiveness with you, so that you may be revered.
>
> —Psalm 130:2-4

READ: Psalm 51:1-17

There is one kind of trouble which has a most painful sting. That is the trouble we bring upon ourselves. There is no feeling quite like it—when you know you should have done a certain thing, but you didn't carry it out, and now it is too late, and you must pay the price for having messed up. Maybe you borrowed a book, and now many years later, you still have it, and you don't know how to find the owner. Or once long ago someone asked you earnestly a question regarding your Christian faith, and you failed to answer. You speak a hurtful word to someone, thereby doing them personal injury, and much as you want to, you can't take it back. Or perhaps some breach of honesty on your part makes you fearful and guilt-ridden. What can one do with such burdens of guilt? Some folk carry around a great deal of this kind of baggage all their lives. Must this be our lot in life?

The confession of sin and guilt found in Psalm 51 can be a vehicle by which we can carry the mistakes of our lives to the very throne of a merciful God, there to confess the mess we've made of things. While the results of our misdoing must remain, the sting of guilt can be removed if we honestly and earnestly seek God's forgiveness. God invites us to confess the mess we've made.

PRAYER: By your grace, most merciful God, help me to go back to the sore spots in my memory and to uncover and admit my sin, confessing it before you. Then may I enjoy your forgiveness. Through Christ. Amen.

~ ~ ~ ~ ~

JULY 24

EXULTING IN GOD

Bless the Lord, O my soul, and all that is within me,
bless his holy name. Bless the Lord, O my soul, and do not
forget all his benefits.

—Psalm 103:1-2

READ: Psalm 66:1-9

As we pass from childhood through youth to adulthood we lose a spontaneity which children posses. The picture comes to mind of a child jumping up and down in exuberant response to something good which has just happened, or in joyous anticipation of something soon to occur. Young people are "cool" and refuse to show enthusiasm, even when they feel it inside. Adults may not feel enthusiasm as intensely or as often as they did in childhood. How sad when life with all its charm and excitement fails to make us jump for joy.

The Psalmist can help us here. In many of the Psalms one senses the exultation of the writer, and the joy of those who sang the Psalms. Use the sixty-sixth Psalm to regain your enthusiasm. Then look at other Psalms in which this sort of unbridled joy and exultation are expressed.

When something really good happens in our lives we

automatically want to share it with someone we love. It is even more satisfying to be able to share one's joy with those who have helped to bring about the circumstances which have brought joy into one's life. When you are overwhelmed by something good in your life, share your joy with God, remembering that every good gift has its origin in God's love for you. Many of the Psalms help one share joy with God in exultation. Read them. Memorize some of those wonderful lines. Try singing them!

PRAYER: I sing your mighty power and your gracious love, O Lord, my God, for you do such marvelous things for me. You brighten my life. In Christ, the Light. Amen

~ ~ ~ ~ ~ ~

JULY 25

DESPAIRING AND LONELY

My God, My God, why have your forsaken me? Why are you so far from helping me, from the words of my groaning? O my God, I cry by day but you do not answer, and by night, but find no rest.

—Psalm 22:1-2

READ: Psalm 22:1-11

Whether we realize it or not, often the "bottom line" of human suffering is the profound sense that God has abandoned us. When we fall into depression or despair, we feel deeply that we have been left alone. We feel cut off from all sources of power, as well as an estrangement from God. We are forced then to admit that our situation is hopeless. Jesus hit that low point on the cross and felt forsaken by God. He used the Psalmists words (22:1) to express his anguish and loneliness.

Somehow, when we are deeply troubled it helps to know that Jesus has been over this same path of sorrow, and that the Psalmists of old had also experienced depression, despair, and loneliness. Reading and praying their words can help us to pass through such valleys when our lives take such turns.

Note now that in the twenty-second Psalm the means by which the Psalmist is lifted out of the pit of despair was to be reminded of what God had done in the past to help him or her personally, as well as for Israel itself.

God may seem to be absent from us in the present moment, but our faith must be firm in our conviction that God has acted powerfully and helpfully in the past—for our own good. If God so acted in the past we can have the faith that God will act on our behalf now and in the future, even though it is difficult to observe divine action in the midst of the turmoil and pain of the moment. This we know, even more surely than the Psalmist knew it, for we know that in the Resurrection of Christ, good has conquered evil for all time and eternity.

PRAYER: Most powerful God, you have been at work from the beginning of time creating and redeeming, loving and guiding, I thank you for the assurance that your love and power are mine today and in my future. In the Risen Christ. Amen.

~ ~ ~ ~ ~ ~

JULY 26

IN PRAISE OF FURRY TAILS AND GREEN LEAVES

You have given them dominion over the works of your
hands; you have put all things under their feet.
—Psalm 8:6

READ: Psalm 8

Scientific evidence is bringing forth evidence that people with pets live longer than people who do not have pets. A child going through the trauma of a hospital experience is helped by a teddy bear which she can hold and cuddle. It is said that stroking a furry cat on your lap is good therapy. From the beginning of human history, apparently, people have developed significant relationships with animals. This kind of relationship is often among the first "friendships" a child will have. To be human is to relate, even to furry friends. One need only refer to the popularity of Beanie Babies over the last few years.

Part of the essence of being human is to relate to other creatures and growing things in God's universe. There is something basically human about surrounding one's home inside and out with vegetation. If it were otherwise, we would pave our yards with green cement and fill our vases with pencils and rulers.

Next time you comb out your dog's coat, cuddle your cat, or water your houseplants, do it knowing that it is an expression of your God-given humanity to care for a portion of God's creation. The wag of your dog's tail, and the purr of your kitten, and the new light green growth on your plant are in response to your caring relationship to them. In this give praise to God. St. Francis wrote in 1225:

> "Dear Mother earth, who day by day
> Unfoldest blessings on our way,
> Oh, praise Him! Alleluia!
> The flowers and fruits that in thee grow,
> Let them his glory also show! Oh praise Him!"

PRAYER: I thank you, O God, for my friends, the birds and the beasts, the flowers and the trees. In Christ. Amen.

~ ~ ~ ~ ~

JULY 27

APPLES COME FROM TREES

"Abide in me as I abide in you. Just as the branch

cannot bear fruit by itself unless it abides in the vine, neither
can you unless you abide in me.

—John 15:4

READ: John 15:1-10

In early spring you can cut off the branches which carry apple
blossoms and bring them inside your house for blossoms, but you
can't make apples that way. The fruit is produced only when the
branch remains connected to the tree as its source of life and
productivity. Unrelated blossoming branches, though fragrant for
a while, will soon rot. Jesus said that we are like such branches. We
need to remain attached to the vine, which is Christ himself. To be
human is to relate.

To be fully human is to be actively related to God. Even though
we are accustomed to thinking of Jesus Christ as divine—and rightly
so, it is also true that he was fully human. In fact Christian thought
affirms that Jesus was the most perfect human person ever to live
upon earth. The writer of Hebrews said that he was like us in every
way, except that he did not sin. That is to say that he did not go
contrary to God at any point in his life. He was what God intended
us to be. In Christ the image of God was unbroken and not
distorted, unchanged by human error. When we relate to Christ,
we are relating to the perfect illustration of our own intended
humanity. So, the better we know Christ, the more we can know
what God wants in us. From the Christian point of view, the essence
of human life is to be fully connected to the vine, which is Christ,
who is indeed God.

As branches of Christ's vine our flowering is not just pretty
and temporary, but productive and lasting.

PRAYER: O living vine of God, from whom I must not separate,
    feed me with the nutrients of faith by which to make me flower
    and bear fruit for you. Through Christ. Amen.

~ ~ ~ ~ ~

JULY 28

HANGING TOUGH

> My grace is sufficient for you, for power is made perfect
> in weakness.
>
> —II Corinthians '12:9

READ: II Corinthians 12:1-10

Oftentimes we do not know what is troubling those around us. It comes as an unwelcome surprise to learn of a physical illness or an emotional problem lodged in the life of a close associate or friend. Only once in all of Paul's writings in our New Testament does he talk about his problem. And then he does not explain what it is. He called it a "thorn in the flesh." The Greek word he uses might more accurately be translated as "stake." A thorn under the skin is an irritant, but a stake wrenching in one's body is quite another matter. What was his problem? John Calvin thought it referred to spiritual temptations. Luther thought it to be persecutions. The Roman Catholic viewpoint for centuries thought it was something sexual. Others have thought it was epilepsy, or headaches, disfigurement, or eye trouble, Or possibly a recurring malaria.

Perhaps it is fortunate that we do not know what plagued Paul, for now each of us can identify his or her own "thorn" and gain from Paul's faith the strength needed to endure it—whatever *it* is. Even though Paul prayed repeatedly for God to remove the problem which bothered him so, his wish was never granted. Instead, God provided Paul; with the strength, patience and endurance to cope with the problem. Thus God enabled Paul to rise above it. Sufficient grace from God was given to match the seriousness of the weakness, whatever it was. That should be good news to us now, in the time to come whenever disease or trouble may intrude upon our lives.

If your distressing life problem is not removed, or removable, do not lose faith. God may very well give you what you need to live through it.

PRAYER: O God, give me the resource I need to endure those difficulties in life which do not go away. Through Christ. Amen.

~ ~ ~ ~ ~

JULY 29

MISSION IMPOSSIBLE

"Is anything too wonderful (impossible) for the Lord?
At the set time I will return to you, in due season, and Sarah shall have a son."
—Genesis 18:14

READ: Genesis 18:1-15

Sometimes we don't ask for help because we don't think such help is possible. "O, he couldn't do that!" we say and continue to try to solve our problem alone. We even doubt God's capability when we fail to seek his help in time of need. Abraham and Sarah doubted God's ability and laughed when they were told in their old age that she would give birth to a child. According to Israel's understanding of God's plan, it was necessary for Abraham to have a son through whom to pass on the line of tribal authority. But he and his wife had no son. And then God accomplished his "mission impossible" and Isaac was born to Sarah.

Don't second-guess what God can or can't do in your life. God wants the best for you, and wants to accomplish his will through your life. Those are two powerful reasons for God to engage in impossible missions in your life. Not everything we want accomplished in our lives will be done, for reasons sometimes beyond our knowing. But more can happen for the good than we have ever imagined. So don't laugh. The next visitor may bring good news of God's gracious and powerful action.

PRAYER: Give me the faith to expect from you, O God, your mighty acts in my life. Through Christ. Amen.

~ ~ ~ ~ ~

JULY 30

THAT'S LIFE

I have learned to be content with whatever I have.
—Philippians 4:11

READ: Philippians 4:10-14

Except for small flames like candles and matches, it is impossible to blow out fires. The more wind you apply the more intensely the fire burns, and the more it will consume. Our desire for possessions is like a fire. The more we try to quench our desire to acquire things, the more brightly the fire of our desire seems to burn, and the more we want to consume. The Stoics of ancient Greece said that, "If you want to make a man happy, add not to his possessions, but take away from his desires." To be content is to be truly wealthy. It was drawing upon the wealth of his contentment which made Paul able to say that he was content in whatever state he found himself.

We live in a culture which believes the opposite—that the more you have, the happier you will be. A belief, by the way, which has never been proven! A great deal of sorrow and tragedy, as well as resentful frustration, have come into the lives of many of us because of our discontent with our own circumstances. Furthermore the goal of ever-increasing consumption has led us to the brink of serious resource depletion. This dangerous drain is begging of us a revision of life-style to a more simple and less wasteful level.

How much happier we would be if we could be content with less, and could say without despair, "That's life," in the face of limitations of any kind which may come to us. Paul was able to say this because he had received the resources from Christ to be content in whatever circumstances came his way in life.

PRAYER: O God, make me content with those situations and circumstances in my life which cannot change. Help me to count Christ as my richest gain. In Him. Amen.

~ ~ ~ ~ ~ ~

JULY 31

RESISTANCE OVERCOME

"Saul, Saul, why are you persecuting me? It hurts you to kick against the goads."

—Acts 26:14

READ: Acts 26:9-18

Some of God's most dynamic work in our lives comes to us as God goads us into unwanted change in our lives. Many times we kick against the goad. The picture here is of a man driving oxen by using a goad, the stick used to force the beasts in the desired direction We don't want God to change the direction of our lives, when God calls us into new adventures. We don't want to be changed We like things pretty much as they are, and we resist unwelcome change.

That certainly was the case with Saul of Tarsus. The introduction of Jesus Christ and his movement into the Judaism of Saul's day presented him with a most unwelcome development. He strongly resisted Christ wherever he could. He kicked against

God's goading! He persecuted Christ's followers hoping thereby to get rid of this hated intrusion upon the settled life he had previously enjoyed. Such angry resistance and bitter opposition was hurting Saul.

However, God stepped in and overcame Saul's resistance. That is what happened to Saul on his way to Damascus. It took a very powerful and dramatic experience to stop Saul in his tracks, to make him quit fighting Christ's call, and to turned him into a follower of Christ.

We need dramatic impact when our resistance becomes strong and we fight the entry of God's word and will into our lives. Some folk resist all their lives and hurt themselves deeply in the process of continued kicking against the goad of God. So check those points in your life at which you resist God. When does your anger flare? What changes are you kicking against? Could these be the very points at which Christ is knocking? On the closed door of your life? Could such a point be the place in your life where God wants to turn you around? "Listen, I am standing at the door knocking; if you hear my voice and open the door. I will come in to you . . ." (Revelation 3:20)

PRAYER: Lower my resistance, O God, and turn me around. Through Christ. Amen

AUGUST

AUGUST 1

ON BEING A CHRISTIAN NEIGHBOR

Be at peace among yourselves. And we urge you,
beloved to admonish the idlers, encourage the faint hearted,
help the weak, be patient with all of them.
—I Thessalonians 5:13-14

READ: I Thessalonians 5:12-24

In the midst of a world in which fighting between ethnic groups is going on, as well as within communities where the spirit of unity has disappeared, Paul urges Christians to be at peace with one another and to respect and assist people in every condition. There is in this passage of Scripture a formula for modeling the Kingdom of God through the kind of fellowship and mutual aid urged by Paul. He was addressing a group of Christians who were experiencing divisions and divisiveness in their congregation. Some of this tension had turned into slander against Paul himself. Some members had begun to despise the law and its authority. And then there were those in the church who had become lazy and were living on the dole, as we would say. Into this mix Paul advises a peaceable Kingdom in which Christians respect one another and pay special attention to the needs of those who are weak or timid.

In our associations with others in our congregations and in our communities, how might we give special care and support to the "little people" who are so often unseen or forgotten because of their timidity? What might we be doing to strengthen those who are powerless—some because of racial or ethnic origin, others because of gender, still others because of cultural differences or appearance. Whatever the obstacle, Christians are called to give special attention and care to the needy. We must open our eyes and ears to discover the weak and the faint hearted. We must open our hearts to want to give aid. We must open our minds to grow in our understanding of how to give meaningful help. We must open our hands to give such aid.

PRAYER: Help me, O Lord, to understand what my neighbor needs from me, and give me the courage to offer caring aid. In Christ. Amen.

〜 〜 〜 〜 〜 〜

AUGUST 2

A HUMILIATING DEMAND REFUSED

But Queen Vashti refused to come at the king's command conveyed by the eunuchs. At this the king was enraged, and his anger burned within him.

—Esther 1:12

READ: Esther 1:10-22 and Galatians 3:26-29

The king was carrying on mightily at a drunken feast and thought he would bring in his queen for a bit of entertainment. When she refuses his humiliating demand he becomes very angry and deposes her. A new queen is chosen and it is Esther who is made queen in place of Vashti.

Poor old King Ahasuerus (Xerxes). He thought he had his wife wrapped around his finger and that he could bring her to his rowdy feast and show off her feminine charms to "the boys." But Vashti had a mind and a dignity of her own and refused to be put on vulgar display. The king was furious. She did not obey him. His friends would think him to be hen-pecked.

How women are regarded in our society is the issue here. The book of Esther assumes the social customs of the ancient orient in which this story takes place. But we see the cruel injustice and the emotional abuse which the king put upon the Queen. We applaud the assertiveness and self-regard of Vashti, because we enjoy a religious and moral point of view which teaches us to regard women as equal to men.

One of the very significant contributions of the Christian faith to our society is the principle of justice which holds men and women as equals. Jesus treated women as beloved of God, and Paul set forth the Christian view point when he wrote to the Galatians: "There is no longer Jew or Greek, there is no longer slave or free, there is no longer male and female; for all of you are one in Christ Jesus." (Galatians 3:28)

PRAYER: Help me to treat everyone as equal and loved by you, O Lord. Through Christ. Amen.

~ ~ ~ ~ ~

AUGUST 3

NO OTHER GOD

> For he had told them that he (Mordecai) was a Jew
> When Haman saw that Mordecai did not bow down or do
> obeisance to him, Haman was infuriated.
> —Esther 3:4-5

READ: Esther 3:1-6, Romans 1:16, and Exodus 20:1-4

When Haman was appointed Prime Minister by the king

of Persia, Haman demanded that others in the royal court bow down to him in an act of worship. Mordecai, a Jew, was member of the court who refused to bow down to Haman because of his allegiance to the commandment to worship no other gods.In his anger over this refusal Haman determined to destroy Mordecai and all the Jews in Persia.

To be a follower of Jesus Christ means that there will be times when you will live in a way that is different from others who do not follow Christ. This is not always easy, for when you are different it bothers other people. So much so that they may even become angry with you for refusing to do something, which they consider acceptable. Mordecai was different. He would not bow down to his boss, Haman, as if Haman were a god. This made Haman so angry that Mordecai's life was in danger. Mordecai was ready to risk danger in order to obey the commandment, "You shall have no other gods before me." (Exodus 20:3)

How much are you willing and ready to risk for Christ? Are you willing to be different, and thus to be ridiculed, or persecuted in some way? Christians in Nazi Germany had to stand up for their faith. At times this put them at risk. One very well known example was Pastor Dietrich Bonhoeffer, who dared to stand up to Hitler. This cost him his freedom when he was sent to a concentration camp, and finally it cost him his life when he was executed by the state.

Paul wrote to the Romans, "I am not ashamed of the gospel." (Romans 1:16) That translates into our lives as "I am not ashamed to be known as a Christian." Because Paul was not ashamed of the Gospel of Christ, many people in his day became Christian. Dare we do less?

PRAYER: Help me, O God, to be willing to stand up for Christ, regardless of the consequences. In his name. Amen.

~ ~ ~ ~ ~ ~

AUGUST 4

IF YOU HAD ONE WISH, WHAT WOULD IT BE?

> Awe came upon everyone, because many wonders and
> signs were being done by the apostles . . . and day by day the
> Lord added to their number those who were being saved.
>
> —Acts 2:43, 47

READ: Esther 7:1-6, 8:7,8,11 and Acts 2:43-47

Queen Esther was asked by the king what her one wish was. She wished that her people, the Jews, be saved from Haman's plans to annihilate them. Not only was her wish granted but in addition, Haman is executed, his sons and more than seventy-five thousand enemies of the Jews throughout Persia are slain by the Jews, and many Persians become Jewish converts. To top it off Mordecai is made Prime Minister to replace Haman.

How many times in your life have you been asked. "If you had one wish, what would it be?" Normally we think up some nice present for ourselves. When the king sought Esther's wish, her chief concern was for her own people who were in mortal danger throughout the empire. She used the kings's offer to grant her wish as her opportunity to intercede on behalf of her people. As a result the Jews were saved from destruction in Persia.

The Christian is committed to doing whatever is possible to serve the needs of others throughout the world. Like Esther our desire should be for those whose lives are in danger. Our greatest desire ought to be for the homeless to find shelter, the starving to be given food, and the oppressed to be released.

One of the results of Esther's wish and its fulfillment was the conversion of many Persians to the Jewish faith. Over the centuries as the Christian church has reached out to serve human need the kingdom of God has been extended and advanced.

PRAYER: Open my heart and mind, O God, so that my fondest wish may be for the welfare and safety of others. Through Christ. Amen.

~ ~ ~ ~ ~ ~

AUGUST 5

AFTER THE VICTORY, THE CELEBRATION

Letters were sent wishing peace and security to all the Jews . . . and giving orders that these days of Purim should be celebrated, observed at their appointed seasons, as the Jew, Mordecai and Queen Esther enjoined on the Jews.

—Esther 9:30-31

READ: Esther 9:29-10:3 and Matthew 5:43-48

The feast instituted by Esther and Mordecai was sort of a "fourth of July" celebration. Very nationalistic, it lifted up the military victory of the Jews over the Persians.

As Christians we celebrate, not so much the victory of one people over another, but the victory of Christ over all who would oppose him. This is really the Easter celebration, when we think about the Risen Christ and his victory over death and defeat. It is then in the spirit of Christ that we turn military victory celebrations inside out and follow Jesus' own words: "You have heard it said, 'You shall love your neighbor and hate your enemy.' But I say unto you, love your enemy and pray for those who persecute you." (Matthew 5:43,45)

While Esther and Mordecai celebrated a love for their own people and a revengeful attitude toward their enemies, the Christian prays for and celebrates God's love for all people, friends and enemies alike. The peace and security which Esther and Mordecai obtained for the Jews in Persia was limited to their own people for a brief period of time. The peace and security which the Risen Christ obtains in God's victory over sin and death is unlimited. It is for all races and peoples for all time.

PRAYER: I celebrate your victory, O God,. for all the world. In Christ. Amen.

∼ ∼ ∼ ∼ ∼ ∼

AUGUST 6

BY WHICH SPIRIT CONTROLLED?

To set the mind on the flesh is death, but to set the mind on the Spirit is life and peace.

—Romans 8:6

READ: Psalm 34:8-18 and Romans 8:5-11

The term "spirit" is used to describe the overall manner and essence of a person. We talk of a person being "mean-spirited" when we observe that much of such a person's relationship to others will be hateful, spiteful, or destructive. Some people seem to have a spirit of sadness about them, while others are high spirited with a zest for life. It seems that a great majority of people in our society today are influenced by what might be called a spirit of worldliness. There is so much emphasis upon fun and excitement, a heavy fixation on money and affluence, and a compelling desire to acquire material things. Instant satisfaction of physical desires of all sorts would seem to describe the spirit under which many live today.

Paul speaks of being controlled by "the flesh," which means human nature. He paints a very bleak picture of the results one can expect of such a spirit. Whether it be clogged arteries from too much fat in the diet, AIDS, spoiled relationships, or financial failure, the results of high living can be pretty tough. Paul concludes that the result is death. On the other hand the result of allowing yourself to be controlled by the Spirit of God, Paul declares, is life and peace.

To be controlled by the Spirit is to live for God and for others, to give ones life for the building up of society, for the good of one's neighbors, and for the care and nurture of family and friendships.

This is what it means to truly live. This is what makes for peace in one's soul.

PRAYER: Help me, O Lord, to submit to the control of your Spirit throughout all my days. In Christ. Amen.

~ ~ ~ ~ ~ ~

AUGUST 7

THIS WAY OR THAT?

Let the peace of Christ rule in your hearts, to which indeed you were called in the one body. And be thankful.
—Colossians 3:15

READ: Psalm 119:137-138, 165-168 and Colossians 3:12-17

How often have you thought when you were facing a dilemma, "If only someone would tell me which way to go!" This way or that! Many a problem seems to have evenly matched options and we go back and forth trying to decide. It helps to have some rule by which to make choices—like the price on a restaurant menu which helps you order fish and chips rather than T—bone. In the important decisions one faces there is a need to have a sure basis for making choices in order to achieve some peace of mind. For it is very unsettling to go over and over a dilemma, not knowing how to decide. One needs an umpire to decide the play, a boss to tell you what to do.

Paul advises that it is the "Peace of Christ" which ought to be the basis for decisions. When we can't tell which way to go let Christ decide for you. When we have submitted our lives to Christ and seek to understand how his influence upon our lives should determine our thoughts, words, and actions, then we can prayerfully ask God to lead us as we make our choices. This is what Paul meant in another of his writings when he used the phrase, "but we have the mind of Christ." (I Corinthians 2:16)

Such decision-making will bring peace in our innermost life and lead to peace in our relationships. "Great peace have those who love your law; nothing can make them stumble." (Psalm 119:165)

PRAYER: In my deciding, give me the peace of having decided your way, O God. Through Christ. Amen.

~ ~ ~ ~ ~

AUGUST 8

NOW, JUST SETTLE DOWN

Finally, brothers and sisters, farewell. Put things in order,
listen to my appeal, agree with one another, live in peace ;
and the God of love and peace will be with you.
—II Corinthians 13:11

READ: Psalm 85:6-10 and I Corinthians 1:1-17

Among Paul's congregations the one in Corinth was the one which wrangled the most. It was to Corinth that Paul wrote his most severe words of advice, advice which could be summarized, "Now, just settle down." There were divisions of opinion based upon differences in experience which kept the congregation from being peaceful. Paul encouraged them to reach common agreement through their love and devotion to Jesus Christ, and by such submission to learn to live at peace with one another.

When we focus upon our own personal experiences and our own prejudices we are bound to disagree with others whose opinions may very well be at odds with ours. Like walking around a room with your eyes fixed upon the floor, you are apt to run into other folk doing the same. What is needed is for one's eyes to be lifted to a higher level in order to get a better perspective on the situation at hand.

Paul encourages us to fix our eyes on Christ—the God outside our own limited orbit of life—and thereby to gain a better attitude toward those with whom we live. Thus, he can say to the Christians in Corinth, "Agree with one another; live in peace." This does not mean a mindless agreement on every detail. The details are shaped by our own personal stories. But agree on the basics: the love of God for all humankind as shown in Jesus Christ. And beyond that live *agreeably*. Then we can live at peace in the church with those who differ on matters of current opinion, like abortion, the right to die, issues of sexuality, or capital punishment. Peace does not come with faked or forced agreement. It comes when each of us aligns our lives with the will of God.

PRAYER: Let me, O God, live agreeably with my neighbor and at peace, despite our differences. In Christ. Amen.

~ ~ ~ ~ ~

AUGUST 9

ALL IT TAKES IS RAIN

I will give you your rains in their season, and the land shall yield its produce, and the trees of the field shall yield their fruit.

—Leviticus 26:4

READ: Job 36:27-33 and Psalm 84:5-7

We don't want it to rain too much during our recreational activities in the summer. We would rather have rain only during the night as in the mythical Camelot. Let's look at rain, and see what lesson it holds for us. Is there a parable in the rain? A good rain turns brown grass into green. The frequent rains in the mountains make patches of green and cause the wild flowers to bloom in the woods and glens. All it takes is rain to bring some color to the earth, and to life.

Psalm 84 was sung by Hebrew worshipers as they walked the dusty roads leading to the Temple in Jerusalem. As they came near the city they passed through the Baca valley which was particularly dry and sterile. But even there the joyous spirit of the people going to worship God made the landscape seem to be revived as with early rain. They might have remembered Isaiah's words, "The wilderness and the dry land shall be glad, the desert shall rejoice and blossom . . ." (Isaiah 35:1) The people of faith experienced God's love as refreshing and life-giving rain showering upon a dry and thirsty land.

Our minds and lives get dry sometimes, uninterested in much of anything, unwilling to do much. We feel tired and lifeless, needing energy. It feels like we are trudging through the badlands looking for a spot of green and a pool of water. God provides us such an oasis filled with his energy and love. Like rain he waters our desert and it comes to life, blossoming with a new spurt of growth and vitality.

PRAYER: O God, come to me now as gentle rain to make me new and alive. In Christ. Amen.

~ ~ ~ ~ ~ ~

AUGUST 10

ROCK OF AGES

The Lord is my rock, my fortress, and my deliverer, My God, my rock in whom I take refuge, my shield, and the horn of my salvation, my stronghold.

—Psalm 18:2

READ: Job 38:3-11, Psalm 18:1-6, and Psalm 61:-1-3

Look at the rocks. Learn what they teach us about God. The psalmist sees God as a rock, and in that metaphor packs an assortment of ideas: fortress, deliverer, refuge, shield, salvation, stronghold. A rock is a strong defense behind which you can hide. A rock is immovable and it will not change. A rock seems to be forever. A rock is strong and will withstand almost everything which could beat on it. God is a rock—changeless and permanent, strong and powerful. Let the rocks you see remind you of a God of power who is your salvation.

There are times when life becomes very confusing. So much is going on. Things change so fast and you become uneasy about the outcome. In fact, sometimes you wonder what there is to hang on to. Look at the rocks in the wind and the storm, in the searing heat and the chilling cold, century after century. They are a parable of God's stability and strength upon which you can depend in good times and bad. The writer of Hebrews affirmed this timeless stability when he wrote: "Jesus Christ is the same yesterday and today and forever." (Hebrews 13:8)

PRAYER: O God, you are the strength and stability I need in times of shifting pressures upon me. You give me power to withstand life's storms. I praise you, the Rock of my salvation. In Christ. Amen

～ ～ ～ ～ ～ ～

AUGUST 11

SUN OF MY SOUL

From the rising of the sun to its setting the name of the Lord is to be praised.
—Psalm 113:3

READ: Job 38:12-14, 19-20 and Psalm 113

There is nothing in our surroundings which is as essential to our survival as the sun. Without it we simply cannot live. It is the source of life for us and for our world. Our utter dependence upon the sun for life is a metaphor for our absolute dependence upon

God, who is the source of our life. For this reason the sun has been considered a God in many primitive religions.

Each new day when the sun rises we ought to think of God, the creator and sustainer of life, and give our praise to God. Many are the blessings of the light of day: illumination by which to see, safety and protection, ultimately the source of all our food. Everything we eat in one way or another derives from the photo-synthetic activity of the sun upon green plants. Finally the sun provides warmth, without which all the earth would freeze over.

The life-giving light of the sun is a parable for the light which Jesus Christ brings to the world, providing salvation to an otherwise dark, sinful, and dreadful existence. Darkness and night have come to symbolize evil and death, while light has come to be a metaphor for purity and redemption. As we depend utterly upon the sun for life, so we depend utterly upon God in Jesus Christ for a new birth of hope and salvation.

The besetting sin of modern technological culture is the delusion of independence. We are so easily convinced that we do not need anyone or anything outside ourselves upon which to depend for survival and for ultimate happiness. It is the affirmation of the Christian faith that each of us needs God in order to live life as it was intended. The Son of God is our Sun.

PRAYER: O Christ, Sun of my life, I depend utterly upon you for my life and for my salvation. Amen.

~ ~ ~ ~ ~ ~

AUGUST 12

WATER SPELLS HOPE

For waters shall break forth in the wilderness, and streams in the desert.

—Isaiah 35:6

READ: Job 38:16-18 and Psalm 65:9-13

To people who live in desert and semi-arid regions of the earth water is always what is sorely needed and hoped for. Biblical visions of the ultimate triumph of God over all that opposes God's will is often pictured as water coming onto dry land, streams in the desert, an oasis in the wilderness. The sound, and then the sight of a rushing mountain stream in the woods spells hope for the hiker who is lost. An isolated service station on a lonely road with its promise of water as well as fuel, spells hope to the motorist whose engine is overheating on a hot summer afternoon.

When you are outside in the summer and come upon a river, a lake or a stream think of the hope for the future which water has traditionally revealed to God's people. Be assured of God's final victory over all that is deadening and evil. Water is a symbol of everything Christians hope for with the assurance of the resurrection of Jesus Christ from the dead.

We live in a world in which warfare and trouble of all kinds prevail. We keep hearing the bad news and wonder if it will ever stop. Sometimes unfortunate turns in the course of life seem to come to us one right after another. And we wish things would smooth out. Many people become negative and dismal in the face of life's tragedies and misfortunes. But people of faith know that God is Lord of history, and that God will ultimately win, even though we cannot see it now. In the meantime let water, wherever you find it, remind you that some day God will bring, "streams in the desert" of life.

PRAYER: I thank you, O God, for the hope you have given me in Christ, that ultimately you will make things right, and my thirst for the good will be quenched with the water of life which you provide. Through Christ. Amen.

~ ~ ~ ~ ~ ~

AUGUST 13

HE KNOWS ME

"Come and see the man who told me everything I have ever done! He cannot be the Messiah, can he?"

—John 4:29

READ: John 4:5-19

Have you ever noticed how good it feels when someone asks you about yourself? Not merely a perfunctory "How are you?" Someone who honestly wants to hear everything you have to say! Have you ever noticed how rare such an opportunity is? It is a mark of well adjusted person when such an honest query is made. And it is good and healthy to be able to share your life story. It is lonely to have to keep everything to yourself. A great deal of counseling and mental health therapy involves simply the sharing of one's life with another human being, the counselor. When one has troubling experiences in life, one often finds it helpful to have someone with whom to disclose these matters, whether such a person is a friend, a loved one, or counselor.

The Samaritan woman found in Jesus' presence one with whom her life could be known. His knowledge of her situation made such an impression upon her that she concluded that he must be the Messiah. She saw in this person not only a friend, but God in human form. Instead of being offended by Jesus' knowledge of her personal life in her checkered past, she was delighted, and perhaps relieved to have Jesus aware of her story. It is frequently a relief to share one's troubles and misgivings with a sympathetic friend.

Perhaps John is showing us a sign of the fulfillment of Isaiah's prophecy of the coming Messiah who would be a "Wonderful Counselor." May Christ be such a friend and counselor to each of us. Then may we be open to the appeal of others who want to share something of themselves with us, as in the phrase, "being little Christs" to one another.

PRAYER: O Lord, make me willing to share myself with others, and grant that I may be open to the lives and experiences of others. Above all let me be open to you, O Christ. Amen

~ ~ ~ ~ ~

AUGUST 14

HE INSPIRES ME

> Then Peter said to Jesus, "Rabbi, it is good for us to be here . . ."
>
> —Mark 9:5

READ: Mark 9:2-9

We speak of being high on something, of a peak experience, or of having a mountain top experience. Many mountain climbers are motivated toward the goal of achieving such a feeling when they reach the top of the mountain. We need not travel far away or climb a high mountain to gain inspiration. For the Christian it is meaningful contact with Jesus Christ which inspires one to new heights of life.

Three of Jesus' disciples had a mountain top experience not because they had been led up a high mountain, but because they came to see Jesus in a new way. In the transfiguration, as it is called, they recognized for the first time that Jesus was a very special messenger of God. Without this peak experience they would have lived their lives in obscurity and boredom. But, because of this exotic manifestation of Christ, their lives were reshaped and they were impelled into new and exciting directions. From that moment onward they were able to say, "it is good to be alive," as they did on the mount that first day of inspiration.

When we have been inspired by God's Holy Spirit to new heights of understanding and motivation, we too, will be saying each day, "How good it is to be alive."

PRAYER: Inspire me, O God, with your Holy Spirit, to see Christ as your divine Son. Make me glad to be alive. In His name, Amen.

~ ~ ~ ~ ~

AUGUST 15

HE CHALLENGES ME

Jesus, looking at him, loved him and said, "You lack one thing: go and sell what you own, and give the money to the poor, and you will have treasure in heaven; then come and follow me.

—Mark 10:21

READ: Mark 10:17-23

The expression,"I don't care," can go either way. That attitude can make it easier to get along with others, or these same words can be harmful. This can mean we are willing to cooperate: "I don't care, I'd like to go along with whatever you want." Or it can mean that we are unconcerned about any potential danger to us or to others. "I don't care. I'll leave my door unlocked. So what if I'm robbed."

More serious is the, "I don't care," we may give to the call of Christ to us. Perhaps we hear his words so frequently that they cease to have an impact. Or perhaps, like the rich young man in the story in Mark 10, we don't want to change our lives. Or maybe, we feel that life is as good as we want it to be. (Not likely!)

Apathy and complacency are the enemies of a life of service to Christ. When we don't care about the needs of others, the shape the world is in, we fail to take seriously Christ's call to help. When we feel that things are really good for us, and that we deserve to be self-satisfied, we will not likely raise a finger for God. Sometimes our daily routine can lull us into indifference. May we awaken to care enough to hear Christ's call and to heed it.

PRAYER: O Christ, open my eyes to see what you see, and my ears to hear the cries of your world. Bend my will to follow your call. Amen.

~ ~ ~ ~ ~

AUGUST 16

PEACE POSITIVE

"Peace I leave with you; my peace I give to you. I do not give to you as the world gives . . ."

—John 14:27

READ: John 14:25-31

Because Jesus Christ comes into our world to redefine human life, there are a number of words which must be redefined in order to fit his level of understanding. When Jesus stood before Pilate he tried to explain to the Roman governor that his definition of "kingdom" was different from that of the people around him. "My kingdom is not of this world," he said. The word "peace," he explains to his disciples is different from the kind of peace people were accustomed to expecting. Peace commonly means the absence of trouble, whether that is noise, or arguing, or warfare. It is peace when such harassment ceases—when the rain finally stops and the over-active youngsters can go back out to play, or when the spouse leaves for work and the tension over some argument is put on hold, or when the U.N. Peacekeeping Force is sent in to a country engaged in civil war to hold back the violence. But these are negatives—merely the absence of trouble.

What Jesus brings is a very positive condition of the spirit which in Hebrew is called, "SHALOM." Such peace involves feeling good about oneself and others. It is to be at ease with God. Shalom is the peace which comes from reconciliation and reunion. It is the enjoyment of life at its fullest, particularly the deep enjoyment of human contact. Such peace cannot even conceive of warfare and violence. This is the peace which only God can give, the peace which passes all understanding. Let us try to receive that gift from Christ. To receive his peace you must extend an open hand, rather than a clenched fist.

PRAYER: For your promise of the gift of peace, I give you humble thanks, O Christ. To you I reach with open hands. Amen.

~ ~ ~ ~ ~

AUGUST 17

WHAT MIGHT HAVE BEEN

O that you paid attention to my commandments! Then your prosperity would have been like a river, and your success like the waves of the sea;

—Isaiah 48:18

READ: 48:17-21

One of the most tragic exclamations in our common experience is, "It might have been . . ." An old man says sadly, "When I was a young kid, I ran off and got married. I had wanted to go to school and become a dentist. But instead I've drifted from one menial job to another all my life. I might have been . . . ."

Isaiah looked upon the exiled Israelites with saddened eyes

and said in effect, "*We might have had peace and prosperity, instead of this abominable exile, if we had only followed God's leading.*" But for Isaiah it was too late. Jerusalem had already been sacked by the Babylonians and its leaders carted off to foreign captivity.

What of us, as a nation? As a world? It is too late? Must we say what might have been? Or can we still work for what could yet be? It is the conviction of the people of the Bible that peace depends upon the obedience of the nation to the commandments of God.

Let us take the time and make the effort needed to discern what God intends for us as a nation.For us in the church. How does God want us to fit into his plan for humankind? As a starting point it should be clear that the one thing God does not want is for us to do anything to risk the annihilation of the human race through instruments of mass destruction. God wants peace for us, and for all the peoples of the world.

PRAYER: Almighty God, divine Peacemaker, show us the way to peace. Through Christ, our Prince of Peace. Amen.

~ ~ ~ ~ ~

AUGUST 18

HOW DO YOU SPELL PEACE?

And the harvest of righteousness is sown in peace for those who make peace.

—James 3:18

READ: James 3:13-18

How do you spell "peace?" You spell the kind of peace Jesus brings: "J U S T I C E." Pope John said, "If you want peace, work for justice." That means that doing right to one another is the way to peace in human relationships on all levels. When we deprive other nations and peoples of food and resources we lose peace.

When we deal unfairly with people in our own society we risk the peace of our society. When we mistreat in any way those in our own families, we risk the peace in marriage and family life. James in the New Testament shares his insight that the enemies of peace are such things as jealousy, bitterness, selfishness, boasting, prejudice, and hypocrisy. We could expand on that list to include the kinds of attitudes and destructive relationships which we have seen as the enemies of peace in human affairs. On the other hand James shows that such attitudes and actions as gentleness, friendliness, compassion, goodness and wisdom produce a "harvest of righteousness," which is peace.

Is it too much to affirm that the peace of the world begins with the way each of us deals with others in justice and right relationships?

PRAYER: Help me, O Lord, to so relate to others that peace grows in our midst. Let your justice fill all our dealings and then spread to the way in which we as a people and a nation relate to the other peoples of the world. Through Christ. Amen

~ ~ ~ ~ ~

AUGUST 19

UNTROUBLED SLEEP

I will both lie down and sleep in peace; for you alone,
O Lord, make me lie down in safety.

—Psalm 4:8

READ: Psalm 4

Some years ago one of the associations devoted to promoting mental health used this phrase in their radio advertising: "Remember that troublesome people are often troubled people." This is a wise and helpful slogan, for often those who disturb the peace are people who do not feel good about themselves. Is that not what we now feel about the neighborhood bully? Interpersonal violence can so easily spring from a painfully low self image on the part of one or more participants in a destructive outbreak.

On the other hand, the Psalmist is aware that peace and inner personal security go hand in hand. In the fourth Psalm there is implied the threat of some kind of interpersonal trouble. The Psalmist turns away from this threat, to affirm faith in God, and that he is secure in himself—that he can sleep at night.

It is a trust in God that dispels fear and makes one feel good about one's self. With such trust and personal security there is simply no need to lash out at others The peace which is not of this world which Jesus brings us is a freedom from fear and an affirmation of self-worth. The interpersonal warfare in our homes and communities would cease if only we could sense God's love and safety more fully.

PRAYER: O Lord, let me rest in you so completely that my fears subside and my sense of worth is restored, and I receive your peace. Through Christ. Amen.

~ ~ ~ ~ ~ ~

AUGUST 20

PEACE IS LIKE A RIVER

Now may the Lord of peace himself give you peace at all times in all ways. The Lord be with all of you.
—II Thessalonians 3:16

READ: Isaiah 32:16-20

When one looks at a beautiful scene in nature, one is taken with the peacefulness of such undisturbed beauty. An array of wild flowers in a field or upon a mountain side with the bright blue summer sky overhead, the trickling brook watering the lush grass and ground cover, leafy trees waving in the breeze—these all reveal a sense of balance and peace in God's creation. Peace comes from fulfilling the plan and intention written into creation. Untouched nature is peaceful because it is carrying out the Creator's plan.

The lesson for us is that peace comes to our lives when we fulfill God's intention for us. In fact it is the witness of the prophets that it is God himself who thus brings peace. Paul, in closing his letter to the Thessalonian Christians, declares that it is the Lord of peace who gives us peace. Peace comes when we are set right with God, in tune with others, and at ease with ourselves. The basis for peace at any level of human life is to be found in the reconciling love of God in Christ. That is why Jesus Christ was hailed as the Prince of Peace.

PRAYER: Reconcile me to yourself, O God, that peace may come into my life . . . Then let peace in each of your children join and flow into a mighty river of peace to water the whole earth. Through Christ. Amen.

~ ~ ~ ~ ~ ~

AUGUST 21

GROWTH

I will open my mouth in a parable; I will utter dark sayings from of old.

—Psalm 78:2

READ: Matthew 13:31-35

"My, how you've grown since I saw you last!" Every child has heard this countless numbers of times, as the adults in his or her extended family come for occasional visits and are surprised at signs of growth in the child. There is something magical about growth. While one cannot see movement or change in a plant, growth is evident from one viewing to the next. Notice the tiny evergreen trees on the forest floor; perhaps only a three inch spine sprouting three little branches. Then look up to the towering parent trees reaching to the sun and sky. That's growth unseen but inevitable.

Jesus used the parables of the mustard seed and of yeast as metaphors for the surprising and unseen growth of the kingdom of God in our midst. Without our knowing it, God is powerfully at work causing dramatic growth in the development and fulfillment of the Divine will on earth.

Think about your life: as it was a year ago, and how it is today. How have you changed during the past twelve months? What do you believe God has accomplished in your life in this past year? How are you more responsive to God's leading? What have you been able to do to give help in the lives of others around you? To be sure, we may wish for greater changes for the better, but let us honestly admit that God has been at work in us, and this has brought about some significant gains in our experience. This is cause for thanksgiving.

Think about the areas in your life in which you truly hope for positive changes and growth, and ask God to help you grow in these ways in the coming weeks and months.

PRAYER: Thank you, O Lord, for the unseen growth in my life. Give me your nurturing love to grow ever more fully into the person you intend for me. In Christ. Amen.

~ ~ ~ ~ ~

AUGUST 22

SCARS

> Who will separate us from the love of Christ? Will hardship, or distress, or persecution, or famine, or nakedness, or peril, or sword
>
> —Romans 8:35

READ: Romans 8:31-39

Most scenes in nature show us not only their beauty but also signs of disruptive events of the past. A portion of gnarled bark on a tree covers an ancient injury. A streak of exposed soil and rock extending down a hillside is left from a torrent of water which swept away growing plants and grasses, leaving a raw scar. A shear ragged rock wall gives evidence of an earthquake in which one portion of the ground shifted violently away from the terrain next to it. An entire mountainside may be devoid of living trees, covered only with blackened or sun bleached trunks, left from a fire in years past. Violent and destructive events occur in the natural world causing scars which show signs of damage from wind or water erosion, fire or earthquake.

Life is like that. Hard things do happen to each of us, and these events of life leave their scars upon us. Of course there are physical scars showing past injuries to our bodies, but there are scars on the feeling side of life as well: hurts, disappointments, tragedies, losses and failures which we have endured. But like the bark on an injured tree we find that we too have gotten over a great deal of adversity and seem to be stronger and wiser for it— oftentimes, but not always.

The apostle Paul endured many difficult times in his life of service to Christ: persecutions, hunger, danger, to mention a few. He testified that in all these events which had befallen him, he felt the love and power of Christ helping him to overcome such adversity. He even sensed fulfillment and victory in the midst of such hardship. Has that been your experience? Can you affirm the power and love of God in the varied course of events in your life? The scars you bear give evidence not only of adverse events but of God's healing power!

PRAYER: Thank you, merciful God, for your healing strength and nurture in time of trouble. In Christ. Amen.

〜 〜 〜 〜 〜

AUGUST 23

COURSE CHANGES

> But more than that, we even boast in God through our
> Lord Jesus Christ, through whom we have now received
> reconciliation.
>
>   —Romans 5:11

READ: Romans 5:1-11

When hiking near a creek or stream you can occasionally find the remains of an abandoned creek bed which is now dry and overgrown with vegetation. For some reason the course of the water changed and now flows in a nearby stream, even though it once followed a different course, However, the direction, and its destination remain the same as it has always been. Some years ago the remains of a Civil War ship was uncovered in a farmer's field almost a mile from the river in which it had sunk in a battle a hundred years earlier. The river underwent drastic changes in the years during which the ancient hull lay rotting.

Life has its course changes, causing us to depart from familiar channels and to enter new routes. This is not always easy, when the old course seemed so comfortable and familiar, and the new one terrifying. Perhaps a new relationship has been established, very different from previous ones which we had enjoyed. Or a new job, so different from former work experiences. When one moves to another town or to a new neighborhood it is a temptation to long for the old course. Some course changes run deeper. An old belief is shattered, or a point of view on an important subject has had to be radically revised when new circumstances emerge. New discoveries about ourselves force us to adopt new attitudes toward others. Life styles must change at various junctures in life.

It is helpful to be aware that despite these course changes God is moving us in a consistent direction. Our destiny remains the same when our basic commitment of God's will remains. The way may change, but the goal is still God's intention for our lives.

PRAYER: Guide me, O God, through life's confusing changes. Give me your course corrections whenever they are needed. In Christ. Amen.

~ ~ ~ ~ ~ ~

AUGUST 24

WIND BOURNE

> But it is written, "what no eye has seen, nor ear heard, nor human heart conceived, what God has prepared for those who love him. These things God has revealed to us through the Spirit."
>
> —I Corinthians 2:9,10

READ: I Corinthians 2:6-16

Though you cannot see the wind, you know it is there because of its effect. The Holy Spirit was understood by our Hebrew ancestors to be like the wind. The Hebrew word used for spirit has the connotation of wind, or breath. If we want to be responsive to God's Spirit we must be willing to be *blown* by him; transported from where we are to where God wants us to be. Notice in the plant life of nature the many different seeds so constructed as to be transported by the wind. Some are light and furry, others have tiny wings, so that they can be easily blown by each gust of wind.

Paul believes that the Christian is responsive to God's Spirit in a special way, so that what the Holy Spirit teaches or urges upon us meets with a certain readiness on our part to be received. This, Paul thought, was to have the mind of Christ. Let us hope that our lives are being so shaped that they can be blown by the Spirit to God's destination.

May we have the mind of Christ to go where he wants us to go, to be what he wants us to be, and to do and say what God wants!

PRAYER: May I be wind-bourne by your Spirit, O God. In Christ. Amen.

~ ~ ~ ~ ~ ~

AUGUST 25

LIFE

What you sow does not come to life unless it dies.

—I Corinthians 15:36

READ: I Corinthians 15:35-50

From out of the dead appearing pine cone of previous years comes the seed for a new young pine tree. In the seemingly dead compost pile are the nutrients to spawn new life for seeds which have drifted into its decaying mass. Seeds found in ancient burial sites have been planted and have grown in today's soil. These are symbols of how life sprouts from death's destruction.

Paul uses this idea of a dead seed as the basis for his teaching about the resurrection. Unless a seed dies it cannot sprout, he declares. Out of a dead log springs the life of a new seedling. There is a basic Christian principle here. God takes the dying aspects of our life and raises up new life in their place. God's new life from the old is seen in the recovery of an alcoholic who is given victory over his/her addiction to emerge as a new person. An unwanted baby destined to personality damage is brought new life by the love of adoptive parents. We think we are at the end of our rope, and then God opens a new door for us. We walk out of the dark into the sunlight of a new beginning. Life from death. Good over evil. Hope replacing despair. Love instead of bitterness and resentment. These are words of resurrection which follow Paul's idea that new life sprouts from old as a result of God's action to bring life out of death. New ways out of old.

PRAYER: Put to death in me, O Lord, what ought to be phased out, and raise in me new ways in Christ. Amen.

~ ~ ~ ~ ~ ~

AUGUST 26

CONTACT

The people who walked in darkness have sen a great light; those who lived in a land of deep darkness—on them the light has shined.

—Isaiah 9:2

READ: John 1:1-9

Have you ever been in a car at night when its headlights failed? That is a frightening experience, especially when there are no other lights to illumine the road. The edge of the road becomes lost in the shadows, curves are imperceptible, and one can lose a sense of direction. This is a metaphor for the way many of us wander about with our "lights off.' The confusion which results is indeed frightening. Do you really know others? Or is there darkness surrounding them which you have not penetrated. Certainly we are often in the dark when it comes to knowing God. Our contact with God is apt to be superficial and infrequent. There is darkness surrounding ourselves. We don't know our ourselves as well as we might. Illusion and self-deception may have taken over. Have you made contact with yourself, your true self? Or are you in the dark about why you are "that way?"

Isaiah's reference to what the Christian faith affirms to be Jesus Christ, described him as light coming into a dark world. The gospel writer, John, declares that Jesus is the true light coming into the world. This means that Jesus illumines our lives so that we can make contact with God, with others, and with ourselves. And with nature as well. Do you really take time to observe all there is to see and hear in the natural world. Our Christian faith opens up the way for us to make contact with nature as well.

Summer time provides us with good opportunity to let the light of Christ help us make contact with nature as well as with ourselves, God and others.

PRAYER: O Light of God, shine in my world, illumine its beauty, brighten the faces and lives of others, make me aware of your presence and show me myself in a new way. Amen.

~ ~ ~ ~ ~ ~

AUGUST 27

CONTACT WITH NATURE

For now the winter is past, the rain is over and gone.
The flowers appear on the earth; the time of singing has come, and the voice of the turtledove is heard in our land.
The fig tree puts forth its figs, and the vines are in blossom; they give forth their fragrance.

—Song of Songs 2:11-13

READ: Psalm 104:1-4, 10-13

It is said that the camera does not lie. Yet when you see a fine nature photo, you can hardly believe that there is such beauty. This surprise comes to us because we see so little when our minds are occupied with other thoughts. We overlook the beauty and detail of the natural world around us. We pass by some of the grandest sights in all the universe without making any contact with such evidence of God's artistry.

Many students of the human condition observe that contact with nature is essential to one's total adjustment to life. We have been created out of the dust of the earth and the earth remains our home. So let us examine nature more fully, making contact with our natural roots. Take time to look deeply at the things of earth and sky. Pause to listen to the sounds of creation: the breeze, the water, the trees, the birds, and the gentle movement of things unseen. Breathe deeply and smell whatever is nearby. Taste some of it. Bite down on a fragrant pine needle, or a blade of grass. And touch. Contact implies touching—getting in touch with nature.

The people of the Bible were in touch not only with nature but with nature's Creator. May we know by our contact with creation, the One who has made it.

PRAYER: Forgive me, Lord, for having taken so much for granted. Help me to gain a new appreciation for all that you have made. Open my eyes and ears, my nostrils, my hands and tongue to perceive your handiwork. Through Christ, the Light which illumines the world. Amen

~ ~ ~ ~ ~

AUGUST 28

CONTACT WITH OTHERS

If we walk in the light as he himself is in the light, we have fellowship with one another.

—I John 1:7

READ: I John 1:5-7; 2:7-14

An old saying decrees that "Good fences make good neighbors." This dictum can be taken too far when fences are put up in such a way to block out others from our consciousness. Like an eight foot high solid wooden fence put up by one's neighbor which casts shade over one's own garden plot, we can screen off so much light that friendships with neighbors whither and have a hard time growing. The number of people any of us knows intimately is limited. In place of open, sunny relationships many are quite superficial, leaving us in the dark about the other person's life. Out contact with others is oftentimes lacking in depth or concern.

Much is written in the New Testament to teach us to love one another, but our modern interpretation of the word "love" seems to keep us from loving. Instead, we tend to be afraid of each other to some extent. John writes, "Perfect love casts out fear," (I John 4:18) and "If we walk in the light—we have fellowship with one another." (I John 1:7) Loving begins with contact in a way that helps us to know each other.

We ought to ask meaningful and sincere questions of each other. We ought not fence off deepening relationships with banal questions and remarks. Rather we ought to "sit in the other person's yard." Such contact is a two-way conversation. Let us make contact in ways which illumine others' lives and our lives as well. Malachi wrote, "Have we not all one father? Has not one God created us? Why then are we faithless to one another?" (Malachi 2:10)

PRAYER: Help me to contact, know and love others whom you bring to me. In Christ. Amen.

~ ~ ~ ~ ~ ~

AUGUST 29

CONTACT WITH MYSELF

Then Jesus said to the Jews who had believed in him,
"If you continue in my word, you are truly my disciples;
and you will know the truth, and the truth will make you free."

—John 8:31-32

READ: Psalm 139

There is a lot of talk these days in popular psychological

movements about, "getting in touch with myself." This, of course, implies that it is not an automatic condition to be in touch with oneself. We tend to work at creating a good impression or at satisfying the expectations of others, and so we create the sort of personage which fulfills these objectives. The more we try to present an imaginary self the more obscured is the true self to others and to ourselves as well. We normally kid ourselves, seldom admitting to our true motives, or our real desires.

Thus, we are actually not in touch with our true selves, while we are busy trying to create a false impression. The New Testament calls such maneuvering, "slavery to sin." Jesus said that when we know the truth (about ourselves) the truth will free us from the slavery of the obligation to create false impressions. We are freed to like the one which is real.

God knows us better that we do. Psalm 139 testifies to God's full knowledge of us. To know God and what God knows about us is to possess the truth of which Jesus speaks, and thus to be in touch with ourselves. John Calvin said, "the knowledge of God and the knowledge of ourselves are bound together in a mutual tie." Through coming to know God in Bible study and prayer, meditation and reflection may we come to know ourselves, and God's unconditional love for us as we are.

PRAYER: O God, show me my true self. Forgive what is not good in me, and cause to grow in me what is good. In Christ. Amen.

~ ~ ~ ~ ~ ~

AUGUST 30

CONTACT WITH GOD

God is spirit, and those who worship him must worship in spirit and truth.

—John 4:24

READ: Job 36:22-33

A cute but embarrassing question small children often ask their minster when he or she is dressed in a clerical gown is, "Are you God?" Of course, the answer must always be, "No." Such an answer frustrates the child. It is a normal human frustration not to be able to have God on our level. No one can see God, nor can anyone have any contact with God through any of the five senses. Contact with God must be on another level. The book of Job struggles with the question of who and where God is in the midst of life's adversities. "Surely God is great and we do not know him. The number of his years is unsearchable." (Job 36:26) The answer which emerges in Job's mind is that you can know God through his actions, particularly in the realm of nature.

Contact with God goes further than knowing his activity as creator and sustainer of the universe. Contact implies a relationship of oneself with God. Worship is this relationship. God is a spirit beyond the world of our senses, but no less real. Worship is initiated by God. God invites us to relate to him. In responding to the invitation to worship God we are given contact with God. This is a very special communication, through which we grow in our understanding of God and the Divine Will for us and all God's creation.

PRAYER: O most holy God, bring me into true relationship with you. Cause me to worship you in spirit and in truth. Through Christ, who reveals you to me. Amen.

~ ~ ~ ~ ~ ~

AUGUST 31

CARING IS UNTO CHRIST

"I was naked and you gave me clothing, I was sick and
you took care of me, I was in prison and you visited me . . .

Truly I tell you, just as you did it to one of the least of these
who are members of my family, you did it to me."

—Matthew 25:36, 40

READ: Matthew 25:34-40

When all is said and done, what is it about one's life that really
counts with God? Usually we answer this with some sort of warning
to be honest, and to be a good person. Matthew places at a very
key position the words of Jesus in the reading today. Just before
Jesus begins his final trek to the Cross he tells his listeners that the
most important activity is helping others. Considering the naked,
the sick, the hungry and thirsty, and those in prison as a "laundry
list" of persons with problems needing care, he shows us that as far
as God is concerned, the bottom line is how much we have done
to help people in need. The scene he sets for this teaching is the
judgement of the nations at the end of history. How well does our
nation fare in such a judgement? How about large corporations
which shut down factories in the interest of preserving profit
margins, thus putting entire towns out of work?

However, more pointedly, the application of this commandment
is for each of us personally. How well do we care for one another?
Do we recognize the needs of others in such a way as to be able to
do something concrete to help them? How well do we discuss
suffering and pain, grief and hurt with our friends and neighbors?
How well do we listen to others as they try to share with us their
innermost needs or outward predicaments? And for that matter,
how are we at sharing our needs with others?

Matthew shows us that by reaching out to others we are making
contact with Jesus in some deep and profound way. Perhaps
knowing that precious insight will make us better care givers.

PRAYER: Help me, O God, to discover needs and to care for those
whose needs have come to my attention. In and for Christ's
sake. Amen

SEPTEMBER

SEPTEMBER 1

A CONVICTION OF HOPE

> For David says concerning him, "I saw the Lord always before me, for he is at my right hand so that I will not be shaken; therefore my heart was glad, and my tongue rejoiced; moreover my flesh will live in hope"
>
> —Acts 2:25-26

READ: Romans 5:1-5 and Acts 2:22-28

Hope is a gift from God to us. The resurrection of Jesus from death is the solid basis for our hope. Peter's sermon on Pentecost clearly roots hope in the raising of Jesus from death to life. If God did so great a thing as that for us, nothing in life can be ultimately dismal. Nothing can be so bad as to leave us with no hope. The raising of Jesus from death to life plants in our hearts the conviction that whatever is "of death" in us will finally be wiped out and replaced by life.

For the disciples of Jesus this hope turned their despair and disappointment on Good Friday to joy on Easter. After the resurrection they could see that Christ's cause was alive and the mission to which they were called would go onward to completion They could hear, with hope in their hearts, Jesus' directive to go into all the world with his message. They now had confidence that God would complete the task Jesus had begun—a task in which his followers are still engaged twenty-one centuries later.

We have been given the hope that whatever work God calls us

to will indeed be completed by God, no matter the set-backs and frustrations we may experience along the way. We hope for the ultimate establishment of peace, justice, freedom and love in all the world—if not on this side of the grave, beyond it.

The resurrection of Jesus has implications both for this world and the next. God is Lord of both. Such hope is unshakable. Apply this to the personal trials you face. Some will be resolved in your life now.

Some diseases will be healed and health restored. In other circumstances hope is to be found in what we anticipate after death in the eternal household of God. Our hope is everlasting! If not now, THEN!

PRAYER: Eternal God, I thank you for the precious gift to me of hope. Through the risen Christ. Amen

~ ~ ~ ~ ~ ~

SEPTEMBER 2

PATIENCE IS A VIRTUE

> May you be made strong with all the strength that comes from his glorious power, and may you be prepared to endure everything with patience, while joyfully giving thanks to the Father, who has enabled you to share in the inheritance of the saints in the light.
>
> —Colossians 1:11-12

READ: Colossians 1:9-14

Patience is one of the words in a cluster of words found frequently in the New Testament. That cluster includes other related ideas: long suffering, endurance, discipline, and forbearance. Taken together these words describe an admirable virtue found only rarely among us. Yet so many of life's turns require of us patience while waiting for a desired change of events, and for the strength to go forward. We may be waiting for our dismissal from a hospital, or for a new job opportunity. Our waiting may be for the return of a loved one, or for some anticipated piece of mail. We may be waiting for some frustrating interpersonal problem to be resolved. Such waiting requires endurance, long suffering, and the discipline of forbearance.

Patience must be received as a gift from God. Surely, only God could have the patience which we need in some of these trials. Paul wished patience for the Christians in Colossae, which he said comes from sharing in the inheritance God has provided us in Christ. Contemplating Jesus' patient endurance on the cross can be the way the gift of patience is offered to each of us.

PRAYER: Give me the inheritance of patience, endurance, long suffering, and the discipline of forbearance, O God Eternal. Through the cross of Christ. Amen

~ ~ ~ ~ ~

SEPTEMBER 3

THE ETHIC OF TRUTH

You desire truth in the inward being; therefore teach me wisdom in my secret heart.

—Psalm 51:6

READ: Romans 7:14-22

Truth is one very significant element which marks us as followers of Christ. Not just that we know the truth about God's redemptive activity for all humankind, but that our lives as Christians are to be characterized by the ethic of truth. That is, we will speak and live the truth. It will be in our inward being as God desires.

Truth in our "inward parts" as the King James puts it is radically different from the usual way of living. Appearance and reality will be one and the same in our lives. We won't put on a show for good effect, or play act for our own benefit. We will be who we are—not phony. We will mean what we say and say what we mean. We will be real, not artificial people.

On the normal course of growing up each of us learns lots of little tricks to keep from being laughed at, or to avoid criticism, to look good and to gain advantage for ourselves over others. Thus we learn to put on a face and to act for effect. The gift of God to Christ's people is the gift of truth. Knowing Christ who testified to the truth in the inward being is to receive the gift of such truth—the ethic of our lives. Knowing that God accepts us as we really are enables us to be who we are—truthfully.

PRAYER: Help me to know the truth in Christ, and grant me the gift of truth in my inner being, by which to live the truth. Through Christ. Amen.

~ ~ ~ ~ ~ ~

SEPTEMBER 4

NOT A STAR—A PLANET

And all of you must clothe yourselves with humility in your dealings with one another, for "God opposes the proud but gives grace to the humble."

—I Peter 5:5

READ: Proverbs 3:27-35 and I Peter 5:1-7

The opposite of humility is pride, and the worst sort of pride is to be proud of one's own goodness. In other words: arrogance and self-righteousness. To be a star! The seductive trap is to delude oneself into thinking that hope, patience, and truth are one's own achievements, and thus these become grounds for boasting. But the fact of the matter is that these conditions of the heart and soul are undeserved gifts from God to us. They are ours through grace. Our boasting has no basis. Rather we should declare the wondrous love of God who grants us hope, instills patience in our lives, and puts truth in our inward beings. If we think in these terms then we are candidates for another gift of God—humility. Can you imagine trying to develop authentic humility—impossible. By definition humility is a gift from God to the unsuspecting.

Once given and received, humility makes a person easy to live with, pleasant to be around, and more than that, one becomes a reflector of God's grace to others. Humility is like being a planet rather than a star. We do not generate our own light and beauty, and thus we are not like a star giving our own performance. Rather, we are reflectors of the light and beauty of God, calling attention to God's love and grace in Christ. In that sense, a planet. Humility does not mean effacing ourselves and saying things to be-rate ourselves. (Back-handed ways of gaining compliments!) It means turning ones attention upon God in such a way that others see God, not us. The best mirror is the one you don't know is there.

PRAYER: Help me to reflect your glory, O God. In Christ. Amen.

~ ~ ~ ~ ~ ~

SEPTEMBER 5

LETTING GO AND TAKING HOLD

> Whoever comes to me and does not hate father and
> mother, wife and children, brothers and sisters, yes, and
> even life itself, cannot be my disciple.
> —Luke 14:26

READ: Matthew 10:34-39 and Exodus 20:1-3

At first these words of Jesus about hating family members seem cruel and heartless. To be against family is to go against a basic human ideal. Family values! But look at it this way: the person who has never grown up and separated from his or her parents remains emotionally a child, and most likely will not become a productive adult. For a healthy and happy marriage "a man must leave his father and mother and cleave unto his wife." There is a principle of human life here. In order to receive one must relinquish. To direct one's life single-mindedly to a goal, one must give up other lesser objectives. Or else we find ourselves going off in all directions and getting nowhere.

The ultimate goal for each of us is to be able to have God's intention realized in us. To do that we must let go of other lesser goals and loyalties so that God's will can become uppermost in our lives. Jesus said that to follow him we must love him more than we do the other significant persons in our lives, most notably— family. The key to what he says here lies in his including one's own self in his list of lesser loyalties. To love Christ with all one's heart is to give up loving one's self in a way that keeps us from receiving Christ into our lives completely. We can't say, "I accept your guidance, but I have other sources of authority and other things that are more important to me." When we give up ourselves to Christ, other loves and interests must take second place. To receive Christ we must relinquish other "gods."

TO TAKE HOLD of Christ, we must LET GO.

PRAYER: Help me to let go, so that I can take hold of Christ. Amen

~ ~ ~ ~ ~

SEPTEMBER 6

YES, BUT

Another said, "I will follow you, Lord; but let me first say farewell to those at my house."

—Luke 9:61

READ: Luke 9:57-10:4

Jesus does not want us to say, "Yes, but . . ." In this, Jesus is directing us to give up certain activities and values in order to receive a new life from God. This means that many of the pet ideas which give us comfort will have to go. Like, "No one loves me," or "I'm not going to amount to much." Or on the other hand, ideas with which we build ourselves up such as, "I'm of the 'so and so' family." "I drive a Mercedes." "My uncle is the mayor." We must give up those deep prejudices which have motivated us for so long like: the prejudice of male superiority, the ethnic racial bias in favor of white European ancestry, the cultural snobbery which makes us think we are better and have finer tastes than those lower than we are, because we read books, or enjoy classical music, or know how to dress,— or whatever.

The Christian must give up the ego-satisfying pettiness of flaunting prejudiced value judgements. Instead we must receive from Christ a just, merciful, and loving empathy for all of our brothers and sisters everywhere.

We do not have a special niche on the social ladder. There isn't a place of importance assigned to us, which others will admire. This is what Jesus meant when he said, "Foxes have holes and birds have nests, but the Son of Man has no place to lie down and rest." Jesus asks us to let go of the world's marks of status and importance and to find meaning in our lives completely in Christ and his lordship over us.

PRAYER: Help me to give up the status symbols which have
    supposedly given comfort, and to receive only Christ's approval.
    In him. Amen.

~ ~ ~ ~ ~ ~

SEPTEMBER 7

A TIME FOR LOSING AND A TIME FOR FINDING

> Then the Lord put out his hand and touched my
> mouth; and the Lord said to me, "Now I have put my words
> in your mouth. See, today I appoint you over nations and
> over kingdoms, to pluck up and to pull down, to destroy
> and overthrow, to build up and to plant."
>
> —Jeremiah 1:9-10

READ: Jeremiah 1:4-10 and Ecclesiastes 3:1-8

Jeremiah had two very important allegiances in his life: to his country, Judah, and to his Lord. In God's call to Jeremiah to prophesy Jeremiah understood that he would have to help his fellow Israelites give up Jerusalem and the life as they had known it in Judah, and further, that God would bring to them a new life and radically new circumstances. The old and comfortable ways would be uprooted and pulled down, destroyed and overthrown, but a new life would be planted and grown by the Lord God.

Jeremiah's faith in God enabled him to let go of his national life and well-being and to move forward in trust toward new life circumstances for himself and his people. As these developments took place Jeremiah accompanied many of his neighbors from Jerusalem into Babylonian exile. There he prepared them to return at a later date to Jerusalem to rebuild it after exile. Jeremiah helped his people to relinquish the old and to receive the new—to lose and to find.

There are times when the circumstances of life cause us to have to give up former surroundings, relationships and life-styles. Death or divorce, economic changes, or other factors intrude upon our lives and we must give up what has been comfortable, meaningful, and precious to us. In many of these periods of disruption and change we discover that God is calling us to let go, and then to receive from God new opportunities, relationships, and life circumstances. When we live close to God we are more ready to give up and to take on, to relinquish and to receive as God leads us. Jesus said. "Those who lose their life for my sake, and for the sake of the gospel, will save it." (Mark 8:35)

PRAYER: Help me to give up what I must, and to receive what you want for me. In Christ. Amen.

~ ~ ~ ~ ~

SEPTEMBER 8

GLORY BE

As for those who in the present age are rich, command them not to be haughty, or to set their hopes on the uncertainty of riches, but rather on God who richly provides us with everything for our enjoyment.

—I Timothy 6:17

READ: Luke 13:10-17

A much used catechism dating from the days of the Reformers, by which children were taught the Christian doctrines, starts with the definition stating that our main purpose in life is to "glorify God and enjoy him forever." The woman in Luke 13 glorified God when she discovered that she had been healed. Bent over by an evil spirit so that she could not walk, now miraculously she could stand straight up and walk. This stimulated her immediate response of glorifying God for what had happened in her life. Going beyond the story, it is fair to guess that from that day onward she enjoyed life more fully than she had before. Contact with Jesus caused her to achieve her main purpose in life according to the Shorter Catechism, "to glorify God, and enjoy him forever."

Have you felt the exhilaration which comes after a sickness has disappeared from your body? Something so simple and common as a headache can leave us almost unnoticed. When we discover that the pain is gone we feel wonderfully buoyant. Life has become enjoyable again. Such is a time to praise God. This comes close to our most primitive purpose, to glorify God. It is sad when healing does not come. But it is also sad when we fail to relate health and wholeness, fun and enjoyment to God, who generously gives us everything for our enjoyment.

How simple it is to achieve our most profound human purpose—to praise God joyfully.

PRAYER: Thank you, O God, for all the good that has come to me, for stopping the pain, or for helping me endure the pain, for strengthening my body and putting joy in my soul. Through Christ. Amen.

~ ~ ~ ~ ~

SEPTEMBER 9

SIMPLY MARVELOUS

When the crowds saw it, they were filled with awe, and they glorified God, who had given such authority to human beings.
—Matthew 9:8

READ: Matthew 9:1-8

Jesus was embroiled in a religious-political controversy with the religious authorities which made them blind to the power of God. In the midst of this argument a paralyzed man was healed and made able to walk. Observers of this who had not been involved in the dispute marveled at the change in the man's body and they glorified God. How long has it been since you truly marveled at anything? And when you did marvel, to whom did you look with admiration?

One of the lessons of this story is that we ought to be ready to marvel at the good things God does all around us, that in marveling we ought to give God the praise for what we observe. So much in life can inspire us to glorify God. But the more we become embroiled in petty disputes and selfish complaints, the less we are able to look up and to see the marvelous works of God in our world. Like hiking on rough terrain we become so preoccupied with the stones and tree roots over which we could stumble that we fail to look up into the beauty of the awesome sky above the graceful lines of the forest ceiling.

Yet our chief purpose is to perceive what God is doing and to glorify God for it. How much more enjoyable life is when we are able to marvel at the wonderful works of God. Would it be too simple to define the Christian as the person who, because of Christ, feels that life is marvelous, and who glorifies God for his wonderful works?

PRAYER: May I sense how marvelous life is and give you the glory, O God, my creator. In Christ. Amen.

~ ~ ~ ~ ~

SEPTEMBER 10

ALL GLORY LAUD AND HONOR TO THEE REDEEMER KING

The shepherds returned, glorifying and praising God
for all they had heard and seen, as it had been told them.
—Luke 2:20

READ: Luke 2:13-20 and Mark 11:1-10

It seems a little early—or late—to be reading the Christmas story. However, it is a shame that we confine these wonderful words to a once-a-year coverage. The shepherds of the Bethlehem hillside ought to be the pace setters for Christians in their instantaneous and enthusiastic expressions of glory to God. These folk returned to their usual routine glorifying God, and most likely enjoying life more fully for having visited Bethlehem and the manger with the infant Jesus in it. The birth of Christ helped them greatly to achieve their main purpose in life, to glorify God and to enjoy God forever.

So it is with us, the presence of Christ in our lives, his redeeming mercy, and his healing strength can turn our thoughts to God in praise and thanksgiving. The forgiveness which is available to us through Jesus Christ can take away much of the negative drag in life which keeps us from enjoyment. When Jesus came to the end of his earthly ministry the crowds accompanying him on his way into Jerusalem glorified God on that Palm Sunday long ago, shouting Hosanna in the highest. In doing so they were echoing the praise of the shepherds and inviting us to glorify God with our lips and our lives because of the enjoyment Jesus brings into our lives through his redeeming grace. No wonder we can sing, "All glory laud and honor, to Thee Redeemer King, to whom the lips of children made sweet hosannas ring."

PRAYER: For Jesus Christ I glorify you, O God. And I thank you for new-found enjoyment through Christ. Amen

~ ~ ~ ~ ~

SEPTEMBER 11

CAUGHT IN THE SYSTEM

". . . no longer a slave but more than a slave, a beloved brother . . . and I, Paul, do this as an old man, and now also as a prisoner of Christ Jesus.
—Philemon 16 & 9

READ: Philemon and I Peter 4:12-19

In modern society it is so easy to get caught in the system. By this is meant that the rules and regulations, the paper work, and the sheer organization of things becomes a system which seems to block one's pathway oftentimes, and sometimes one's initiative. Try to put through a complicated insurance claim, or try to fight "city hall" in order to remodel your house. One keen observer once commented that whenever something goes wrong on a mail order, there seems to be no end to the mistakes and confusion which follow as one tries to straighten out the matter in an attempt to receive the items ordered in the first place.

The letter of Paul to Philemon regarding Onesimus, the slave, is about the system. Both Paul and Onesimus, as well as Philemon were caught in a system which today we would call evil. Onesimus was a slave, the property of Philemon. He had tried to fight the system by running away, but now was about to be sent back—to re-enter the system. Paul was a prisoner, not because he had been convicted of anything criminal, but because he had gone contrary to the religious/political system. Philemon, a Christian, was forced by the system to own another man's life—a relationship which years later would be deemed wrong for Christians as well as for anybody else.

Yet, Paul, while living under an evil system, remained faithful to Christ and carried on evangelistic and pastoral work. Being in prison did not keep him from offering Christ to Onesimus, or from interceding on behalf of Onesimus.

Regardless of whatever system we must endure the example of Paul teaches us to remain faithful to

Christ in whatever circumstances we may find ourselves.

PRAYER: O Lord, make me faithful and effective for Christ. Amen

~ ~ ~ ~ ~

SEPTEMBER 12

ALL IN THE FAMILY

I am appealing to you for my child, Onesimus, whose father I have become during my imprisonment.
—Philemon 10

READ: Philemon 8-10 and John 15:11-17

One can well imagine how strange a place Rome must have been for Paul when he arrived there as a prisoner. Also for Onesimus, the runaway slave who not only did not know people, but who had reason to fear everyone he saw, because he was a renegade outside the law. For both men the anonymity and loneliness of the large city must have been nearly overwhelming. Yet in the midst of such social isolation Paul and Onesimus not only found each other but came to feel that they were in a family together. Each with his profound devotion to Jesus Christ was a member of the same family, so to speak. Paul, because of his long years as a Christian became a father to the new Christian, Onesimus. We would use the term "mentor" these days. What a joy for both men.

What a joy it is for someone entering a new town or city to find a church whose fellowship is warm, into which one is easily drawn and integrated. The fellowship which we enjoy in Christ goes a long way to off-set the loneliness and isolation of modern society. The opening and closing words of Philemon bear witness to this Christian fellowship which we enjoy to this day. This stems from Jesus' words, "No longer do I call you servants but I have called you friends."

PRAYER: Thank you, O God, for the friendship we enjoy with one another in Christ. Amen

~ ~ ~ ~ ~ ~

SEPTEMBER 13

CHRISTIAN FAITH WORKS

Formerly he was useless to you, but now he is indeed useful both to you and to me.

—Philemon 11

READ: Philemon 11-16 and John 14:12-16

There is an old story about a little girl who used her piety
to avoid work. Every time her mother asked her to do the dishes
her reply was, "I can't, Mother. I'm reading my Bible." And
what solicitous mother would obstruct such exemplary
behavior? A little boy was expelled from school in a North
Carolina town because his extreme form of evangelistic religion
made him into a bothersome, noisy child preacher who resisted
school authorities on the grounds that they were not Christian.
It is a misunderstanding of Christian faith to think that it takes
us away from the necessary and proper work and regulations of
the world.

Paul declares that the conversion of Onesimus to Christ made
him a better worker both for his owner, Philemon and for Paul
himself. The runaway slave had been anything but helpful to
Philemon. Now as a new Christian, Onesimus would be a
cooperative worker.

True Christian faith has a way of making us more responsible
and reliable workers and citizens in a world which requires the
contribution and effort of each one of us. Jesus promised his disciples
the power of the Holy Spirit to make them better workers for God,
not only in church related efforts, but in all legitimate and necessary
work in the world. One's work is a way of exercising Christian
stewardship. Through the efforts of our minds and our hands we
carry out our tasks a stewards of God's creation for the betterment
of all.

PRAYER: Help me to be a good worker in whatever work I am
engaged, as a good steward of my time and talents. In Christ.
Amen.

~ ~ ~ ~ ~ ~

SEPTEMBER 14

KNOWLEDGE IS POWER

For this reason, though I am bold enough in Christ to command you to do your duty, yet I would rather appeal to you on the basis of love.

—Philemon 8,9

READ: Philemon 17-20 and Matthew 16:13-19

Perhaps the most surprising sentence in Philemon is the one singled out for today—that Paul would have the power to order Philemon to do something. That, however, was the power Paul possessed. The source of such power was God. The exercise of that power appropriately was in order to carry out God's purposes, not Paul's.

It is indeed surprising to hear Jesus give Peter the power to forgive people's sins as reported in Matthew 16. The history of the church has been influenced strongly by this word to Peter. As a result the Roman Catholic Church established structures and methods by which to dispense forgiveness to the faithful. The confession of sin and assurance of pardon in many orders of worship represent a modern expression of this power to forgive granted to Peter, now offered in the church to its worshipers.

The knowledge of God's truth and the understanding of his purposes provide the Christian power over some of life's difficulties. Such knowledge and understanding helps one to control his/her own life according to God's will. While Christ humbles each of us, he grants a new sense of self confidence to us as well. This gives us power to live more orderly and effective lives for Christ.

PRAYER: Help me to understand your will, O God,. and to know myself in such a way that knowing my need for your forgiveness and strength, I may have the confidence to live effectively for Christ in my dealings with others. In him. Amen.

~ ~ ~ ~ ~ ~

SEPTEMBER 15

ON THE WINGS OF INSECTS

"You know how to interpret the appearance of the sky, but you cannot interpret the signs of the times.
—Matthew 16:3

READ: Joel 1:1-4 and Matthew 16:1-4

"The grasshoppers were so thick that I had to stop and brush them out of my radiator. And the highway was actually slippery, there were so many of them crushed on it. The best crop we've had in years, and now the hoppers are ruining the harvest". So the ran the commentary about the hoppers of the summer of 1986 in eastern Montana! The closest to a theological interpretation of the plague was, "that's the way it goes—always something."

Not so with the ancient Israelites during a similar summer. On the wings of insects they heard the voice of God. Or at least Joel, the prophet, did. He made his interpretation known in his prophecy, later recorded in the book of Joel. He begins his statement: "Hear this, O elders, give ear, all inhabitants of the land! Has such a thing happened in your days, or in the days of your ancestors? Let all the inhabitants of the land tremble, for the day of the Lord is coming, it is near—" (Joel 1:2, & 2:1)

It was one of the most significant functions of the prophets to interpret the signs of the times. They offered a theological interpretation of current events by declaring what God was saying to the people through the things that were happening. Thus, the wings of locusts carried the message of God to the people.

Jesus once chided his followers for not reading the signs of their times, thus missing the significance of his appearing in the world. How about us? Are we attuned to the message of God so that when events unfold and circumstances change we are able to learn what God is telling us through these situations? God did not cause the locust plague, nor any other tragedy. But when such things happen, God may very well have insights to share with us through such events . . . on the wings of insects, so to speak.

PRAYER: Help me to hear your voice, O God, speaking to me in the midst of current events. In Christ. Amen.

~ ~ ~ ~ ~ ~

SEPTEMBER 16

THE GUILT EDGE OF TROUBLE

As he walked along he saw a man blind from birth. His disciples asked him, "Rabbi, who sinned, this man or his parents, that he was born blind?"

—John 9:1-2

READ: Joel 2:12-17 and John 9:1-3

There is a universal connection deep in our minds between trouble and guilt. Whenever tragedy, accident or disease strike us, we are apt to ponder our own failings, or sin, and to feel pangs of conscience. We seem automatically to feel that we are the cause of our trouble. Many a person lying on a hospital bed after some sudden physical crisis, confides in his or her pastor, "I haven't been going to church as regularly as I know I should have." Jesus' disciples questioned Jesus about sin when they came upon a blind person. Because the condition had existed from birth they wondered if the problem originated with the blind person's parents.

Joel declared to the people in the midst of the horrible locust plague that they must repent, "Yet, even now, says the Lord, return to me with all your heart, with fasting, with weeping, and with mourning.

(Joel 2:12) The time of national devastation would be an occasion for reviewing Judah's disobedience to God and the covenant the nation had with God. Trouble brought pangs of conscience to Joel and the people of God.

There was a time when many mental health professionals were highly critical of churches for inducing guilt in the minds of people, which it was thought injured their mental health. But now the more enlightened position is to recognize the universal character of guilt and to see that religion helps people identify and define their guilt, and that religion is not the cause of it. The Christian faith helps us to understand that our natural human tendency to live as if God does not exist, is guilt-producing. Through Christ we are invited to confess this tendency to God and to be forgiven.

The guilt edge of trouble may very well help us to approach God in a spirit of confession, and to work through our guilt in response to Christ's offer of forgiveness and redemption. It is not so much a question of who sinned?" as it is a question how God is leading me from guilt to forgiveness during this time of trouble in my life?

PRAYER: Speak to me in my times of distress, and show me your mercy in the midst of my own shortcomings. Through Christ. Amen.

~ ~ ~ ~ ~ ~

SEPTEMBER 17

THE LAST ACT: Sometime later in the valley.

When the Son of Man comes in his glory, and all the angels with him, then he will sit on the throne of his glory.

All the nations will be gathered before him, and he will separate people one from another as a shepherd separates the sheep from the goats.

—Matthew 25:31-32

READ: Joel 3:1-2, 12-15, and Matthew 25:31-33

"He lives as if there were no tomorrow!" This is a phrase we use to describe someone who lives recklessly without thought of the consequences of his behavior. Such an attitude is not rare these days. In fact, our entire culture seems to have lost its awareness of a final act in the human drama in which there will be an accounting. However, widespread trouble has a way of calling us to account.

Joel interpreted the locust plague as a signal for God's judgement, "For then in those days, and at that time, when I restore the fortunes of Judah and Jerusalem, I will gather all the nations and bring them down to the valley of Jehoshaphat, and I will enter into judgement with them there." (Joel 3:1,2) Joel believed that the last act would take place sometime later in the Valley of Jehoshaphat, meaning this would be the Lord's judgement.

We live in a day when many do not believe there will be a last act other than one's own personal death, and that ones's own behavior is to be evaluated only on the basis of whether or not it makes one feel good and does not hurt anyone else. It is felt that no one else is to determine this. Each of us is to be his own judge, many would say. Not so, says Joel. God is the judge. To God alone we are accountable. Jesus refers to this as the time when the sheep and goats are separated.

The message in this for us is that it makes a difference to God how each of us lives, and if that is so, we ought to consult him now, before the last act—sometime later in the valley of judgement.

PRAYER: Direct me, O God. Show me the pathway for my life which is according to your will. In Christ. Amen.

~ ~ ~ ~ ~ ~

SEPTEMBER 18

WHEN THE GOING GETS ROUGH . . . REST

"Come to me, all you that are weary and are carrying
heavy burdens, and I will give you rest. Take my yoke upon
you and learn from me . . . ."

—Matthew 11:28-29

READ: Joel 2:10-13, Psalm 37:3-8 and Matthew 11:28-30

The Christian approach to life is often so wonderfully opposite
the normal behavior patterns. A very typical American slogan says,
"When the going gets tough, the tough get going." It was a very
tough time when Joel prophesied but he did not counsel people to
toughen up against the adversity of a locust plague. Rather, he
offered the hope of a vision of God to inspire the people. Jesus'
offer to the weary and over-burdened people is not an added dose
of adrenalin. He offered rest. How very opposite! What he said
next is a clue to understanding what he is offering to each of us. By
promising that his yoke is easy he is contrasting his own way to
the selfish way of life which is so tiring.

It is tiring to continually try to prove oneself worthy in the
sight of others and deserving in the sight of God. Everybody is
wearing themselves out trying to make a big impression, it seems.
In place of such futile efforts Jesus is suggesting that to follow him
is really easier. To put at rest all of one's vain attempts to make it
on one's own is really a relief. To say in effect to Christ, "You take
over. Lead me in the best path for my life," is to rest in the Lord
and to wait patiently for him.

Sometimes it is a life crisis which encourages us finally to put
our complete trust in God. When all other supports have failed us,
then it becomes plain that trusting faith in God is the most restful
route to take. That, after all, is what Joel counseled.

PRAYER: Help me to put my whole trust in you, O God. Place
me under the yoke of Christ. In   . Amen.

~ ~ ~ ~ ~

SEPTEMBER 19

BEING REAL

One who gives an honest answer gives a kiss on the lips.
—Proverbs 24:26

READ: Proverbs 8:1-10 and Matthew 12:38-42

A baffle is an object placed in a stream to redirect the course of its flow. People can be baffling when they obstruct our understanding of them. It is difficult to develop deep friendships with those who screen themselves off from us, diverting attention from the real self behind the baffle, to something false. The ancient teachers of wisdom knew this truth about human affairs when they said that the honest answer was a way to intimate friendship.

Jesus was aware of the wise teachings of the Jewish tradition which was often attributed to King Solomon. Jesus did not deny the value of such teachings. Rather, he proclaimed that an even greater teaching was coming. Indeed, it was his very life which gave the world understanding which goes beyond the wisdom of the Old Testament.

How can one decide to be honest and to give an honest answer when we are so conditioned to protect ourselves through a set of baffles by which to avoid real contact with others? In other words, how can we enter into true friendship with others? Only when we feel good about ourselves and no longer fearful of attack from others. The saving grace of Christ makes us able to have such self-assurance. When we recognize through Christ that God loves us as we are, we can begin to feel OK about ourselves—that is what it means to be redeemed. Then we can dare to give honest answers, to remove the baffles, and to be real to others. True friendship, like a kiss on the lips, will result.

PRAYER: Help me to be real, O God. Make me less baffling to others. In Christ let me be a true friend to others. In him. Amen.

~ ~ ~ ~ ~

SEPTEMBER 20

PEACE OF MIND

A tranquil mind gives life to the flesh, but passion
makes the bones rot.

—Proverbs 14:30

READ: Proverbs 8:11-20 and Matthew 6:19-21

The wisdom of the ancient Israelites pre-dates modern holistic medicine by tens of centuries. Yet the wise of those ancient times understood its principle. What you do with your mind and emotions has a direct affect upon your physical health. A mind at ease makes for a healthy body. Uptight emotions can do damage to the body. A frenzied, anxious, tense life filled with stress and conflict inside and out is a life which does violence to the physical body, causing a greater incidence of certain diseases.

Jesus was getting at this same principle when he spoke of treasure. Whatever it is that you concentrate upon and direct your life toward—that is—your treasure—will somehow determine the outcome of your life. If you give in to resentment, hatred, jealousy, small-mindedness and envy, you will lose in the long run. Jesus said, "Those who want to save their life will lose it." (Luke 9:24) If you eat your heart out in negative and destructive passions, your heart my be literally eaten out.

On the other hand peace of mind, being at ease with God through receiving Christ's love and grace could very well go a long way in setting things right in your life, both mentally and physically, as well as spiritually.

PRAYER: Peace of mind, O God, is what I want and need. Let me know the love of Christ so fully that I begin to experience that peace he promised. In him. Amen.

~ ~ ~ ~ ~

SEPTEMBER 21

THE SOURCE OF JUSTICE

The evil do not understand justice, but those who seek
the Lord understand it completely.

—Proverbs 28:5

READ: Proverbs 8:22-31 and John 1:1-5

The "wisdom literature" in the Old Testament, most notably, the Book of Proverbs affirms that *Wisdom* is at the beginning of all God's acts, as Proverbs 8:22 states. Wisdom is seen as the underlying foundation of all that is. John affirms this and calls this elemental influence, "the Word," and goes on to identify the Word with Christ. Thus to worship the Lord who laid down the rules of creation, is to understand God's justice. To forsake God is to forget what is just.

Look at our world today. Examine your own interpersonal relationships. See the connection! To the extent that we acknowledge God as our Source, we will deal with others as equals, who themselves are God's creation, and loved by God. This understanding is the beginning of justice. Without acknowledging our common origin in God, we fall prey to the human temptation of separating ourselves from others, and creating levels of perceived worth among people. This leads inevitably to treating others as less than human. Such dehumanizing is the beginning of injustice. Where there is a prevalence of dehumanizing actions and customs there may well be an absence of true worship.

If the universe has been organized on the basis of wisdom, as an underlying principle, then it is surely necessary for us to try to understand wisdom, and to comprehend what justice demands of us in human relationships. To understand justice and wisdom completely we must turn to Christ the Word, the source of wisdom and justice.

PRAYER: O God, make me wise and just in all my ways. Through Christ the Word. Amen

~ ~ ~ ~ ~ ~

SEPTEMBER 22

LOVE'S BLIND EYE

Hatred stirs up strife, but love covers all offenses.

—Proverbs 10:12

READ: Proverbs 8:32-36 and I Peter 4:7-11

Fault-finding is an unhappy business. It makes the one who has made the mistake unhappy, and it breeds and feeds on the unhappiness of the finder as well. Consider what criticism and judgement do to the fabric of happiness in a family. When parents pick at the children for every little thing, when brothers and sisters are forever attacking each other, or when husbands and wives are quick to point out every fault in the spouse, there is bound to be strife. "Hatred stirs up strife . . ." But the rest of the verse is, "but love covers all offenses." (Proverbs 10:12)

The New Testament also provides this insight into what might be called "love's blind eye." "Above all, maintain constant love for one another, for love covers a multitude of sins." (I Peter 4:8) The setting into which Peter introduces this idea is the fellowship of the church, where it is also true that when a loving group of people overlooks the faults in each other, there is peace and harmony in the church. But, on the other hand, when human foibles are the constant subject of conversation, there can be little true happiness and peace. Nor church growth either! Jesus said, "Blessed (happy) are the merciful . . . Blessed (happy) are the peacemakers . . ." (Matthew 5:7,9)

PRAYER: Grant me a blind eye to the faults of others, and let me relate to them in love, knowing that you are the just and loving judge of all your children, including me. In the mercy of Christ. Amen.

~ ~ ~ ~ ~ ~

SEPTEMBER 23

COMMITMENT IS COURAGE

> I will know that . . . you are in no way intimidated by your opponents.
>
> —Philippians 1:27,28

READ: Philippians 1:27-30

The late William Barclay re-told the story of a French soldier newly recruited, who was trembling with fear as he faced a desperate situation. He was given courage when a much older veteran came along and said to him, "Come, son, and you and I will do something fine for France!" Besides much needed companionship the veteran gave to the recruit a sense of commitment, and with that motivation he was given courage to face the fire.

When our commitment to Christ and his cause is strong, and when we sense that we are not alone, one of the essential results is courage. Many an imprisoned missionary of the Cross could testify to this fact of faith.

While most of us do not have to face gunfire, or the persecution of hostile political authorities for our faith, we have countless other opportunities to show courage as soldiers of the Gospel. It takes courage to stand firm against popular opinion and to speak on behalf of someone who has taken a stand for Christ. It takes courage to attempt to change the thinking of a friend or loved one whose position you feel is contrary to the will of God. It takes courage to share your innermost thoughts and feelings with someone whom you think could grow in faith because of your witness. It takes courage to say, "No," when everyone else is saying, "Yes."

The courage we need for such acts of personal valor derives from a strong commitment to Christ: and such a commitment is nurtured by continual and meaningful contact with others of faith. That's one reason church is important to one's Christian life.

PRAYER: Make me courageous, O Lord, that I may more firmly stand for you. Through Christ who stood firm for my sake. Amen.

~ ~ ~ ~ ~

SEPTEMBER 24

COMMITMENT AND HUMILITY

> Do nothing from selfish ambition of conceit, but in humility regard others as better than yourselves. Let each one of you look not to your own interests, but to the interests of others.
>
> —Philippians 2:3-4

READ: Philippians 2:1-11

Humility, like happiness, is difficult to create in oneself. We recognize that it is a by-product of something else and cannot be the object of one's striving. What is that something else which brings humility to one's life? The answer to that question is commitment. When we commit ourselves to someone else and become truly concerned for their good, our self concern drops in proportion. The end result of that transformation is true humility. According to one dictionary definition, "To be humble is to be made meek and submissive to the divine will." Commitment to Christ brings humility.

In many ways commitment, humility and love are faces of the same reality. When you love someone you commit yourself to the good of the one loved and thereby reduce your own self-concern and pride. That is true humility. Paul urged us to be humble toward one another and to look out for the interests of the other person. This attitude is like that of Jesus Christ. Jesus said that the humble will be happy and receive what God promises. It all fits together.

PRAYER: O Lord, by your grace may I commit myself to Christ anew this day, and in so doing give myself to the good to others. In him. Amen.

~ ~ ~ ~ ~

SEPTEMBER 25

COMMITMENT IS DISCIPLINE

But our citizenship is in heaven, and it is from there
that we are expecting a Savior, the Lord Jesus Christ.
—Philippians 3:20

READ: Philippians 3:12-21

Why is a Christian like a spy? Have you ever wondered? Probably not. But there is a very basic similarity between one who is deeply committed to Christ and a secret agent for a foreign country. Each lives in a host country while serving a different governing authority. Paul called the Christians in Philippi "Citizens of heaven." Like a foreign agent we take our orders from a source of authority other than from the host society itself. The spy serves a foreign government. The Christian serves Jesus Christ. In each case that commitment disciplines his or her every decision.

On a personal level it is the Christian's commitment to values outside the self which disciplines his or her actions. Discipline is doing what one would not ordinarily or naturally want to do. The line of least resistance may very well be the opposite of the decision one would make under the direction and discipline of Christ. We live in a society that says, 'Whatever is best for you, you should do." As citizens of Christ's kingdom we cannot allow so shallow and self-serving a rule to guide our decisions. Rather we must discipline ourselves to ask, "What does my commitment to Jesus Christ require of me in this instance?" And, like it or not, that is what we must do. It is necessary for each Christian to determine how this underlying commitment to Christ translates into the many day-to-day, as well as long term commitments which are made in life. Marriage commitment, job commitments, commitments to ones community, the nation, or cause, all must be examined in the light of the basic Christian commitment. Then decisions must be made under such discipline as Christ seeks from us.

PRAYER: O Christ, I am under oath to you. Give me strength to discipline my life accordingly. Amen.

〜 〜 〜 〜 〜 〜

SEPTEMBER 26

COMMITMENT IS JOY

Rejoice in the Lord always; again I will say, Rejoice.
—Philippians 4:4

READ: Philippians 4:4-9

"I'm coming unglued," is a colorful phrase one hears occasionally. Earlier the same feeling was expressed in such phrases as "coming apart at the seams," or "pulled in a thousand directions." These ideas depict a very normal human feeling associated with some degree of disintegration. When there are many conflicting claims upon us, or when we seem not to have any unifying purpose in life, or when life crises come at us too rapidly, we feel anxious and as if we may not hold together much longer. Astronomers and other scientists say that the normal tendency in the universe is toward disintegration. Things just naturally want to fly apart. And how easy it is for life to fall in a heap. Such experiences produce despair and gloom.

But on the other hand, the Christian faith promises joy. How can that be? Notice that Paul associated joy with union with Christ. Commitment to someone outside oneself and some measure of union with that person produces happiness and joy. A good marriage in which there is mutual commitment, and union with one another is indeed a source of joy. This can also be the case in a close friendship in which we are truly committed to the welfare of the other person. Thus united in our efforts, we find joy in common projects and concerns.

Our ultimate commitment is to God. Such commitment re-integrates one's whole being. Union with Christ pulls together the many strands of one's own life and re-directs all of life toward a common purpose—service to Christ. In this way Christ helps us "put it all together." That is indeed a joyful process.

PRAYER: O Christ, help me put my life back together through committing myself to you. Amen.

~ ~ ~ ~ ~ ~

SEPTEMBER 27

PLYWOOD, GUMBO, AND CRAB GRASS

"But as for what was sown on good soil, this is the one who hears the word and understands it, who indeed bears fruit and yields, in one case a hundredfold, in another sixty, and in another thirty."

—Matthew 13:23

READ: Matthew 13:1-9, 18-23

A new homeowner putting in a new lawn very faithfully watered the newly sprouting seeds. Soon the grass had come up and the sun gave it nourishment to flourish. Finally a lush green carpet appeared—almost. In the midst of the green was a rectangular yellow spot. No amount of water would make it green. Finally the owner dug up the spot and found an inch beneath the surface a discarded piece of plywood left over from the builders. The roots couldn't penetrate the wood. In the same yard the carrots planted in the garden were always stunted. The cause was similar. The tender new growth wasn't able to penetrate the patch of gumbo beneath the thin layer of topsoil. And elsewhere in the same new yard the only thing green was crab grass. How like Jesus' parable of the sower and the soils.

The parable of the sower is the only parable for which Jesus gives an explanation of its meaning, so far as the record in the Bible is concerned. Through this story Jesus is pointing to some common problems we have in adequately hearing and accepting his message for us, just as one's yard and garden may have a difficult time providing for everything to grow properly. He is telling us that we might not be ready to hear the Gospel. We may not sense a need for God's action in our lives, thinking that we can handle everything on our own. He is pointing out that once heard, the Good News needs to be studied and pondered until it becomes a growing part of our lives. Jesus is warning us further that many other interests and loyalties can crowd out the message of God's love, until we barely think of God through the day.

But on the positive side, the parable of the sower and the soils compares the productive Christian to good soil in which the message of Christ can easily flourish.

PRAYER: O God, plant your message in my life. May I be ready to hear and understand. May I so study your word that I become able to produce good fruit for Christ. In his name. Amen.

~ ~ ~ ~ ~ ~

SEPTEMBER 28

PERENNIAL DELIGHTS

". . . and the seed would sprout and grow, he does not know how."

—Mark 4:27

READ: Mark 4:26-29

Among the perennial delights of an established yard and garden are the perennials! How anything can survive the sub-zero temperatures of winter and come out of it in the spring stronger and more full of beauty than the summer before is a mystery. And yet there they are: the flowering plants, put in the soil years ago blazing with color each springtime. On many a deserted rural landscape one can find perennial bushes still alive and blooming long after the old homestead was vacated and torn down

Jesus assures us that no matter how severe the winter of our existence or temporary our frail human structures, there is growing in our very midst something so strong it will live forever, so full of beauty that it will bring pleasure to the entire human race. It has such a growth potential that it will never be thwarted, and yet it is so hidden that it cannot readily be seen. That mighty and vital perennial is the Kingdom of God, Jesus tells us.

Translated into our terms what does it mean for the Kingdom of God to be a perennial? It means that wherever people obey God, and acknowledge Christ as King and Lord of their lives, God's will is growing. Wherever the reconciling love of God is found to bring people together, and wherever God's mercy and forgiveness is re-uniting people with God, there is the growing vital reality which is beautiful to behold. It means that the strength and destiny of God's perennial Kingdom assures it of ultimately becoming the only plant in the garden. "And he shall reign for ever and ever! King of Kings! And Lord of Lords."

PRAYER: O God, thank you for growing in our midst your Kingdom of Love and Beauty. Through Christ the King. Amen.

~ ~ ~ ~ ~

SEPTEMBER 29

NO NEED TO HOE YET

"Let both of them grow together until the harvest; and at harvest time I will tell the reapers, 'Collect the weeds first and bind them in bundles to be burned, but gather the wheat into my barn.'"

—Matthew 13:30

READ: Matthew 13:24-30

Weeds are a fact of life in the lawn and garden. Chemical herbicides, biological control, and hoeing are the three main foes of weeds. But most yards will still have weeds. Jesus assumed that life was like a yard and garden with the inevitable weeds. He said in effect, "No need to hoe yet. Let the weeds go, and in the harvest we'll take care of them."

How we would like to be perfectionists when it comes to life. We would like to rid the world of every sin and remove all the wrongs and injustices from society right now. Furthermore, we are sometimes discouraged by "weeds" in our lives—the wrongs we do, and the good we fail to produce. Sometimes we even dare to become impatient with God and ask why God doesn't remove some person or problem from the face of the earth. Jesus provides us a perspective on these questions when he tells us of the wheat and the weeds growing together until harvest. There will always be evil, but God is in charge of the final harvest when the good wheat will be saved for God's storehouse. In the final accounting the weeds will be destroyed.

It is therefore our task to set our minds on the things of eternal value in a world which worships temporary self-seeking objectives. We must contribute to justice in the midst of continuing injustice. We must be peacemakers in a world bent on its own insane destruction. It is God's task to harvest the justice, peace and righteousness, and ultimately to do away with all that is contrary to God's will.

PRAYER: O most patient Lord, grant me patience to see things from your perspective and to serve you accordingly. In Christ. Amen.

~ ~ ~ ~ ~ ~

SEPTEMBER 30

ONLY GOD CAN MAKE A TREE

> It is the smallest of all the seeds, but when it has grown
> it is the greatest of shrubs and becomes a tree, so that the
> birds of the air come and make nests in its branches."
> —Matthew 13:32

READ: Matthew 13:31-32

After many years a former resident returned to the yard in which her children had once played. The small spruce tree her children had once jumped over, had become a forty foot tree much to her amazement. Add to such amazement the fact that earlier the spruce had begun as a tiny seed. Our highly complex and sophisticated technology has accomplished a great deal "to the moon and back," but we have never been able to create life and growth, as in the case of a tree or a plant of any kind. That secret remains in the mind of God.

It was this miracle of extraordinary growth which Jesus cited in order to assure us that the Kingdom of God is indeed growing in our midst, and that finally it will be the greatest of all kingdoms, offering support and protection beyond our power to replicate. The bringing of God's kingdom is beyond our power. However, we can be assured that Jesus' coming into the world is God's announcement of the Kingdom of God. The resurrection of Christ is God's assurance of the ultimate triumph of God's kingdom over all evil in the world.

When we become frustrated with our own feeble efforts to improve the world situation, or to straighten out local problems, it is good to know that "only God can make a tree." God will bring order out of chaos and God's righteousness will finally win out. This assurance, however, ought not to keep us from doing everything we possibly can to cooperate in God's reconciling work in the world both far away and close to home.

PRAYER: God of creation I thank you for the assurance of your ultimate triumph over evil. Help me to join in the effort to overcome wrong in human life. Through the risen Christ. Amen

OCTOBER

OCTOBER 1

FAITH FOR NO REASON

> The Lord said to Satan, "Have you considered my servant, Job? There is no one like him on the earth, a blameless and upright man who fears God and turns away from evil." Then Satan answered the Lord, "Does Job fear God for nothing?"
>
> —Job 1:8-9

READ: Job 1:6-11, 2:7-10 and Luke 9:57-62

"I haven't seen Dave in church since his wife died."

"No, he's not been there. Wasn't that tragic? Only thirty-nine, and those poor children she left!"

"You know, He told me he'd prayed so hard during her illness, feeling that his faith would make her well."

"Yeah, that would be enough to make me lose my faith."

Sadly, faith that is tied to results or rewards is false faith, and it is easily lost when the results are tragic. Job was tested at this very point. Would Job lose his faith when things got really bad for him—when he lost his property, his children and family, and finally his health? Instead, could it be that Job fears God (has faith) for nothing, for no reason? The message of the parable of Job is that Job's faith was not built upon expected good results, or upon continuing blessings and security. His faith was true faith—based upon God only. Job's *faith for no reason* remained with him strongly throughout a lifetime of adverse circumstances.

Luke tells us of people who promised to follow Jesus, but who had concerns of their own which they put first. This was false faith. Jesus declared that true faith would not bring comforts, but hardships instead.

True faith is a gift from God which is its own reward. Such a faith is our dependence upon God's grace for our every moment regardless of the difficult circumstances we may have to endure.

PRAYER: Grant me such a faith as Job was given, O God. Through Christ. Amen.

~ ~ ~ ~ ~

OCTOBER 2

FAITH THAT GOD CARES

What are human beings that you make so much of them, that you set your mind on them.

—Job 7:17

READ: Job 7:1-6 and Luke 12:22-31

"Oh, I have faith in God," he said. "God made the universe and is in charge of the grand design, but more than that—No. God is like 'The Force.' Whatever happens now is up to us, and our genes, you might say—and nature. God's much too distant to be involved in day to day happenings. Current events are our responsibility, not God's."

There are a great many people in modern times who were schooled in the "clock-works" theory of the universe. That God designed the world as a clock maker would. Then God wound it up and is letting it run on its own now. They do not believe that God is directly involved. He created the universe, set ups the rules and now it's on its own. This idea leads to a vague belief in God which really is not faith at all, for it requires self-reliance apart from God.

Job was overwhelmed by the conviction that God cares for humanity, and for himself personally, despite the magnitude of God's creative power over all the universe. The writer of Job echoed the affirmation of true faith found in Psalm 8: "When I look at your heavens, the work of your fingers, the moon and the stars that you have established; what are human beings that you are mindful of them, mortals that you care for them?" (Psalm 8:3-4)

True faith runs counter to the prevailing notion in the behavioral sciences that humankind is but one more specie in the diverse list of growing things in the universe. Thus humanity is seen as limited to the laws and dynamics of nature. Instead of this mechanistic and determined view of our life, Christian faith knows God's particular care and concern for humanity—indeed for oneself. This is a powerful element in the consciousness of the Christian's sense of identity.

In the Luke passage cited above, Jesus declares, "Of how much more value are you than the birds." (Luke 12:24) The person with true faith knows God's love and concern no matter what comes in life.

PRAYER: I pray for faith, the sure awareness of your care for me, O God. Through Christ. Amen.

~ ~ ~ ~ ~

OCTOBER 3

FAITH'S AWARENESS OF SIN

> "Then call, and I will answer; or let me speak, and you reply to me. How many are my iniquities and my sins? Make me know my transgression and my sin."
>
> —Job 13:22-23

READ: Job 13:20-25 and Luke 18:9-14

"I wish I had such a faith as Pastor Jones has. He is so sure of his forgiveness when he witnesses to his religious experience. All those sins when he was young, and now he is no longer a sinner like he was. Only little sins now is how he puts it. If I could only have a faith like that."

Jesus told of such a person when he compared the Pharisee who claimed to have no sin, with the tax collector who knew himself to be a sinner. The one who is aware of his own sin is the one with faith. Faith is the assurance of God's love, not of our goodness.

Sometimes assurance of goodness takes the form of denying that there is such a thing as sin. Common in our society is the use of the word "indiscretion," which is used instead of "sin." This switch in terminology is used especially often when celebrities of one sort or another are caught in an "indiscretion."—not in a "sin." Faith is the willingness to admit one's own sin against God and the desire to pray for forgiveness, to repent and to be overwhelmed by the fact of God's undeserved mercy.

Sin can keep one from faith when we do not seek forgiveness, and thus keeps us separated from God. Job and the tax collector should be models of true faith as we see each of these two men painfully aware of his shortcomings, and at the same time conscious of God's forgiveness.

PRAYER: Forgive me for my sin, O God. In faith I accept your mercy through Christ. Amen

~ ~ ~ ~ ~

OCTOBER 4

FAITH WITHOUT PROOF

For I know that my Redeemer lives, and that at the last he will stand upon the earth.

—Job 19:25

READ: Job 19:23-27 and John 20:24-29

Speaking on a panel of scientists on "The Faith of the Scientist," a nuclear physicist said: "I used to say that unless I could observe concrete evidence of God through my five senses I could not believe. But now my research is much more sophisticated. When I can derive through my computer, mathematical proof for a divine power, then I'll have faith—but only then."

In many ways the highest expression of faith for Job is the phrase set to music by Handel: "I know that my redeemer liveth." This faith was not based upon the proof of the eye or ear—or computer. Such true faith is in the inner being, as an assurance. A knowing which cannot be shaken by life's developments, good or bad.

The disciple, Thomas, was known as "doubting Thomas," which may not be fair to him. It comes from the story in John cited above. More important is the concluding statement by Jesus, "Blessed are those who have not seen and yet have come to believe." (John 20:29)

Some people speak of hearing God's voice audibly, or of seeing a vision of Jesus. When we hear of such experiences we are tempted to envy them, feeling that if only we could have such an experience we would have stronger faith. The testimony of Job and of John is that authentic faith does not rely upon such proofs. It is a gift of God to the inner heart of a person which makes us able to trust in God no matter what.

PRAYER: God, grant me faith in my inner being. Make my trust in you unshakeable. Through Christ. Amen.

~ ~ ~ ~ ~

OCTOBER 5

FAITH'S REALITY

"Therefore I have uttered what I did not understand,
things too wonderful for me, which I did not know I

had heard of you by the hearing of the ear, but now my eye sees you."

—Job 42:3,5

READ: Job 42:1-6 And Luke 24:13-32

When asked to define faith she answered, "I don't know. Faith is sort of like knowing that there is a God and that Jesus was God's Son, and that God wants me to live a moral life, and that I should do my best." Though a fairly typical answer, this is not true faith. Rather it is a belief in God, and that is about all. It is not a very real faith.

Job finally affirms the reality of his faith when he concludes, "Now my eye sees you." The disciples on the walk to Emmaus felt their "hearts burning" within them as they walked with Jesus to supper. After seeing him sitting at the table with them they reflected on the reality of their faith even before seeing Jesus with their eyes.

The reality of authentic faith is found in the inner warmth and enthusiasm we feel when we contemplate God and sense Christ's call and presence. Real faith is assured of the certain hope of a final face to face encounter with the Master. Later in the Bible Paul declared this when he wrote: "For now we see in a mirror, dimly, but then we will see face to face. Now I know in part; then I will know fully, even as I have been fully known." (I Corinthians 13:12)

True faith is knowing with burning hearts that each day is a day closer for us to that face to face meeting with God.

PRAYER: Thank you, Lord, for the burning heart within me, and for the promise of seeing your face. In Christ. Amen.

~ ~ ~ ~ ~ ~

OCTOBER 6

LIFE ON A FLOOD PLANE

And if he (God) did not spare the ancient world,
even though he saved Noah, a herald of righteousness,
with seven others, when he brought a flood on a world
of the ungodly."

—II Peter 2:5

READ: Isaiah 54:9-14 and II Peter 2:1-9

It keeps us both humbled and encouraged to remember Noah. Humbled because the story reminds us that we live on a flood plane and that untruth and wrongdoing will ultimately sink us. That is what happened in Noah's time. But the encouragement in the story is that God does ultimately side with the faithful. Peter reminds us that God rescued Lot, and he rescued Noah. The writer of Isaiah 54 reminds his hearers of Noah and God's promise not to destroy his people. This was very good news to the people in Isaiah's time because they were suffering from what seemed to be an endless exile in Babylon. Isaiah helped them to have hope for a return to their homeland by reminding them of the return to safety which God gave to Noah in the flood. If God did it for Noah, God will do it for us. Life on a flood plane—but life with a divine rescuer promised. Life in exile—but life with a hope for homecoming.

There are times in each of our lives when we feel inundated with a flood of troubles, or a high tide of conflicting claims upon our lives. In such times it is helpful to remember that God led Noah through the flood to dry land. There are times when we feel exiled, away from the security of home, when people criticize us, or ridicule us, or ignore us, and we feel "out of it." Like the Jews in exile it is helpful to be reminded that God promised Noah that no matter how bad the flood he would offer a life saver. Remembering helps us to create a hopeful future.

PRAYER: Help me to remember your promise of saving grace, O Lord. In Christ. Amen.

~ ~ ~ ~ ~ ~

OCTOBER 7

HOPE UNREASONABLE

> By faith he received power of procreation, even though he was too old—and Sarah herself was barren—because he considered him faithful who had promised.
>
> —Hebrews 11:11

READ: Isaiah 51:1-6 and Hebrews 11:11-16

The exiles from Jerusalem had no reason to believe that they would ever see their homeland again. Nothing in the current news of the day gave them any hope. Like hostages held for political purposes there often isn't reasonable hope for their release and return. Isaiah offered hope unreasonable to the exiles by reminding them of the unreasonable event in the life of Sarah and Abraham. She gave birth late in life in defiance of medical wisdom then and now. In remembering Sarah the exiled Jews were given the courage to hope for the unreasonable in their situation—release from captivity and return to their native land. In a curious way their memory helped to create the very future they dared not hope for.

Are their desired changes or developments in your life which you hesitate to hope for, because it seems unreasonable to expect such? Even though not everything can change as we would wish, can you remember especially helpful developments in your own past which came as a surprise and for which you can now thank God? Remembering how God has blessed you in the past will help you to hold on to hope of future blessings.

PRAYER: Remind me, O God, of all that you have done in my life and create in me a hopeful attitude toward my future, because of your continued grace. In Christ. Amen.

~ ~ ~ ~ ~

OCTOBER 8

LESSON FROM THE WHEAT FIELDS

> And he said to them, "Have you never read what David did when he and his companions were hungry and in need of food?"
>
> —Mark 2:25

READ: Isaiah 55:3-9 and Mark 2:23-28

When you are feeling weak, confused or frustrated remember King David. This is what Isaiah said to the exiles around 500 B.C.E. He revealed to the people that God was saying to them: "Incline your ear, and come to me; listen, so that you may live. I will make with you an everlasting covenant, my steadfast, sure love for David." (Isaiah 55:3) It must have been a great encouragement to Israel to remember the golden age of King David, when God's power was evident in David's reign, and to be told that such a power would be available to them in their time of exile.

During periods when we feel weak, it is very helpful to remember incidents when we felt that we had been given God's power. Perhaps a crisis through which you had to pass was a time when you felt that God gave you the strength to overcome obstacles. In your present circumstances it helps to remember such divine help. Such a cycle of TROUBLE—REMEMBERING—HOPE can be found frequently throughout the Psalms.

Jesus was teaching his disciples a new way of looking at the Law in order to prepare them for the gift of grace and freedom. Having been raised as legalistic Jews they were afraid to break out of the bonds of a long list of "do's and don'ts." When Jesus plucked grain on the Sabbath his disciples feared the authorities. Jesus reminded them of the courage of David who did something similar.

When you are facing new situations, it helps to be reminded of the power and guidance of God which has helped you in such situations in the past.

PRAYER: Help me to remember your grace in the past so that I may know of your grace now, O God. In Christ. Amen.

~ ~ ~ ~ ~ ~

OCTOBER 9

REMEMBERING THE DAY OF REMEMBRANCE

Remember the sabbath day, and keep it holy.
—Exodus 20:8

READ: Exodus 20:8-11 and I Corinthians 11:23-34

When Jesus came near to the day of his death, his concern was for his disciples. To give them a continuing source of strength and to provide for continuous contact with him, he instituted the sacrament of the Lord's Supper. "Do this in remembrance of me," (I Corinthians 11:24) he said. In this way he planned for them to remember him whenever they ate the bread or drank from the cup.

We gain strength for our journey of life when we remember those who have gone before and who have been strong and courageous. Many an adult child has survived hardship through remembering the love and courage of his or her own parents, in times when they had faced difficulties in their lives.

As Christians we must constantly remember Christ in our daily lives, so that our decisions and our actions may reflect his presence in our world. The communion service in Christian worship is a resource for such remembrance. From the sacrament we gain strength for living through contact with Christ.

For our Hebrew forebears the sabbath provided strength as they observed it weekly, affirming God's creative power and God's day of rest on the seventh day of creation. Sabbath rest and Communion remembrance can be the way we remind ourselves of God's power through Christ to recreate our lives.

PRAYER: We remember your creative power, O God, and your saving grace through Christ's death on the cross for each of us. In Him. Amen.

~ ~ ~ ~ ~ ~

OCTOBER 10

LIKE A STRING AROUND YOUR FINGER

Then they remembered his words, and returning from
the tomb, they told all this to the eleven and to all the rest.
—Luke 24:8-9

READ: Deuteronomy 6:1-9 and Luke 24:1-12

Tying a string around your finger is an old fashioned, but seldom seen, method of reminding oneself of something important. We have other means now, like putting a note on a refrigerator door held by a small magnet. There are hand held mini-computers which remind us of appointments, or digital watches with tiny alarm buzzers to sound at a prescribed time. The ancient Israelites tied little boxes to their foreheads, on their forearms and on their door posts to remind them of the Lord, the only God of all the world. It would seem that many today need a little box tied on someplace on the body to remind them of a forgotten God.

When the women arrived at the tomb early on that first Easter morning they found it empty. At first they were confused by this unbelievable fact. They wondered where Jesus' body had been taken. To clear up their confusion they were advised to remember Jesus' own words about how he was to rise from the dead after three days. When they remembered that, their fear and confusion was turned into joy and exultation.

We need to remember always the words of Jesus and the actual fact of his resurrection.

Whenever the evil and tragedy of this world get us down, we must remember God's victory over evil, which is demonstrated in Christ's resurrection from his death which had been perpetrated by the forces of evil. Whenever we are confused about life's inequities, or the failures of human frailty and sin, we need to remember Jesus' words, his teaching, his comfort to the needy, and above all his triumph over all that opposed him—the resurrection.

PRAYER: Help me always to remember Christ's resurrection and your triumph, O God. Amen.

~ ~ ~ ~ ~ ~

OCTOBER 11

IN A KINGDOM WHERE UP IS DOWN

"For I have set you an example, that you also should do as I have done to you.

—John 13:15

READ: John 13:3-17 and Luke 22:24-27

If the stories of Jesus were not so familiar to us we would find many of them to be quite fantastic. Not just the miracles but the way Jesus related to people and met their needs. The world of Jesus is truly an "Alice in wonderland" sort of Kingdom, where up is down! John tells us about what Jesus did at the Last Supper when he took a basin and a towel and performed the servant's lowliest duty by washing the dirty, smelly feet of his disciples. And even more fantastic—he instructed them to do the same to each other from that time on. How do you read that in any other way than as a surprising, radical turn-around? And yet the implication is that we are to do the same. Foot washing is not the issue. That does not figure into how we do things for each other today when we have good shoes and pavement. But the fact remains, we are being asked to be servants to one another. What must you and I do to be servants to others in our day?

Earlier, Jesus was confronting his disciples on this same subject when he answered their requests for special position and privilege in the new kingdom. Luke tells us that Jesus showed that their desire for greatness was the way things are done in the world, but that with his people the greatest would be the least and that the leader must be the servant. Up is down! That is to say that there is to be no jockeying for position in the kingdom over which Jesus rules. It doesn't matter who you are. Whoever you are, you are to serve others. No one is to be considered above or below. Instead of the normal human ambition—intensified in our society today— to "better ourselves," we are to have compassion for those around us. What will this reversal mean in our lives? How does Jesus want you to change?

PRAYER: Christ, my King, help me to serve others as my equals— as you have served me. Amen

~ ~ ~ ~ ~ ~

OCTOBER 12

RICH IS POOR AND POOR IS RICH

For you know the generous act of our Lord Jesus Christ,
that though he was rich, yet for your sakes he became poor,
so that by his poverty we might become rich.
                                                —II Corinthians 8:9

READ: Luke 12:13-34 and Leviticus 25:10

One of the most deplorable facts of most societies, ours included, is the vast difference in wealth between the very rich and the very poor. There are indications today that this gap is widening in our nation. By contrast, in the society Jesus establishes, the disparity between rich and poor is dissolved. A symbol for this is Paul's description of Jesus' own action . . . "though he was rich, yet for your sakes he became poor."(II Corinthians 8:9) Jesus calls you and me into a kingdom of new relationships in which the sharing of resources with each other overcomes the injustice of unequal distribution of wealth and power.

In Old Testament Law the Sabbath year and the year of Jubilee were designed to keep the wealth gap from compounding. Every seventh year slaves were to be released, and every fiftieth year people were to be restored to their ancestral lands, even though indebtedness and foreclosure had removed them in the intervening years. In Jesus' re-institution of this concept those of us in his new kingdom are to make our resources available to those who have need for them. In place of piling up riches, we are not to worry. "Sell your possessions, and give alms." (Luke 12:33)

How hard it is for us to take Jesus' words to heart and to put them into action. But we must try. Let us begin by letting go of wealth and possessions as a sign of worth and importance. Let us learn to ignore the world's signs of success, and to concentrate on the marks of success in Jesus' kingdom: compassion, sharing, love, justice, and obedience to Christ.

PRAYER: Make me rich in compassion and poor in my dependence upon material things, O Christ. Amen.

~ ~ ~ ~ ~

OCTOBER 13

LITTLE IS BIG

"All who exalt themselves will be humbled, and all who humble themselves will be exalted.
—Matthew 23:12

READ: Matthew 23:1-12 and Mark 10:13-16

One of the refreshing things about small children is their innocence of our generally held views of greatness. They simply don't know and don't care who "Mr. Big" or "Mrs. Great" are. They will just as easily jump onto the lap of a president as into the arms of their Aunt Emma, or take the hand of an intruding burglar as readily as that of a trusted neighbor. In their innocence they don't draw the distinctions we draw. So what does this mean to us if we take Jesus' command seriously, "Truly I tell you, whoever does not receive the kingdom of God as a little child will never enter it." (Luke 10:15)

In Christ's kingdom we are not to defer to one another according to human-made distinctions which normally divide people, setting some higher and greater than others. Translating this principle into church life, it means that no one is any greater than anyone else. The newest member is as great as the charter member. The smallest child is as noteworthy as the pastor. The church officer and high schooler are of equal status in the the church. If we can drop the common distinctions which divide us, perhaps we can relate to one another in loving and caring ways, which will be a sign to the world around us of what kind of a society Christ wants for the world.

Jesus modeled this new social way when he he corrected the disciples by asking them to let the children come to him. Let this be our model as well, as we allow *little* to be *big*.

PRAYER: Help me, O God, to treat others as equals and keep me from drawing artificial distinctions which hurt others. In Christ. Amen.

～ ～ ～ ～ ～

OCTOBER 14

OUTSIDERS IN

There is no longer Jew or Greek, there is no longer slave or free, there is no longer male or female; for all of you are one in Christ Jesus.

—Galatians 3:28

READ: Luke 4: 25-30 and Galatians 3:23-29

Among middle class American youth brands have become extremely important. High schoolers wouldn't be caught dead in an off-brand pair of jeans. Middle schoolers have closets filled with clothing from GAP or Old Navy. Everyone wants to be IN. It is tough to be an outsider, so tough that some youths have been driven to suicide because of social ostracism. While it is normal and inevitable to enjoy being with people whose tastes and interests are similar to our own, it is painfully divisive to cut people out because of their failure to come up to our standards of fashion or taste.

The New Testament labels it sin when we place ourselves in exclusive groupings, while keeping others out who do not carry the same symbols of belonging as we do. Jesus came to erase the lines which divide us, to tear down the walls of separation. "Neither Jew nor Greek, slave nor free, male nor female." (Galatians 3:28) In Christ's kingdom outsiders are in.

How will this change the way we relate to people? It places us squarely in favor of racial and gender equality, and impels us, as Christ's followers, to work for equal rights for racial, ethnic, and other minority persons in our society. Fortunately our society has come a long way in this direction. Curb cuts for handicapped and handicapped parking places near business entryways, keep this effort ever before us. We have, however, a long way to go in bringing racial and ethnic persons up to speed, and providing women equal economic footing. Beyond these obvious disparities, we are called to erase the subtle distinctions of taste, background, and lifestyle which keep people out of our own circles. In Christ's kingdom those who bowl and those who play polo will sit down at the same table.

PRAYER: Help me to accept my neighbor as myself. In Christ. Amen,

~ ~ ~ ~ ~ ~

OCTOBER 15

EAST IS WEST AND NORTH IS SOUTH

"For I tell you, that unless your righteousness exceeds that of the scribes and Pharisees, you will never enter the kingdom of heaven."

—Matthew 5:20

READ: Luke 6:27-36 and Matthew 5:14-20

To be in Christ's kingdom is not something beyond life, as we have customarily felt. The Kingdom requirements which we read so glibly from Jesus' teachings get filed in the *"To do later"* box, because we think the Kingdom is in heaven. But it many ways, as we have been considering, Jesus' description of the Kingdom way of living is applicable to Christians in this life. As such, the fellowship of Christ's followers becomes a model for the rest of the society around us. "You are the light of the world. A city set on a hill cannot be hid." (Matthew 5:14) As loyal subjects of Christ's kingdom we have learned that we are not to draw distinctions on the basis of wealth, power, position, age or social class. We are all one, equal in God's sight regardless of race, taste, or life-style.

In some ways, the most difficult gap to bridge is the gulf which comes between us and our enemies. But even this difference is to be overcome if we are to be part of Christ's kingdom. "Love you enemies, do good to those who hate you." (Luke 6:27) This means the neighbor who has harassed you with noise or litter, and the business person who has cheated you, or mislead you. It means the member of your own family who has in one way or another "written you off." It means the boss who is unfair and insensitive, or a team member who isn't carrying his/her share of the load. *Anyone* who mistreats you in *anyway,* Love them, and do good to them. This is the way of the Kingdom of Christ.

PRAYER: I pray for those who have mistreated me, O Christ. Help me to love them. Amen.

~ ~ ~ ~ ~

OCTOBER 16

GIVING AND GETTING THE RIGHT ANSWER

> These are the things that you should do: Speak the truth to one another, render in your gates judgements that are true and make for peace.
>
> —Zechariah 8:16

READ: Zechariah 8:14-17 and Ephesians 4:17-25

In a large unabridged dictionary the word, "right," takes

up almost two columns, for it is a term which has multiple meanings. First of all "right" means true or correct, as in true factual answers on test questions in school—the right answer. Even more important is the giving and getting of right answers to questions we ask of each other in day to day living. Our common life together in families and in society depends utterly upon the communicating of truth among us. Without assurance that the truth will be spoken, the fabric of society will be torn and will disintegrate. When truth between spouses erodes, their marriage is in serious, if not terminal, trouble. Parents must have truth from their children, and it is essential for a child to expect truth from his/her parents.

Our understanding of nature and history is based upon the pursuit of truth and its honest telling. We are justifiably critical of those countries who allow their ideology to affect how they write and re-write their history. When a scientist allows conclusions to be shaped by special interests, like those who have provided a grant for the project, it is not science anymore. It is dangerous to tamper with truth, because our life and welfare depend upon the giving and getting of truth to and from each other.

God, the Author of truth, requires of his people minds and voices committed to truth. We acknowledge that when we speak the truth we are somehow in touch with the God of truth. We are followers of Christ who is the Way, the TRUTH, and the life.

PRAYER: Help me to know and tell the truth in all my living and
dealing with others. In Christ. Amen.

~ ~ ~ ~ ~ ~

OCTOBER 17

DOING THE RIGHT THING

Stand therefore, and fasten the belt of truth around
your waist, and put on the breastplate of righteousness.
—Ephesians 6:14

READ: John 1:16-17 and I John 21-8

The word "right" also means "good," in a moral or ethical sense. "He did the right thing," is a way of observing that one has done something morally good, or has taken an ethical step. However, knowing what is right and wrong in human behavior these days is a difficult process, for there are a lot of opinions on these matters, and it depends upon to whom you talk. In our society today we have allowed right and wrong to become relative terms, for we live in an age in which authority is challenged and absolutes are questioned. We have removed the divine judge from the bench and we grant authority to the most appealing voice. Truth and goodness have become relative terms. "Whatever you want to do is up to you," is another way of stating this point of view, this state of affairs we to which we have come.

As Christians we believe that righteousness comes from God and that in Jesus Christ we are given the capacity to do right in a moral sense. Paul spoke of the law as a "schoolmaster" helping us to grow in our understanding of what is right and good. Now through the grace of God as granted to us in Christ we are called to live our lives "doing the right thing."

PRAYER: Help me, O God, to live in such a way that I am doing the right thing in my life. In Christ. Amen.

~ ~ ~ ~ ~ ~

OCTOBER 18

THE RIGHT MAY BE WRONG

"See, I am sending you out like sheep into the midst of wolves; so be wise as serpents and innocent as doves."
—Matthew 10:16

READ: Matthew 7:1-6 and Romans 14:1-10

Not everything that is right is right! What does this mean? Something may be correct or morally good, yet it simply isn't right for the occasion. For example: You may be called to the bedside of someone who is very sick, one who may not survive the illness. It might be true, that if the person had followed a more healthful diet, and had exercised more, or had not been a smoker, this condition would not be so serious. Furthermore, it would be morally good to give such advice in order to help prolong a life. But, at this particular moment it would not be right to offer such a lecture on diet and life style to the person gravely ill. The time and the situation make the right—wrong! Jesus said we must be wise as serpents, harmless as doves. Prudent restraint would make us both wise and harmless at the bedside of such a dying friend.

A third way of understanding the word, "right," is to think of it in terms of what is appropriate. What is fitting and helpful in a given situation? Our goal is not just to be correct factually or righteous morally. Our goal as Christian folk is to do the will of God in as many of life's instances as possible. Oftentimes prudence must take precedence so that we do or say the appropriate thing in hope of fulfilling God's purposes. Ecclesiastes notes that there is "a time to keep silence, and a time to speak;" (Ecclesiastes 3:7) Good advice! Sometimes talk would be casting pearls before swine and sometimes silence is golden. But at other times our witness to the truth and the morally right action is required; and then silence would be betrayal.

PRAYER: O God, give me prudence so that I may know what is appropriate, patience when silence is required, and courage to speak at the right time. Through Christ. Amen

～ ～ ～ ～ ～

OCTOBER 19

ARE YOU RIGHT WITH GOD?"

> Much more surely then, now that we have been justified
> by his blood, will we be saved through him from the wrath
> of God.
>
> —Romans 5:9

READ: John 8:31-32 and Romans 5:1-11

A fourth meaning of the word, "right," is more difficult to pin down In some ways it represents a summary of the true, the good and the appropriate. There is a curious phrase used when observing how a street is laid out, or how a building is situated on a site. When the street or house is at an angle not conforming to one of the four points on the compass we say it isn't "right with the world." Descriptions such as: straight, level, consistent, uniform, well-balanced, sound, sane, justified, help us to see "right" in this fourth way. The page of a book looks right when both the left and right margins are vertically even.

When Paul wrote to the Roman Christians to declare that through the death and resurrection of Jesus Christ we are put right with God, he was using the term, "right," in the sense of being justified. Things are straight between ourselves and God. We are on course and not askew. Thus we are right with God now, not out of line with God's intentions for us. That is a very good feeling—to be right with God, and incidentally that makes one right with the world as well.

As with the printed page which is justified, so it is attractive to be justified and right with God. There is comfort in knowing that our life is level, sound, sane, well-balanced and straight. That's what it means, in part, to be right with God and right with the world. Such is the gift we have in Christ.

PRAYER: Thank you, God, for putting me right. Amen.

~ ~ ~ ~ ~ ~

OCTOBER 20

RIGHT ON

And he stood up, and immediately took the mat and
went out before all of them; so that they were all amazed
and glorified God, saying, "We have never seen anything
like this."

—Mark 2:12

READ: Mark 10: 46-52; Acts 10:29-33 and Luke 9:51-62

There are no "couch potatoes" in the New Testament.
Rather, there is an excitement, an air of immediacy found in
its pages. Things happen fast. People are cured and immediately
jump up. Peter came at once to the home of Cornelius and
immediately a serious life-changing conversation between Peter
and Cornelius takes place. Things happen right now in the
New Testament. Jesus and his disciples move about from place
to place, going to one town after another. The modern term,
"right on," could be used to describe what the Gospel writers
tell us about Jesus' movement.

And so here is the fifth, and final use of the term, "right."
Right denotes immediacy. Right away, right now, right on. If you
want to follow Jesus, you had better be ready to get "right with it."

Toward the end of Jesus' time with his disciples there is a
growing sense of urgency as he prepares them for his mission. It is
at this point that we must accept some of this urgency as we feel
his call to us to join him in his mission—to go "right on" with
Christ's work. He needs your talent and effort right now. Such is
the urgency of Christ's mission in the world. Such is the immediacy
of his challenge to us to obey. He wants us to be able to say to him
when he calls us to his work: "RIGHT ON!"

PRAYER: Help me to get right with it—to obey Christ's commands each day as I hear his call to me. In his name. Amen.

~ ~ ~ ~ ~ ~

OCTOBER 21

OUT OF DARKNESS—LIGHT

So then you are no longer strangers and aliens, but you are citizens with the saints and also members of the household of God.

—Ephesians 2:19

READ: Psalm 39:2 and II Corinthians 4:6-8

Have you ever been in the midst of a "gloom and doom" conversation with a group of people when everyone is downcast except one? When in the midst of such a group one person seems to be strangely joyful, the comment is sometimes made about the one positive person, "She must know something we don't!" The Christian is someone who knows something which produces joy in the midst of an otherwise dismal world. When one seems to be crushed with despair, feeling alone and hurt, the Christian Faith has a way of lifting one to another level of reality on which there is hope and joy like a light shining in the darkness.

Paul offers a perspective upon life which helps us to realize that the really important and lasting values in life are unseen, while the actual events of life are quite temporary. Thus one becomes aware that in terms of life's final accounting, love and right relationships with God and with one's fellow human beings are far more important and lasting than physical ease, the acquiring of wealth, or the piling up of various experiences.

It is relatively easy to keep this perspective while things are going well, but more difficult when troubles come. But the time of trouble is precisely the time when it is most helpful to keep one's mind fixed upon the words of Paul, "For this slight momentary affliction is preparing us for an eternal weight of glory beyond all measure, because we look not to what can be seen but at what cannot be seen; for what is seen is temporary, but what cannot be seen is eternal."

(II Corinthians 4:17-18) We do know something which others may not know—the eternal perspective given by grace.

PRAYER: Help me to keep a perspective on life which reminds me of your eternal values. In Christ. Amen.

~ ~ ~ ~ ~ ~

OCTOBER 22

STRAIGHT FOR THE GOAL

> Beloved, I do not consider that I have made it my own;
> but this one thing I do: forgetting what lies behind and
> straining forward to what lies ahead, I press on toward the
> goal for the prize of the heavenly call of God in Christ Jesus.
> —Philippians 3:13-14

READ: Philippians 3:12-21

Events in one's own past can render one immobile. The death of a loved one can keep one from productive activity until such a painful loss can be resolved. During periods of doubt and unhappiness one's re-living the past can blunt one's ability to work on present difficult realities. The common excuse for studying history is to avoid re-living it. On the other hand, the constant memorializing of the past can be a futile attempt to make it happen again in order to make it come out more favorably.

Paul affirmed a forward direction for his life as he declared to the church at Philippi that he had let the past go in order to press on toward the goal to which Christ was calling him. For Paul this was not a rejection of the past so much as it was a placing of former glories in their proper perspective. It was, after all, his earlier personal confrontation with the risen Christ which now motivated his own movement forward into a world beyond his present horizon. He felt that what Jesus Christ had done in his life had made him a citizen of a new world toward which he was now drawn. This was in contrast to the limits others placed upon their own lives by remaining exclusively committed to serving their own desires.

Jesus Christ provides the leverage we need to be lifted out of the oppressive limits in which normal human existence confines us. He sets us upon a new direction leading us to a fuller citizenship in heaven. In plain terms—if life is getting you down, let the call of Christ to a new direction lift you up and lead you to new heights of human life.

PRAYER: Lift me, O Christ, so that I may enter the new citizenship in your Kingdom, even now while I still live here on earth. Amen.

~ ~ ~ ~ ~ ~

OCTOBER 23

THE SECRET CENTER

When Christ who is your life is revealed, then you also will be revealed with him in glory.

—Colossians 3:4

READ: Colossians 3:1-17

In the Northern Hemisphere the North Star is the one fixed point which does not move while all the other stars and planets rotate throughout each twenty-four period. Thus, the North Star is the navigators' center upon which to plot their course across the sea. In the Southern Hemisphere no such star shines. In its place the Southern Cross is always visible and rotates around a hiddeen center which coincides with the South Pole. So navigation can be charted by the. Southern Cross as it goes around its secret center. The ordered life of a Christian rotates around a secret center, which Paul declares to be Christ. Because Christ points to the absolute Lord of the universe our course is sure, if it is related to the certainty of that secret center, Christ himself.

Disorder occurs when our lives rotate around other shifting points, like using an art compass which has lost hold of its center point causing it to slip, and it is no longer able to make a perfect circle.

Paul urges us to keep our lives fixed upon the one true center available to us—Jesus Christ of the cross. Christ is true because he is the manifestation of the God who ordered the world. As Christians we look forward to the day when Christ will be fully revealed as the center of the universe. Meanwhile we have the Cross, as navigators in the Southern Hemisphere have the Southern Cross.

PRAYER: Help me, O God, to live with Christ as the center by which my life will be ordered. In Him. Amen.

~ ~ ~ ~ ~

OCTOBER 24

GOD'S WORK OF ART

For we are what he has made us, created in Jesus Christ for good works, which God prepared beforehand to be our way of life.

—Ephesians 2:10

READ: Ephesians 2:1-10

People who know art can look at a painting and determine who the artist was who painted it. Many people in Montana can look at a piece of western art and tell whether or not it is by Charlie

Russell, a favorite of Montanans. Does your life reveal the artist who created you? The Jerusalem Bible translation opens Ephesians 2:10 with the phrase, "We are God's work of art." Is there any evidence that you are God's work of art? If not, whose creation are you?

It is a very normal human tendency to allow others to determine the shape of ones life, to give to others the privilege of being a strong influence over one's life. We easily allow ourselves to be the canvas upon which someone else paints an image. Those who allow others to hold such power over them often do so by their constant deference to what others will think of them. Fear of ridicule or avoidance of criticism often are the reasons we grant others power to shape our lives. Our society likes to give such power to the rich and the famous, subtly urging us to model our lives after theirs— or what we think theirs is like. This is what Paul calls following the course of this world. He invites us, rather, to give to God such rightful power to the shape our lives, the privilege of being the artist who paints us. In this way we become God's work of art.

God's intended way for us as revealed in Jesus Christ is an alternative to the mass confusion of models in today's world. Popular psychology urges each of us to be his/her own person. The Christian Faith goes a step further to affirm that the way to become one's own person is to go back to the drawing board and ask the one who created us in the first place what He had in mind and to let God complete the painting—which is YOU.

PRAYER: O Christ, paint me the way you want me! Amen

~ ~ ~ ~ ~ ~

OCTOBER 25

A NEW VIEW OF THINGS

.... that the creation itself will be set free from its
bondage to decay and will obtain the freedom of the glory

WORDS for Thinking and Thoughts for Meditation

of the children of God. We know that the whole creation
has been groaning in labor pains until now.

—Romans 8:21-22

READ: Romans 8:1-2, 18-22

Typical of the new view of things, the people of Salt Lake City
had been focusing their binoculars on a family of peregrine falcons
nesting high up the side of Hotel Utah. An endangered species,
these birds were not only being watched by the public, but
protected by wildlife biologists in the area. In an earlier age such
care would not have been offered these falcons, or to any other
aspect of creation. But it is different now that we are aware to some
extent of what Paul meant by the hope that creation would be set
free of the bondage of decay.

A new view of things!

How we view things is strongly affected by the spirit which
dominates our thinking. In former years, especially in America,
the earth was viewed in the spirit of conquest, something to be
exploited as the source of riches to be had for the taking.

Paul says that when one is controlled by the Spirit of God, one
understands that nature too is in need of renovation and care,
while for the time being things are not right. There are earthquakes
which devastate, floods which severely damage, and fires which
destroy, accidents which happen indiscriminately.

When we are faced with physical diseases and natural disasters
the Spirit helps us to endure the results of such imperfections in life,
knowing that ultimately God will conquer all evil and will stand by
us in the meantime to uphold us in time of trouble and tragedy.

The care which the falcon family in Salt Lake City has been
given is a metaphor for the care God wants to extend to us when
we are endangered.

PRAYER: When physical things close in on me, O God, and my
health and survival are endangered, reveal to me your care and
concern for things which affect me. In Christ. Amen.

~ ~ ~ ~ ~ ~

OCTOBER 26

WAITING IN THE CONSTRUCTION ZONE

But if we hope for what we do not see, we wait for it
with patience.

—Romans 8:25

READ: Romans 8:3-9, 22-25

If you drove anywhere on the highway this past summer you probably endured more than one construction delay. First the red-orange sign, then the line of stopped cars, It is especially exasperating when you notice that the motors in the cars ahead of you have been turned off, and people are out of their cars and looking up ahead as best as they can. You crane your neck and can't see a thing. No sign of activity up ahead, no trucks coming down the other lane—nothing! That's when waiting is so hard to endure, when you can't see any known reason for the delay. Then patience is slight.

Quite the opposite of this normal human tendency to lose patience when you can't see, is Paul's claim that when we hope for what we can't see, we wait patiently. How can such a claim be made among Christians? Because we are now affected radically by the Spirit of God who assures us that God is in charge of the reconstruction project and it will be completed in due time. No need to worry therefore.

Because our thinking is dominated by God's Spirit, we know that the unseen end of things is in God's loving hands. This is a resurrection faith by which Christians are assured of God's ultimate victory over every power which opposes the divine will. If we live with that assurance we can endure the trials of life in the meanwhile. When death leaves us lonely we know that ultimately our fellowship with one another will be re-created. When physical limitations cripple us we know that our spirits nevertheless are free to soar to new heights. When misunderstanding spoils human relationships and erodes our own self confidence we are aware of God's perfect knowledge of us and of our needs. With such knowledge of the unseen blessings of God's construction we are able to endure the waiting in the meanwhile.

PRAYER: Be with me while I wait, O God. In Christ. Amen.

~ ~ ~ ~ ~ ~

OCTOBER 27

PRAYER'S BODY-LANGUAGE

> And God, who searches the heart, knows what is the
> mind of the Spirit, because the Spirit intercedes for the
> saints according to the will of God.
> —Romans 8:27

READ: Romans 8:9-11, 26-27

A considerable amount of attention is given these days to non verbal communication or body-language, by which we reveal to some extent what is on our minds and hearts. Unconsciously we "read" each other on this level more fully than we are usually aware. Have you ever seen a meeting around a table at which all are facing the speaker at the head of the table, except one person whose legs are crossed away from the speaker and who is looking out a window? What do you conclude that member is unconsciously communicating to the group? In some very strenuous human circumstances words are inadequate to express one's true feelings, and so non-verbal communication is capable of speaking the truth in us. Take for example the grief-laden hug just inside the door of the funeral chapel.

In earnest prayer we often do not have words which seem

adequate to reveal to God what's going on in us. Normally such frustration can thwart real prayer. When one is in touch with the Spirit of God it is the Spirit's own non-verbal communication which lifts our own spirits into the presence of God. "... but that very Spirit intercedes with sighs too deep for words." (Romans 8:26) In the moment of interaction with the Spirit we are made able to offer God our inarticulate groans in authentic prayer.

Let your own true emotions carry the revelation of your true self into God's presence whether that be fear or dread, joy or sorrow, distress or delight.

PRAYER: O God, by the sighing of your Spirit, receive my deepest feelings. Through Christ. Amen.

~ ~ ~ ~ ~

OCTOBER 28

WATCHING FOR OTHER NEWS

We know that all things work together for good for
those who love God, who are called according to his purpose.
—Romans 8:28

READ: Romans 8:12-13, 28-30

The day Martin Luther King, Jr. was assassinated, a young black dancer, Arthur Mitchell saw a report of it on TV while en route to a dance engagement. That ignominious event changed Mitchell's life, and subsequently the lives of many black youths growing up in Harlem. As a result of the high drama of that day Arthur Mitchell developed a dance studio in Harlem dedicated to the purpose of lifting children and youth out of the hopelessness of the black ghetto and into a world of professional dance. From that stage many have moved on to other stages and areas of productive living—as a result of the life of "Brother Martin," which unfortunately was cut short. Similarly the city of Boston began making available the funds to every one of its high school graduates for a college education.

In the midst of all the bad news there is the outcropping of other news, evidence of God's power at work in every event. When our minds are in constant conversation with the Spirit we are sharpened in our ability to identify the action of God intermingled with all the other strands which make up the news. Invite the Spirit to watch the evening news with you. Have fun as He helps you spot the evidence of God's hand in it!

Then let your creative interchange with the Spirit center upon your own affairs and let the Spirit help you identify where God is at work in your own life. Careful though! Not everything that happens is God's action or will. That would be too easy. God's action is intermingled with other factors and forces, not all of which are in accord with God's intention. Ultimately what develops out of this intermingling is good.

PRAYER: O Holy Spirit, point out God's work to me, and intermingle God's action in all that plays a part in my life. Bring about what is GOOD. In Christ. Amen.

~ ~ ~ ~ ~ ~

OCTOBER 29

LIFTING THE QUARANTINE

If children then heirs, heirs of God and joint heirs with Christ—if, in fact, we suffer with him so that we may also be glorified with him.

—Romans 8:17

READ: Romans 8:14-18, 31-39

Trouble has a way of separating people from one another, despite the common belief that it draws people together. After the early rallying which comes after tragedy or disaster strike, sooner or later the victim of misfortune is very apt to feel isolated, oftentimes simply because others have had to return to their own lives and concerns. There are also times when the victim is intentionally put under a kind of quarantine when others want to separate their own lives from trouble. The invalid is forced to spend many hours alone. The new widow finally must pick up the broken pieces and return to her routine alone.

While loneliness may be the normal result of trouble, and cause some of its own suffering, life in the Spirit provides us with the Comforter to go with us through the narrow trails of trouble. The Spirit helps us to consider the action of God in Christ on the cross on our behalf, enabling us to understand the pain God endures for us. The Spirit enables us to recognize God's victory over death in the resurrection, teaching us that nothing is too devastating for God. Interacting with the Spirit in this way leads us to share in Christ's suffering. As in counseling, it helps a great deal to share our burdens with others, thereby lifting the quarantine.

PRAYER: Go with me, O God, through the narrow places in which
    I feel alone and isolated. In Christ. Amen.

~ ~ ~ ~ ~ ~

OCTOBER 30

ON YOUR MARK, GET SET, LET GO

Be still and know that I am God!
—Psalm 46:10

READ: Colossians 3:5-17 and I Kings 19:11-12

The darker it is, the more you can see; the more quiet it is the more you can hear. These seemingly contradictory statements are true in a certain sense. Millions of people in the modern world rarely see the stars anymore. Of, if they do, they occasionally see only a few bright ones. As more and more people have moved into well-lighted urban areas the accumulated night illumination and the growing smog of cities, obscure the starry night sky. What a treat it is on camping trips in the mountains to stand outside at night and take in the millions of stars in the great dark dome overhead.

Similarly modern life is noisy, keeping us from hearing the subtle quiet sounds of nature. Again it is a treat to camp in a quiet spot away from the crowds and hear the sounds of birds and insects, water-falls and gently bending branches, the rustling of leaves and the sigh of the breeze.

When we do not seem to be able to "find God" in our daily lives we should start by letting go of the sights and sounds of modern life, the voices and thoughts which usually congest our consciousness and drown out God's stirring. The Psalmist said, "Be still, and know that I am God."(Psalm 46:10) Other Bible translations put it this way: "Give in and admit that I am God," "Stop fighting," or "Let it be then, and learn that I am God." The first step in finding God is to let go of all the things which clutter our minds, and in silent, wordless meditation to focus as much of one's attention as possible upon the darkness and the silence, and then to listen for remembered sounds: some beautiful sound which carries God's "voice" to us, perhaps the strains of a hymn, or a great classical theme of music. Maybe the earnest melody of a folk song. And under the dome of darkness imagine a beautiful tranquil scene, some view of nature not far removed from the creator's touch. The sunlit blade of grass or the cascading mountain white water. Then perhaps God will draw into your thoughts in a new and vivid way. "and after the (wind, earthquake) fire, a sound of sheer silence."(I Kings 19:12)

PRAYER: Help me to let go, to still the sounds and to dim the glaring lights. May your presence come forth under the quiet dome of darkness, O God. In Christ. Amen.

~ ~ ~ ~ ~ ~

OCTOBER 31

TRY TO REMEMBER

My mouth will tell of your righteous acts, of your deeds
of salvation all day long, though their number is past my
knowledge. I will come praising the mighty deeds of the
Lord God, I will praise your righteousness, yours alone.
                                                —Psalm 71:15-16

READ: Hebrews 11:1-2 and Psalm 77:7-15

Much of the Bible can be seen as a book of memories. Like a
family album the Bible contains pictures of times past when
members of "our family" were happily involved in the events of
their daily lives

Remembering God's wonderful deeds is one way of seeking
the Divine presence in our lives here and now, even though God
may have seemed absent from your awareness. In the midst of our
own confusion and turmoil over problems both personal and world-
wide, we can pause to remember what we believe to be God's
influence on past events in our personal lives and in world events.

Some of the Psalms go through this helpful exercise of
remembering. After complaining about how bad things are, the
Psalmist declares, "I consider the days of old, and remember the
years of long ago." (Psalm 77:5)

However, not all of us have happy memories of days gone by.
Those who do are fortunate. By turning the pages back to those
days when God showered blessings on us, we are likely to discover
that God is with us in our present struggles. Or if our own personal
memories do not point to God's activity it may be helpful to come
to know the activity of God with the people of God in other settings
from the Bible. The study of the Bible will reveal a long history of
God's loving and reconciling work in the story of Israel and the

accounts of the early church. The healings of Jesus as he went about Palestine provide us with a sign and indication of how God helped people in the past through Christ. In this way we may very well find God reaching into our lives today to help us in ways appropriate to our needs.

Try to remember the things God has done in your life and in the lives of people you know. Be aware that God is still at work in our lives today.

PRAYER: Help me to remember your deeds, O Lord. Through Christ. Amen.

NOVEMBER

NOVEMBER 1

THERE BUT FOR THE GRACE OF GOD

When they kept on questioning him, he straightened
up and said to them, "Let anyone among you who is without
sin be the first to throw a stone at her."

—John 8:7

READ: John 8:1-11 and I John 4:7-10

The gift of Christian community is presented to us in many of
the events and teachings of Jesus' life among us. In John's story of
the woman caught in adultery Jesus lays the ground for true
fellowship. All who truly understand themselves as having fallen
short of the intention of God for their lives come confessing their
sin, and with their desire to be turned around by Christ. This
mood of humble repentance puts us all on the same footing, and
none can claim to be better in any way than the other. God bestows
upon each of us the full measure of forgiveness and grace to do
better tomorrow. Not one of us can claim to have an edge on the
achievement of greatness or perfection. We all kneel at the foot of
the Cross seeking God's forgiveness through Christ. There is deep
fellowship given to those who so kneel together, as at the communion
rail.

Unfortunately we give up the gift of community when we make
claims for our own moral achievements and look "down our noses"
at others whom we think are less worthy than we. It is a human
tendency to so look at others. It is sin. We must admit that we are

prone to look for the bad in others and to exalt the good in ourselves. But that is not the gift of community which Christ gives us. Let us return to the true Christian position in relation to one another— that of kneeling beside each other before the Cross.

PRAYER: Forgive me, O Lord, for the sin of self-righteousness. Grant me the gift of true Christian fellowship. In Christ. Amen.

~ ~ ~ ~ ~

NOVEMBER 2

BLEST BE THE TIE THAT BINDS

". . . to sit at my right hand or at my left is not mine to grant, but it is for those for whom it has been prepared."
—Mark 10:40

READ: Mark 10:35-40 and Luke 22:24-30

As Jesus' ministry was winding down and he soon would turn over the administration of his mission to his disciples, he experienced a break in the fabric of fellowship among his closest followers. They began jockeying for position. Certain disciples wanted to be chosen for key positions, leaving others behind. While all human organizations require some amount of distinction between leaders and followers, and must place power in the hands of certain members of the organization, Jesus declared that such inequity would not appear among his followers. There would be differences in function but not in rank. Because God would call each one to a particular task, each would be equal to every other follower.

In Jesus' reply to James and John he gave to his church the mandate for democracy among us, and for an equality as we together stand before God. How deep would be our fellowship if we could hold on to this concept.

Jesus came among us as one who serves, giving us the example of how each of us is asked to carry out Christian life in the fellowship of faith. We are to be a community in which each serves the needs of the others. In such mutual service there is to be a caring concern for one another which presents to the world outside the church a model for the kind of humanity God intends.

PRAYER: O Lord, help us to care for one another in the fellowship or your church. Through Christ. Amen.

~ ~ ~ ~ ~ ~

NOVEMBER 3

I NEVER DISCUSS RELIGION OR POLITICS

> Now I appeal to you, brothers and sisters, by the name of our Lord Jesus Christ, that all of you be in agreement and that there be no divisions among you, but that you be united in the same mind and the same purpose.
> —I Corinthians 1:10

READ: I Corinthians 1:4-17 and John 13:31-35

The words of the old adage, "I never discuss religion or politics," are often repeated as an effective conversation stopper. Have you ever wondered why so many people feel this way? One reason may be that both subjects have a way of heating up emotions, because each of these areas of life require commitment on our part. There may be another reason for avoiding religious arguments. They simply never get anywhere. There is something about arguing over religious beliefs which has a way of keeping one from actively practicing the religion in question. An active faith commitment becomes a sterile intellectual platform.

Paul discovered that the members of the Christian congregation in Corinth were arguing religion. Apparently it was a sort of interdenominational argument with each side claiming to have been following the correct way, or the authentic leader in the church. "I belong to Paul . . . I belong to Apollos . . . I belong to Cephas . . . I belong to Christ." Often such arguments include this last statement in the form of "I am a *real* Christian." Such a haughty claim usually ends the argument in a stand-off.

Christ is not divided, and so such argumentation is out of place and it is debilitating. Instead of such in-fighting let us get on with the task of sharing Christ's love in the world. The way to share that love in the world includes demonstrating the love we have for one another within the church. Arguing blurs that message, often destroying it. Paul said, "God is faithful; by him you were called into the fellowship of his Son, Jesus Christ our Lord." (I Corinthians 1:9)

PRAYER: We thank you, O God, for our oneness in Christ. Help us to show such unity in love for one another. In Christ. Amen.

~ ~ ~ ~ ~

NOVEMBER 4

GOD'S THE GENERAL CONTRACTOR

So neither the one who plants nor the one who waters
is anything, but only God who gives the growth.
—I Corinthians 3:7

READ: I Corinthians 3:1-9 and I Peter 2:1-6

We have gotten so accustomed to organizing, supervising, controlling and making things work that it is hard to let go and give God the credit. Sometimes in congregations we fall into the trap of claiming credit for ourselves for various developments in the church's life. We like to take credit for the new church building or the redecorated nursery, the fine organ and the great choir. We hold on to the ideas, gifts and opinions which we have contributed to the church in the past, claiming ownership over these against all odds. Some years ago a church remodeling caused considerable conflict when the oak paneling in the chancel was removed and replaced with more modern material, without consulting the man who had originally given the money for the oak construction. Because of such tenacious sense of ownership trouble can brew over such matters in church life.

Paul reminded the Corinthian Christians that it is God who matters in the development of the church and its program. God is the one who causes the church to grow and develop. We are instruments in the hand of the Divine Builder. When each of us is reminded of God's creative and sustaining power in the life of the church we are bonded together in response to God' work among us. God is the general contractor. We are the brick layers.

PRAYER: We thank you, God, for your creative power by which our Christian fellowship is given and maintained. In Christ. Amen.

~ ~ ~ ~ ~ ~

NOVEMBER 5

AT EASE—CLOTHED—AND RIGHT MINDED

> They came to Jesus and saw the demoniac sitting there,
> clothed and in his right mind.
> —Mark 5:15

READ: Mark 5:1-20

There is no enslavement in modern society more hideous than addiction to drugs or alcohol. Like the demoniac in the story in Mark for whom no restraints were effective while his disease caused him to mutilate himself, the one who has fallen into self-destructive addiction no longer can live freely in any sense of the word. This can be true not only for those bound in chemical addiction but for all those who are caught up in some form of compulsive behavior. Folk, who with the apostle Paul would say, "That which I do not want to do, I do." If outside influences, forces, or persons have a hold upon you, and compel you to do things you really do not want to do, perhaps you need the intervention which Jesus Christ brings when he says, "Come out of the man you unclean spirit."

There has been a tendency to interpret Christ's liberation as a release from moral or legalistic restraints. Such a person, we say, is free to do whatever he/she pleases. Look again at the demoniac, who because of his illness could not live at ease with himself or with others. When the liberation of Christ came to him, he was able to sit still, remain clothed, and conduct himself in his right mind—hardly a prescription for an immoral, libertarian sort of life. His freedom led to the mental attitude of an ordered, civil, and acceptable life. Freedom leads to order as we use our freedom to fulfil the intentions and expectations of God which have been "written into our genes" since our very creation.

Are you at ease with God and with life? What is it in your life which binds you and keeps you from fulfilling God's best wishes for your life? Perhaps this is what the focus of your prayer for healing might be.

PRAYER: Break the chains, O Christ, which bind me, and which keep me from an ordered life of faith, fulfilling your expectations of me. Amen.

~ ~ ~ ~ ~

NOVEMBER 6

NO LONGER LAME

The man went away and told the Jews that it was Jesus who had made him well.

—John 5:15

READ: John 5:1-15

One of the most well-known phrases from the healing stories of Jesus is: "Stand up, take up your mat and walk." (John 5:8) This story stimulates our imagination. The man had been ill for thirty-eight years. Yet all it took was one command from Jesus—"get up and walk." Then the poor man ran into the authorities, who criticized him for walking on the Sabbath. After thirty-eight years of imprisonment from a physical handicap, the new-found ability to walk took precedence over the weekly Sabbath prohibitions. It is tempting to speculate about how Jesus healed the man. Perhaps it was his encouragement to the man to use what resources he had for his own release from lameness. Whatever it was, it was the power of Jesus that liberated him and gave him a new life.

For us the message is that the power of Christ is offered to us to release us from the restrictions which keep us from being fully human. Sometimes these restrictions are physical. The healing power of God acts upon such a condition, not always to remove the physical limitation, but nevertheless to bring new life to the victim. Even more deeply than physical healing, the power of God in Christ unlocks our spirits so that we need no longer be crippled in mind and spirit because of our physical problems. The Christ, who rose from the dead, is able to help us to rise above our disabilities.

The story has been televised of a major league pitcher who lost a pitching arm and shoulder to cancer. In it he testified that his Christian faith has made him able to triumph over this most tragic devastation in his life. Instead of pitching he now is able to share the message of faith with people all across the country. Jesus gave him the incentive and power to "rise, take up his bed and walk." Jesus Christ can do that for us as well in the midst of whatever restrictions we may be experiencing.

PRAYER: O Christ, help me to "walk" no matter how lame I may be in whatever way. Amen.

~ ~ ~ ~ ~

NOVEMBER 7

THIS ONE WASN'T HEALED

When he heard this, he was shocked and went away grieving for he had many possessions.—Mark 10:22

READ: Mark 10:17-22 and Luke 14:16-24

We are accustomed to thinking of both of these stories in reference to receiving or not receiving our reward in heaven. In the case of the rich man we conclude that money gets in the way of going to heaven. Perhaps this interpretation is too narrow and we need to see that what the man was missing was meaning and quality in life. For him life was not a great banquet and he wanted to know how to find what he was missing. He had a hunger of the soul which was not being satisfied. Jesus directed him to let loose of his possessions and to turn his love and attention to those in need. He asked the man to turn inside out. Then he would find meaning in life. In the parable of the great banquet Jesus points out that those who put other concerns first, before their love for God, will miss the eternal dimension of life, which comes from knowing God.

What this adds up to for us is that God wants first place in our affections. God wants our love exclusively. God wants us to place our other commitments in a secondary position—money—work—community affairs—patriotism—even family. This is what the Old Testament means when it refers to God as a "jealous God." "You shall have no other gods before me." (Exodus 20:3)

When other values are placed higher than Christ in our lives, we become captivated by them and coerced into serving "other gods" causing us to miss the banquet, and to go hungry—spiritually, so to speak. When other commitments block our commitment to Christ we will go away grieving!.

PRAYER: Help me to love you first, O God. Through Christ. Amen

~ ~ ~ ~ ~ ~

NOVEMBER 8

OH TO BE REMEMBERED

So God created humankind in his image, in the image
of God he created them.—Genesis 1:27 The Lord God
took the man and put him in the garden of Eden to till it
and keep it.

—Genesis 2:15

READ: Psalm 8

When Voyager I wings its way into limitless space beyond
Saturn and ultimately beyond our galaxy, it carries a gold disc
with a description of who we are, so that intelligent life somewhere
in space and time may come to know us. There is something both
heroic and futile about such a blind effort to be remembered.

There is in the human heart the desire to be eternal, or at the
very least to be remembered. In the midst of the endless black
canyons of astronomical space, and the unimaginable extension of
time, it is very difficult to feel eternal, considering our brief span
of four decades more or less.

But the good news is that God lifts us to a position in the
universe which is so special that we do have a relationship with the
Eternal. Worship and prayer in human life form the link to eternity
providing us with a sense of significance and meaning. As we wing
our way through the seemingly endless round of life's activities we
travel with the imprint of the Eternal Creator upon us. "So God
created humankind in his image, in the image of God he created
them." (Genesis 1:27)

PRAYER: O God, give me a new sense of meaning, as you reveal to
me your imprint upon my life. In Christ. Amen.

~ ~ ~ ~ ~ ~

NOVEMBER 9

AND SPEAK TO THE PEOPLE, AND TELL THEM

"Go, stand in the temple and tell the people the whole
message about this life." When they heard this, they entered
the temple at daybreak and went on with their teaching.

—Acts 5:20-21

READ: Acts 5:12-42

It isn't unusual for people who have been associated with each
other in the community or at work for a long time, to discover
after years together that each is an active Christian affiliated with a
church. In such cases over many years of professional and
community association the subject never came up.

We so often keep our religious commitment under tight wraps.
For some reason we tend to view religion as a private matter, and
we tend to keep it secret. What a loss of significant sharing we
cause by our spiritual secrecy. We lose out on the insights and
experiences others could offer us, as well as the deeply rewarding
excitement of sharing with another person what is closest to our
heart—faith in God and our relationship to Christ.

Isn't it curious that we, who face no real threat of persecution for
speaking of Christ are so silent, while those who have faced serious
peril have dared to proclaim their faith. Beginning with the apostles
in the New Testament, men and women have often felt compelled to
speak the truth of God's action in their lives. Dare we do less?

PRAYER: O God, give me the courage to share my faith and
experience with others. Help me to discover the opportunities
in which I might be an instrument of your Word in the life of
someone I know, In Christ. Amen

~ ~ ~ ~ ~ ~

NOVEMBER 10

THEY HAVE MADE THEMSELVES AN IMAGE

He took the gold from them, and formed it in a mold, and cast an image of a calf; and they said, "These are your gods, O Israel, who brought you up out of the land of Egypt."

—Exodus 32:4

READ: Exodus 32:1-10

We look at the story of Israel and the Golden Calf as quaint, colorful and not too relevant. But on the other hand look at the ways in which we use certain items to bring us good luck. There was a time some years ago when a rabbit's foot was a popular good luck charm. Like the four leaf clover it was supposed to do the wearer good. An athlete wears a special pendant to give her success in the race or game. We may not be as far removed from a heritage of superstition and magic as we think!

It is especially tempting in times of frustration and impending disaster to fashion "gods" to bail us out. Sometimes these are physical items we clutch or place around our neck. Other times they may be certain phrases which we speak to give us good luck or perhaps even a certain prayer which we believe will automatically benefit our future. But such human efforts to determine the future must forever remain less than God. Idols, it would seem. Like the golden calf which Aaron had made in a time of national frustration, our images and little formulas cannot be identified with the Lord God Almighty, Maker of heaven and earth. God alone is to be worshiped precisely because God cannot be brought down, and melted into an image of something else which we have shaped.

Our Christian hope for our nation and for our world, as well as for ourselves, lies in the conviction that God is above all human inventions of the mind or hand, and that it is God who will ultimately shape our future.

PRAYER: Keep me from putting my trust in something I have devised. By your grace may I dare to trust in You alone, O God. In Christ. Amen.

~ ~ ~ ~ ~

NOVEMBER 11

ENEMIES? WHO ME?

"Father, if you are willing, remove this cup from me;
yet not my will but yours be done."

—Luke 22:42

READ: Luke 6:27, 32-36 and 23: 32-39

In polite society most of us feel that we simply don't have any enemies. So we conclude that all the Christian talk about loving one's enemies doesn't exactly apply, unless we mean the Terrorists. But the principle still stands. Christians, like Christ himself, are to love their enemies. That is, indeed, a reversal of how everybody else lives. In Gethsemane Jesus was tempted to take our natural point of view—that is to save himself. In the taunts of those who witnessed his death by crucifixion this common view-point found repeated expression in the question, "Are you not the Messiah? Save yourself and us!" (Luke 23:39) Earlier Pilate had tried to give Jesus a chance to seek a reprieve, but Jesus did not take it. Rather, Jesus faced his own death loving the very enemies who put him on the cross, praying for them to be forgiven. Jesus clearly modeled this reversed way of thinking by submitting to death at the hands of enemies—enemies whom he loved.

How can this help us when we feel we do not have enemies? What about those who disagree with you? What about those who oppose you in one way or another? Or those who resist you, distance themselves from you, and remain aloof? To some extent these are examples of enemies. Anyone who threatens you in any way or challenges your position or power is in effect your enemy. How one deals with opposition, resistance, threats, disagreement or rejection depends upon whether one loves or hates one's enemies. Jesus directs us to love those who disagree and in any way reject us. How much easier it is to get along with such folk when one honestly loves them!

PRAYER: Help me to love my enemies. O Lord. In Christ. Amen.

~ ~ ~ ~ ~ ~

NOVEMBER 12

NOT EVEN SUPPOSED TO GET EVEN

"But I say to you that listen, Love your enemies, do good to those who hate you, bless those who curse you, pray for those who abuse you."

—Luke 6:27-28

READ: John 18:33-37 and Romans 12:14-21

It is commonly thought that a criminal must be caught in order to bring him/her to justice; but underneath such words there frequently lurks the human desire to "get even." It is not unusual to find the family of a murder victim spending huge sums of money over a long period of time to find the murder in order to see justice done. Some persist long after law enforcement has given up and filed away the case. Could it be that the motive is vengeance rather than justice?

The desire to "get even" is the way of the world. In matters far less serious than murder we strike back at those who mistreat us. Someone intentionally mis-states your opinion or tells an untruth about someone in your family. From that time onward you have little use for them and you find ways of getting back at them. You are ignored by someone whom you know and the next time you find yourself looking the other way to avoid recognizing them. Normal, human, and quite common among us. But it is not the way of Christ.

When Jesus was asked by Pilate about his kingdom, Jesus said that his kingdom was not of this world. In fact, the more seriously you study Jesus' teachings, the more you realize that his way was the opposite of the world's ways. Instead of getting even he instructs us to pray for those who mistreat, misquote, or ignore us. This is one way in which he asks us to take a very different approach to human relationships—very different from the common way of vengeance.

Think about the people who have hurt you. Now soften up toward them. Pray for them. Love them. Do good to them.

PRAYER: O God, I pray for my enemies: _____ In Christ. Amen.

~ ~ ~ ~ ~ ~

NOVEMBER 13

SEED-TIME AND HARVEST . . . OF PEACE

> "If anyone strikes you on the cheek, offer him the other also . . ."
>
> —Luke 6:29

READ: Matthew 26:47-56 and Galatians 6:7-10

A U.S. jet carrying hundreds of innocent passengers explodes in the air and all are plunged to their deaths. An anonymous phone call comes in to U.S. officials from a terrorist organization claiming credit for the tragedy. Our military presence is beefed up at all U.S. embassies in the region. Another hostage is taken, while reports of the death of a long-time hostage are circulated. And Jesus' words ring true: "All who take the sword will perish by the sword."

(Matthew 26:52) And Paul's words come true: "for you reap whatever you sow." (Galatians 6:7) "But they were innocent people on that plane!" You say. Yes, but do you and I share in the complicity with death and destruction in which our nation is involved? So many adult Americans played "war" when they were little kids in the neighborhood. Now all of us play "big people's war games." When will it stop!

Jesus called upon his people to stop the war games when he warned his disciples not to use the sword against his captors in the Garden of Gethsemane. It cost Jesus his life to stop the killing process, but by his sacrifice we now know another way. If we carry the name of Christ how can we help our world put down the sword? Are their instances in your own life in which you can stand on the side of peace instead of violence? Can you become a peacemaker close to home? Such seeds of peace planted in your own backyard will reap a harvest of peace, we are promised.

PRAYER: Help me, O God, to find ways of planting seeds of peace. In Christ, the peacemaker. Amen.

~ ~ ~ ~ ~ ~

NOVEMBER 14

NEITHER SNOB NOR HUMBLE BE

"Do to others as you would have them do to you."
—Luke 6:31

READ: Matthew 7:1-12 and John 15:12-17

Jesus' second great commandment is the focus of Jesus' words which are today's text: "You shall love your neighbor as yourself." (Matthew 19:19) This is at the foundation stone of our effort to relate to others without violence, but instead in a sharing manner. If we could just enter into the lives of others sensitively and appreciatively so that we could begin to feel what it is like to be that other person, to think his/her thoughts, and to experience life as he/she does, it would be easier to love them as ourselves.

Normally we classify others as different and distant from us, labeling some as enemies or competitors, or at the very least as strangers. Holding others at a distance allows us to position ourselves above or below them socially or psychologically. "Looking down our nose" at them or "looking up" to them are approaches which keep us from sensitively relating to one another as friends. Jesus presents us with another way of relating by urging us to see others as we see ourselves, to care about others as we care about ourselves. Then we will find ourselves able to act toward others in a way which is loving and helpful—just as we wish others would act toward us.

Can you put away all pretense? Can you let go of your snobbishness, or your inferiority feelings and just relate to others humanly—sensitively—and lovingly? That's living in a new Kingdom.

PRAYER: Help me, O God, to love others as I know I love myself. In Christ who did that. Amen

~ ~ ~ ~ ~ ~

NOVEMBER 15

MEDDLING WITH MY BANK ACCOUNT

"... and from anyone who takes away your coat do not withhold even your shirt.

—Luke 6:29

READ: Matthew 6:7-14, and Matthew 10:40-42

When the preacher starts talking about your pocketbook, he is apt to hear: "Now you're meddling, Reverend." We really accept

Jesus' teaching about peacemaking. But when he challenges us to share our material wealth we bristle. And yet the way of Christ is the way of total sharing. That is difficult to do.

There are some deep seated ideas in our American way of life which make these words of Jesus especially difficult. His words are so opposite to prevailing values. We hold high the right of private property and with it the idea that each person must work diligently for his/her own material things. Those who work eat. The indigent will (ought to) go hungry. "I have mine. You work for yours." Doesn't sound like what a Christian should think, does it? But these are some of the values upon which our society has been built. During a recent hurricane the TV cameras focused upon a store owner standing outside his shop holding a rifle to keep looters away. Instead Jesus says "When someone takes away your coat, do not withhold even your shirt." (Luke 6:29) Closer to home, when a pan-handler comes with a story of personal loss you know is not true, you feel abused. And yet, Jesus commands us to share. Could it be that looting and pan-handling are negative results of our fixation on private property? In more primitive societies sharing is a value which seems to replace private property. Are such ways closer to Christ's way?

PRAYER: Help me to share with others, O God, even when I don't think they deserve it. In Christ. Amen.

~ ~ ~ ~ ~

NOVEMBER 16

TIME TO REMEMBER

Sing praises to the Lord, O you his faithful ones, and give thanks to his holy name.

—Psalm 30:4

READ: Psalm 30:1-12

November is a time to remember. It is a time of rustic recollection of the warmth of other years, the scent of burning leaves, new crispness in the night air, and the yellow moon of harvest. Time to think long thoughts of days gone by. One of the Chicago newspapers used to print each year at this time a famous cartoon sketch of Autumn in which an old man and a young boy sit gazing into the smoky fire of burning leaves, which they have raked into a pile. As the smoke gently unfurls the corn stalks in the distance turn into Indian tepees and the dancing flames produce an image of braves dancing before their tents. Surely that fleeting "fall feeling" does indeed bring back images of experiences of earlier times in our lives—ones about which we feel good. And sometimes we wish we could return to some of those experiences in our lives. November is the time to pretend for a moment or two that we are "back there, and then" re-living days gone by.

It is fitting that November is Thanksgiving time. Give thanks for precious memories, for brief moments of exquisite recollection, when the pressure of today's activity is suspended. For a moment we enjoy again old sights, voices long since hushed, a delicate aroma almost forgotten, the sense of God's goodness through a closeness of family or friends, and an awareness of God's presence in the quiet stillness of bare tree limbs against a clear moonlit night sky.

God is good. Let us praise God for good memories. Let us give God thanks for what he has done for us in "those good old days," and in all the months and years since!

PRAYER: I am thankful, O God, for those times of remembering when you bring back good thoughts so that I might "sing praises to the Lord, and give thanks to your holy name." Through Christ. Amen.

~ ~ ~ ~ ~

NOVEMBER 17

A CAN OF STRING BEANS AND A SONG IN THE HALL

> I will sing to the Lord, because he has dealt bountifully
> with me.
>
> —Psalm 13:6

READ: Psalm 65: 9-13

In the days before religious celebrations were banned from public schools children were often involved in school Thanksgiving programs which were unashamedly Christian. In some of these celebrations children brought food items to share with the needy in their town. In one of these programs the children marched through the halls and down the stairwells toward the gymnasium where the program was to be held. As they marched along carrying their food items they sang, "Come, ye thankful people, come./ Raise the song of harvest home./ All is safely gathered in, 'ere the winter storms begin./ God, our Maker doth provide, for our wants to be supplied./ Come to God's own temple come. Raise the song of harvest home." Children carrying their cans of string beans sang lustily carrying God's gifts, as the Pilgrims had done before.

In an affluent age, when it is so easy to take everything we have for granted, it is difficult to keep in mind the fact that God is our source of survival and the generous provider of our luxuries as well. Thanksgiving gives us one time in the year when we are encouraged to count our blessings and to give God our thanks. In modern urban society most of us are so far away from any kind of seed-time and harvest cycle that thanksgiving as a response to God's gift of survival for us is easily passed over, except for the very day of Thanksgiving. Perhaps we should adopt a custom of giving a silent prayer of thanksgiving every time we enter a modern super market with all its abundance ready for our "harvesting!"

The words of Paul to the Christians in Thessalonica should be pasted on our every wall: "Give thanks in all circumstances, for this is the will of God in Christ Jesus for you." (I Thessalonians 5:18)

PRAYER: For every good thing, all of which come from you, O Lord, I give you thanks today, and every day. In Christ. Amen.

~ ~ ~ ~ ~ ~

NOVEMBER 18

A CHILL WIND BLOWING

"Where, O death, is your victory? Where, O death is your sting?"

—I Corinthians 15:55

READ: I Corinthians 15:55-57

November is a time when the end is in sight. The chill winds of fall are blowing, bringing a dark foreboding of the icy blasts of winter. With the loss of leaves and the freezing to brown and gray of the colorful summer flowers we are aware of death as a normal and inevitable stage in the cycle of life. You can cover your tomatoes each night for only so long! Then you must face up to the reality of a chill wind blowing. Only then can you live through another winter.

In the story of Joni Ereckson autumn came early in the young life of a vivacious seventeen year old girl when a diving accident fractured her neck suddenly turning her into a quadriplegic. This must have felt like an instant killer frost bringing death to the brightest blossoms of summer. Her young spirit chilled, she was forced to depend upon others for her every need. She wanted to die, but couldn't even do that alone. Then her premature November turned into April when she prayed, asking God to show her how to live. Finding new faith in Christ she began to blossom again. God took the *given* in her life and turned it into a *gift*, when she learned to paint by holding the brush in her mouth, and when she began to share the message of faith in Christ in her writing for others.

When the chill winds of autumn cause a measure of death in your life God can take the *given* in your life and make it a *gift*. A form of resurrection! An illness, or the loss of a loved one; perhaps a failure of some kind, or a broken relationship; facing up to a critical limitation in your life—these are the chill winds blowing, which sometimes bring the killer frost. These may be the *givens* in your life which cannot be changed, even through prayer. Joni prayed to be healed but her spinal cord remains forever severed. What God did instead was turn the *given* into a *gift*. This, God will do for you!

PRAYER: O, most merciful God, help me to accept the *given* in my life. Then grant me the courage and the wisdom and the faith by which your grace can provide me the gift of the new life of another spring-time in my life. Through Christ. Amen

～ ～ ～ ～ ～

NOVEMBER 19

FREEDOM AND THANKSGIVING GO HAND IN HAND

When he saw that he was healed, turned back, praising God with a loud voice. He prostrated himself at Jesus' feet and thanked him.

—Luke 17:15-16

READ: Luke 17:11-19

Toward the end of November our thoughts turn to Thanksgiving Day and to giving thanks to God. Customarily we think of the things for which we are thankful like food and shelter. For the leper in Luke's story, his thanksgiving was for healing. More deeply his thanksgiving was for freedom. As a leper he had not been free to associate with other people. He had been held hostage by his disease. He had been kept outside the gate of the city. Now, after his healing he could enter the social life of his community and be with other people. This was new life. This was freedom.

Thanksgiving for the early Pilgrims was for the harvest which promised to sustain them through another winter. But, more deeply their thanksgiving was for new-found freedom which was allowing them to establish a new society in a new land on their own terms. Terms which were in many ways set by God.

If Christ's liberation is the most important result of his Gospel of Love, then thanksgiving is the most important response on our part. Like the leper who was set free from his social imprisonment, who gave thanks with a loud voice, so we give thanks to God for the freeing power of Christ.

From what has Christ set you free? From worry—from guilt—from low self-esteem—from fear—from shyness or social clumsiness—from old resentments or endless disputes—from??? In your life what has locked you in its grip, and now has been removed? Such a removal—such a healing—is cause for profound thanksgiving to God. We have pictures etched in our consciousness of American hostages stepping off the plane in Germany on their way home to freedom with thanksgiving in their hearts. In Christ we are freed hostages. Let us give thanks with a loud voice.

PRAYER: I thank you, O Lord, for setting me free from fear and guilt, from the unfair power others exert over me and for whatever else you have done for me. For _____
_____. In Christ. Amen.

～ ～ ～ ～ ～ ～

NOVEMBER 20

MAKE FRIENDS FOR YOURSELVES
(Luke 16:9)

Love one another with mutual affection.
—Romans 12:10

READ: Romans 12:9-13 and Colossians 3:15-17

One of the childhood surprises about the traditional story of the Pilgrims at the first Thanksgiving was that they invited the Indians to dinner. Why did they do that? Weren't they the enemy? No, they may very well have been the cause of Thanksgiving, for it was their help on which the survival of the Europeans depended. Those first native Americans were the ones who taught the Pilgrim farmers to put a fish in each mound of seed corn. They were the first county extension agents in a manner of speaking!

You can't be thankful alone. Once you begin to count your blessings you realize the extent to which the richest dimensions of your life have to do with other people. Thanksgiving dinner needs to have family and friends at the table as much, or maybe even more, than it needs the turkey.

Autumn is a time to strengthen relationships. After having been engaged in various summer pursuits now that fall is here you begin to get involved with others in church and community activities. It is a privilege to become better and better acquainted with others and to share with them your own story. It is so helpful to find a person who has had some of the same experiences as you have gone through. It is refreshing to develop relationships in which there is a mutual and honest exchange of ideas and feelings.

The Apostle Paul hoped that his congregations would provide the environment in which brotherly and sisterly love would unite those Christians in their fellowship. John talked often of the love Christians should have for one another. One of the marks of the early Christians was their mutual love.

PRAYER: O Lord, we thank you for each other. May we develop relationships which reflect your love for us. In Christ. Amen.

~ ~ ~ ~ ~ ~

NOVEMBER 21

PRAISE AND THE PARA-MEDIC

"In the same way, let your light shine before others, so that they may see your good works, and give glory to your Father in heaven."

—Matthew 5:16

READ: Matthew 5:13-16

Some years ago when little Jessica McClure was lifted out of the well shaft into which she had fallen and had become trapped for two and a half days, the town of Midland, Texas cheered. This brought joy to people all over the world who had heard about her plight. When the man who went down to carry her up was interviewed afterward, he refused to accept the praise and deferred that to the many others in the community who had helped so valiantly. Others in the community said that the incident had done a great deal to bring the town together.

The effects of heroic and dramatic acts on the human scene seem to have a far-reaching effect beyond the few who are closely involved. A single act of love can open a wider reservoir of community good will.

When Jesus encouraged his followers to show his love in their words and deeds he promised the "pay-off" would be that people would give praise. But that praise, he said, would be offered to God, instead of to the human actors. Instead of the para-medic in Midland, Texas taking all the praise, he wanted it to go to the entire community. As Christians, Christ asks us to be signs of God's love for humanity. And so our actions ought to cause people to take note of God's goodness and power. Do we do things that are signs of God?

PRAYER: Help me, O God, to live in such a way that others become aware of your love. In Christ. Amen,

~ ~ ~ ~ ~ ~

NOVEMBER 22

WHAT DOES YOUR SIGN SAY?

And they went out and proclaimed the good news everywhere, while the Lord worked with them and confirmed the message by the signs that accompanied it.
—Mark 16:20

READ: Matthew 28:16-20

The last few verses in Matthew are called The Great Commission, by which the missionary activity of the church has been motivated for generations. These words of command to individual Christians often challenge us to speak and act in ways that hopefully will bring people to know Christ better. But we wonder if we do as good a job as we should in following his command. Oftentimes it is very difficult to gauge ones success in this venture of discipleship.

Mark adds an idea which may help us to know whether we are accomplishing something for God. "The Lord worked with them, and confirmed the message by the signs that accompanied it." (Mark 16:20) What this means for us in our day, at least in part, is that when the message we share verbally is reflected in how we live, what we say will be authenticated in the minds and hearts of observers. This confirmation God will bring to the minds of those with whom we share the gospel. Sadly, the opposite is also true. When a person does not live up to his or her own preaching, people are quick to call that person a hypocrite. And that spells the end of effectiveness of such preaching.

Does the life we live reflect the message of God's love and saving grace? Are we signs of God's kingdom?

PRAYER: O God, help me to live worthy of your Word, which I want to speak. In Christ, the Word. Amen

~ ~ ~ ~ ~

NOVEMBER 23

HEROES OF RESISTANCE

> Conduct yourselves honorably among the Gentiles, so that, though they malign you as evildoers, they may see your honorable deeds and glorify God when he comes to judge.
>
> —I Peter 2:12

READ: I Peter 2:9-17

Time has a way of proving the truth. Staunch Christians in Germany during the Nazi era were frequently denounced and often put in detention camps for their Christian acts against the Hitler regime. But their behavior in those trying times eventually proved them to be acting for God authentically. They are now seen as heroes of the resistance. It is not easy in any age to act in a Christian way when others in the community do not agree, but such behavior becomes a sign of God's rule, which ultimately will rightly reign.

There were Christian people in America in the 1950's who recommended U.S. recognition of Red China, who were severely denounced for such "un-American thoughts." But the passage of time has proved them right as the U.S. now relates more openly with China.

Many times in our relationships with those who depend upon

us emotionally too heavily, to their own detriment, we must give them "tough love," by withdrawing our support when such action prolongs the problem. This may be seen by others as cruel, but in the long run this kind of love is a real sign of God's way with those who need to become strong.

Let us behave in such a way that ultimately others will thank God for our love and courage in dealing with them.

PRAYER: O God, help me to be strong when that requires unpopular stands, or actions which may be misinterpreted. In Christ. Amen

~ ~ ~ ~ ~

NOVEMBER 24

IS IT IN THE BOOK?

"You that are Israelites, listen to what I have to say: Jesus of Nazareth, a man attested to you by God with deeds of power, wonders, and signs that God did through him among you, as you yourselves know."

—Acts 2:22

READ: Acts 2:14-24

Religious pluralism describes America. There are all sorts of religious groups, some of which are Christian, many of which do not claim to be. You meet adherents of such groups in airports, on your doorstep, on television and radio. It is very confusing, if not dangerous to fall into the trap which tolerance sets and to conclude, "If it's religious it must be ok." How are we to judge which groups to listen to, or more critical yet—to contribute to and to follow?

In Jerusalem on the day of Pentecost following Jesus' crucifixion there were Jews in town who showed signs of being very religious. However, some of the onlookers thought they were drunk. How could one determine whether the frenzied speaking of that group truly was inspired by God? Peter's answer was to affirm that these folk were authentic because what they were doing is what the Scriptures had predicted, and that they were following Jesus, who himself showed the proper credentials.

Our standard of judgement is whether an idea or an experience is consistent with the Bible. Does the message or life-style in question go along with what we know to be the biblical way. This is not always easy to determine, but the more one prayerfully studies the Scriptures the more readily can one judge whether it is "in the Book."

PRAYER: O God, help me to know the Bible well enough to be able to follow only those whom you have truly inspired. In Christ. Amen.

ↄ ↄ ↄ ↄ ↄ ↄ

NOVEMBER 25

BY THE HAND

"Truly I tell you, unless you change and become like children, you will never enter the kingdom of heaven."
—Matthew 18:3

READ: Matthew 18:1-5

Being a parent of children growing up in these high-tech times is a humbling business. They know their way around the confusing world of computers and other electronic devices so much better than many of their elders. It is particularly humbling to be advised by another family member to ask your child to help you get the VCR programmed properly. Advice is always hard to take from someone your equal, and harder still from someone "beneath" you. And yet there is something mature about the person who can accept good advice gracefully, no matter from whom.

Is this what Jesus meant when he said, "Unless you change

and become like little children . . . ?" Among other child-like characteristics is the child's willingness to be led, to which Jesus is pointing as a necessary requirement for entering the Kingdom. How else could we be expected to find our way into God's realm? Only by humbly accepting God's advice and following God's directions can we find our way through the maze of conflicting loyalties into the place in which a single-minded allegiance to Christ is the "law of the land?"

The eagerness with which a small child places her hand in her mother's and her willingness to follow give us a picture of what Jesus wants us to do in accepting his lordship over our lives. Such trusting eagerness and desire to follow Christ is the changed outlook he is asking of us as he invites us to become as little children in order to enter his realm.

PRAYER: Humbly do I accept your leadership, O Christ. Let me follow you eagerly and expectantly. Take me by the hand! Amen

~ ~ ~ ~ ~

NOVEMBER 26

TELLING IT LIKE IT IS

When Jesus saw Nathanael coming toward him, he said of him, "Here is truly an Israelite in whom there is no deceit!"

—John 1:47

READ: John 1:43-51

Among the many changes in the turbulent 1960's was a new emphasis upon being brutally honest—telling it like it is. By this was meant an attitude and approach to each other which refuses to exchange nice falsities in the interest of keeping things smooth. Among the disciples of Jesus, Nathanael stands out as a child of the 60's, so to speak. When Philip hurried to find Nathanael to tell him the Messiah had been found, and that he came from Nazareth, Nathanael's honest reaction was to say, "Nazareth—YUK! What good can come from that place?" Instead of taking offense at such a statement, Jesus praised Nathanael for his honesty—one in whom there is no guile. Then, when Nathanael became aware of Jesus' insight, he showed his honesty again, by telling it like it is—"Wow! You really are God's son!"

Here is another characteristic of the child whom Jesus identified as of value in his kingdom: honesty—the absence of deceit or sham. This is the naivete of a child which Jesus found attractive in Nathanael.

In Christ's kingdom people are asked to relate to each other honestly, without social sham, but in love for one another. This is to be our way, instead of engaging in the kind of game playing which tends to obscure the true person, thus destroying meaningful conversation between one another.

PRAYER: Open me, to a new honesty as I relate to others in love, O Christ. Amen.

~ ~ ~ ~ ~

NOVEMBER 27

WITH MALICE TOWARD NONE

Rid yourselves, therefore, of all malice, and all guile, insincerity, envy, and all slander. Like newborn infants, long for the pure, spiritual milk, so that by it you may grow into salvation.

—I Peter 2:1-2

READ: I Peter 1:22-2:3

There is a moral innocense possessed by small children which Peter holds up as needed by true followers of Christ. It is the absence of malice, or evil. A child may be bad at times and cause all sorts of trouble, but it isn't malice. Child psychologists may identify what is going on in the child and devise ways of helping the child modify his or her behavior. But malice is of a different order. While bad behavior is in some sense a conditioned response to factors beyond the child's control, malice is intentional. It is ill-will toward another person or toward the world. It is not a matter of emotions gone awry. It is the will of a person bent upon doing harm to another. It is what must be put away in the life of a Christian.

To look at the world without malice is to have no desire for harm to anyone, even to enemies. This is what Jesus meant by asking us to love our enemies and to pray for those who persecute us. The remarkable witness of Christians who have been imprisoned for their faith or taken hostage has been their lack of hatred or recrimination toward their captors. Instead of such malice there has often been sensitivity and caring for those who have held them captive. That is what living without malice is like!

Can we put away such evil and long for spiritual milk? Peter holds up the innocence of the infant as a model for Christian discipleship.

PRAYER: Strip from me all malice, O Christ. Amen

~ ~ ~ ~ ~ ~

NOVEMBER 28

INITIALIZING THE DISC

Jesus answered him, "Very truly, I tell you, no one can see the kingdom of God without being born from above."
—John 3:3

READ: John 3:1-8

It used to be that one had to initialize a new disc for the computer before it could accept newly printed material from the word processor. It had to be prepared for the operating language of a particular computer. That's what Jesus said—believe it or not! You cannot see the kingdom unless you've been born again— prepared to accept the operating language of the new kingdom, so to speak. You must be initialized—born again.

To come into Christ's kingdom is to be given a new start in life, a new birth. The old program must be erased, like a used disc is erased in order to accept new material. One must get rid of a lot of one's own "stuff" in the form of pre-existing attitudes and habitual ways of thinking and acting, in order to have a clean disc for Christ's new program. In the traditional language of Christian theology this process of arriving at a clean slate is what is meant by confession, repentance and forgiveness, which prepare us for the new life in Christ. Initializing the disc. Then we can handle God's language—God's word—for our new citizenship in the Kingdom.

What do you need to have erased, so that you can enter a new era in your life? What are the old patterns of thought and behavior which you would like to get rid of? Let Christ's reclaiming mercy strip you of all the old "stuff" and prepare you to handle the new program.

PRAYER: Dear Lord and Savior erase the old and install the new in me! In Christ. Amen.

~ ~ ~ ~ ~ ~

NOVEMBER 29

GETTING INVOLVED

> Bear one another's burdens, and in this way you will fulfill the law of Christ.
>
> —Galatians 6:2

READ: Galatians 6:1-10

"I'm sorry, that's *your* problem," is one of the more cruel statements we make to one another. It stems from an attitude of uninvolvement. We consciously steer clear of getting involved with other people's problems and pain. What a hard world it is when each of us must shoulder his or her own load, when no one else will listen or even sense that we are in pain.

Not so with those who seek to fulfill the law of Christ. We are to bear one another's burdens. Our way is to get involved, to try to know something of the needs of other and to offer to share in the solving of their problems. It is the way of Christ to offer healing, forgiveness and new life to those lives which are shriveled with disease, sin or despair. As followers of Christ we must seek to alleviate human suffering wherever we find it. On a day to day basis this means responding to pleas for help from friend and neighbor, and from those in our own families. It means being willing to get involved in helping others through their difficult times. It means being a good listener, and sometimes to be a silent companion standing with someone who is experiencing grief

How thankful we can be that there are Christian friends and loved ones in our own lives who are willing to help us bear our burdens from time to time. Those who pass through the "valley of the shadow of death" during serious illness know the depth of caring and prayerful fellowship which their church provides them in such times.

PRAYER: Help me, Lord, to get involved in the lives of others when they experience pain and suffering. And I thank you for the caring love I receive from others. In Christ. Amen

⌐ ⌐ ⌐ ⌐ ⌐ ⌐

NOVEMBER 30

PRAYER IS BEING AWARE

Pray without ceasing.
—I Thessalonians 5:17

READ: I Thessalonians 5:9-28 and Psalm 90:1-2

It is a normal human trait to want to be near people we like, and it is the highest of human desires to want always to be with the one we love. When that is not possible we make phone calls, write letters, e-mail, or do whatever else we can to approximate being together. Indeed the presence of the one we love often pervades our life whether the loved one is near or far.

So it is with the Christian's relationship with God. Our love for God should make us want to be with God all the time, to keep in constant communication with God. If our love for God is strong the divine presence becomes a pervasive reality in our lives twenty-four hours a day.

When Paul wrote to the Christians in Thessalonica to instruct them to pray continually, he was thinking of the way in which the Christian can be constantly aware of God's presence. This is not so much a special signal or some sort of holy glow, as it is an underlying assumption or recognition that God is involved in my life all the time. To pray without ceasing is to keep such a thought alive, to cultivate one's consciousness in such a way as to consider more and more frequently God's Being, and God's loving care and guidance, so that no matter what is going on in one's life, the divine dimension figures into our thinking, and our decision-making. The Old Testament often affirms God as our "dwelling place." "Lord, you have been our dwelling place in all generations." (Psalm 90:1) The late Paul Tillich, referred to God as the Ground of our being."

And so, we pray continually, thus relating always to the One who loves us, and whom we love.

PRAYER: For your constancy, I give you thanks, O Lord. You are always with me. In Christ. Amen.

DECEMBER

DECEMBER 1

IMMANUEL

Therefore the Lord himself will give you a sign. Look, the young woman is with child and shall bear a son, and shall name him Immanuel.

—Isaiah 7:14

READ: Isaiah 7:10-17

One of the most basic of human needs is a spiritual one. It is to experience a closeness to God. Some have found a partial answer to this need in mountain climbing. Others find some closeness after long periods of fasting and meditation. Still others seek to experience the divine dimension of life through various kinds of "New Age" techniques and group experiences.

The happy thing about anticipating Christmas is that through it we declare that God comes to us in a very special and complete way. God chose to come and to be with us through the person of Jesus Christ. Long before Christmas, the prophet, Isaiah, realized that God would some day assist us in our quest by appearing in our midst as Immanuel—God with us. Now with December here the season of Advent is being celebrated. In this season of expectation we joyously look forward to a renewed closeness to God to be found in the coming of Jesus into our lives.

While you begin to think of plans and preparations for the Christmas season, let the celebration of Advent keep your mind firmly set upon the anticipation of God's greatest gift to humankind, the gift of God's Son, Jesus Christ, our Lord and Savior. Let the word from the prophet, Isaiah, IMMANUEL, ring in your mind and heart as your December song!

"O come, O come, Emmanuel . . . ."

PRAYER: Come into our lives, O God, through your son, our Lord Jesus Christ. Help us to see you more clearly as you come to us in Jesus' advent. In Christ. Amen.

~ ~ ~ ~ ~ ~

DECEMBER 2

THE LORD IS OUR RIGHTEOUSNESS

> In those days Judah will be saved and Jerusalem will live in safety. And this is the name by which it will be called: "The Lord is our righteousness."
>
> —Jeremiah 33:16

READ: Jeremiah 33:14-16

There are so many tragic items in the news to consider each day. The most distressing news stories have to do with hurt and injustice which people and nations bring upon each other, doing violence, or dealing unfairly in one way or another. Sometimes we come to the point of wondering if there are any good people left, and whether good will ever triumph over evil. The good news of the advent of Christmas is that God promises and assures us that ultimately good will conquer evil, justice will be done, love will be victorious over hatred, and right will win over wrong. That is what the coming of God's Son, Christ, means to us. Jesus Christ is the one perfect human being, through whom God brings his righteousness and shows perfect love in a world needing justice, goodness, and love.

Jeremiah looked forward to this hope, when he declared that

God's action (God's Son) would be named "RIGHTEOUSNESS." For Jeremiah this meant the restoration of the nation, Judah, and the safety of Jerusalem. For us this means the restoration of right relationship with God and reconciliation with each other. What better Christmas gift to anticipate!

PRAYER: Bring your goodness to us, O God. Show us your loving kindness. Bring your justice into our world, your righteousness into our lives. Through Christ, our Lord. Amen.

~ ~ ~ ~ ~ ~

DECEMBER 3

WONDERFUL COUNSELOR, MIGHTY GOD
EVERLASTING FATHER, PRINCE OF PEACE

For a child has been born for us, a son given to us; authority rests upon his shoulders; and he is named Wonderful Counselor, Mighty God, Everlasting Father, Prince of Peace.

—Isaiah 9:6

READ: Isaiah 9:2-7 and Philippians 2:9-11

The apostle Paul knew that the name of Jesus was the greatest name in all the world, because of what God does for the world through Jesus Christ. In Christ God saves us. In Jesus God comes to us providing a closeness to himself, and through Christ God brings goodness and love to humankind. For we believe that Jesus Christ is in fact God!

Isaiah proclaimed that Jesus is the Wonderful Counselor, Mighty God, Everlasting Father, Prince of Peace. What more can be said? As counselor Jesus meets us in our own lives and assists us with our personal problems. With power everlasting Christ rules the world and promises to bring peace.

During this wonderful time of Advent we anticipate the coming of God's power and love, God's redeeming grace and guiding force, through which ultimate justice and peace will be given.

PRAYER: Glory to you, O God. Humbly, we look forward to the gift of your love in the Christ Child. In Christ. Amen.

~ ~ ~ ~ ~ ~

DECEMBER 4

AMOS AND JOHN

Again Jesus spoke to them, saying, "I am the light of the world. Whoever follows me will never walk in darkness but will have the light of life."

—John 8:12

READ: Amos 5:14-20 And John 8:12-18

Darkness can be dangerous and confusing. If you have ever had to drive somewhere in the darkness of a severe dust storm or through dense fog, you know how confusing it is not to know where the road is, and to realize that in any moment you could hit another vehicle. Or worse yet, a pedestrian. When the dust settles or the fog clears the light of day makes all the difference. With a clear view ahead you are safe and you know the way to go.

The prophet Amos used the image of darkness to describe how it feels to be separated from God and to live in a way that God does not want. Dark and gloomy days do make one feel unhappy and sad. That is how it feels to disappoint God when we forget about him or do not do as he intends for us. Without God's Word we live in darkness, because we find it difficult to know God and to do God's will.

Jesus uses the idea of darkness and light to show us that he has come into the world to reveal to us how to live as God intends us to live. In this way Jesus brings light into our lives and into our world. Without him it is dark, dangerous and confusing. With Jesus it is light, safe, and guided. In that light we have joy because we know God's intention for us, and in Christ we can seek to fulfill God's will.

PRAYER: O Christ, Light of the world, shine into my heart and mind today, as I prepare for your birth. Amen

~ ~ ~ ~ ~ ~

DECEMBER 5

JEREMIAH AND PAUL

> But Jesus has now obtained a more excellent ministry,
> and to that degree he is the mediator of a better covenant,
> which has been enacted through better promises.
>
> —Hebrews 8:6

READ: Jeremiah 31:31-34 and I Corinthians 11:23-26

The Old Testament is filled with many detailed rules and regulations which were thought to be necessary for pleasing God. By the time of the prophet Jeremiah, many of the rules had been broken and people were not loving God or each other as God had intended. Jeremiah said that the time would come when God would speak to the hearts of people and help them to follow God's will. Pleasing God would be a matter of the heart, not of regulations.

This is a very precious promise, for that is exactly what we desire. We want to know in our hearts how God wants us to live and to have implanted in our wills the desire to follow God's leading.

Before Jesus was crucified he gave his disciples a special way of staying in touch with him. We call this Communion. When he announced what this Holy Supper would mean he took the idea which Jeremiah had spoken of, the idea of a new covenant between us and God, in which Jesus promises to come into our hearts and to bind us to God in a special way. In this way we can know God more fully. In Advent we eagerly anticipate the new covenant which is initiated in Jesus' birth.

PRAYER: Come into our hearts Lord Jesus. Bind us to you and reveal your will for our living. Amen.

~ ~ ~ ~ ~ ~

DECEMBER 6

EZEKIEL AND JOHN

"I am the good shepherd. The good shepherd lays down his life for the sheep."

—John 10:11

READ: Ezekiel 34:7-16 and John 10:7-18

The prophet Ezekiel felt that the leaders of his people had not taken good care of the nation. They had been like bad shepherds who did not protect their sheep from wild animals or keep them from wandering away and becoming lost. The people depended upon their leaders to keep them in good relationship to God. The leaders had failed them.

We depend upon ministers and Bible teachers to help us understand God's will, and we trust them to do a good job. It is tragic when the leaders whom we trust fail us. When such a failure occurred Ezekiel promised that God would be our good shepherd.

As we look forward to Jesus' birth, we are reminded of the many ways in which he takes care of our deepest needs. Jesus declared that he was the good shepherd, and that we are his sheep. In this way Jesus leads us through life, protects us from the many hazards in life, and loves us as a shepherd loves his sheep.

In Advent we anticipate the Good Shepherd who fulfills all our needs and desires.

PRAYER: Thank you, Lord, for being my good shepherd. In Christ. Amen.

~ ~ ~ ~ ~ ~

DECEMBER 7

ISAIAH AND JOHN

> "Peace I leave with you; my peace I give to you. I do not give to you as the world gives. Do not let your hearts be troubled and do not let them be afraid."
>
> —John 14:27

READ: Isaiah 52:7-12 and John 14:25-31

Before modern communications technologies, which began with the telegraph, messages had to come in person by heralds or messengers. The last of such personal messengers were the Western Union messengers who brought telegrams to one's door. In Isaiah's time the people under Babylonian captivity looked for messengers to bring good news. The prophet Isaiah announced that such a joyful message was coming! "How beautiful upon the mountains are the feet of the messenger who announces peace, who brings good news . . . ." (Isaiah 52:7) Such good news meant that the people would soon be free to go back to Jerusalem. The exiles, the hostages, could soon return home.

The most beautiful messenger of peace is Jesus Christ. He brings us an inner peace that can't be found in any other way. He sets us at ease with God, makes us feel good about ourselves, and gives us the mind and attitude with which to love each other. Anticipating Christmas is looking forward to peace, reconciliation with God and our brothers and sisters. "And on earth peace!" sang the angels.

PRAYER: Let there be peace, O Lord, and let it begin with Jesus' birth. In Christ. Amen.

~ ~ ~ ~ ~

DECEMBER 8

THE RED GLOW OF EARLIEST DAWNING

> But the angel said to him, "Do not be afraid, Zechariah,
> for your prayer has been heard. Your wife Elizabeth will
> bear you a son, and you will name him John."
> —Luke 1:13

READ: Luke 1:1-17

The liturgical colors for Advent worship should really be red, orange, yellow and gold. These are the colors of the advent of each day—sunrise as it progresses into the fullness of day. Red is the first sign of dawning, especially when there are clouds in the sky. In fact the most beautiful of sunrises are those when there are some clouds to illuminate and reflect. The clouds of pre-dawn which stretch across the horizon provide the canvas upon which the sun paints its streaks of red, as its first choice of color from its pallet for the day.

Traditionally red has symbolized courage and sacrifice, for we have connected these attributes of the human spirit to the color of blood. As the sunrise symbolizes the coming of Christ, red points ahead to his courageous sacrifice upon the cross to show God's unlimited and unconditional love for each of us. Older theologies emphasized the blood of Christ in his sacrifice by which forgiveness is purchased. The anticipation of that sacrifice was seen in many references to blood in the Old Testament.

The clouds upon which the colors of the sunrise are most beautifully painted symbolize for us the troubled and turbulent horizons of our lives. One's sky is never completely cloudless for any of us. But it is the light of Christ which shines upon our troubles that brings the beauty of the red glow of earliest dawning. This is the beauty of Advent.

PRAYER: O, coming Christ, dawn upon our troubled lives ad turn our turbulence into the red glow of courage for a new day. Amen.

~ ~ ~ ~ ~

DECEMBER 9

THE FIERY ORANGE OF SUNRISE

> The angel replied, "I am Gabriel. I stand in the presence of God, and I have been sent to speak to you and to bring you this good news."
>
> —Luke 1:19

READ: Luke 1:18-35

In announcing the birth of John, Luke prepares us for the coming of Christ, who is Jesus of Nazareth, the cousin of John. Those to whom Luke first wrote the story of John's birth knew of John the Baptist's preaching in the wilderness, "Repent, for the kingdom of heaven has come near." (Matthew 3:2) He was a fiery preacher and did indeed fire up many followers who changed their ways and became prepared to accept the new message of life which Jesus would bring to them. His fiery prophetic preaching also inflamed the King who ultimately executed him for his fire!

It is appropriate to see the orange of the sunrise as symbolizing the fiery message by which John preached repentance and the coming of Christ to bring in his new kingdom of the forgiven. The message of repentance is a message of radical transformation, like the change from night to day at sunrise. In the orange of sunrise the inevitable day is foreseen. There will be no turning back to night now. Unlike sunset, sunrise points to the bright light of day which is coming very soon. This is the advent of the kingdom of light coming.

The coming of Christ in Advent begs life change in each of us. When Christ enters your life things will be different, never again to return to the old corridors of darkness. The fiery orange of sunrise has a way of purging us of the last grip of sleep, as it awakens us to new vigor. So with the advent of Christ!

In the beauty of sunrise is the fiery orange of transformation from dark to light, from sin to salvation, from the kingdoms of this world to the kingdom of God.

PRAYER: O coming Christ, bring the fiery orange of the transforming sunrise into my life so that my heart might burn with love for you and for the world. Amen.

~ ~ ~ ~ ~ ~

DECEMBER 10

THE YELLOW RAYS OF DAYBREAK

His mercy is for those who fear him from generation to generation.

—Luke 1:50

READ: Luke 1:39-56

One of the most poetic expressions of our anticipation of Christ's coming into the world is Mary's Song. Luke gives it to us in his first chapter. She sings of great things which God causes to happen in the coming of Christ: justice and mercy would be brought to the human condition. Into a world darkened by greed, injustice, warfare and hatred, the bright yellow rays of daybreak are shining forth as Christ enters in fulfillment of God's promises.

Although the sky was darkened at the time of Jesus' crucifixion, three days later when the yellow rays of daybreak filled the sky, the resurrection of Christ changed the course of human history.

During Advent God's people anticipate Jesus Christ. He will ultimately defeat the forces of evil in the world through his death and resurrection. Advent gives us the assurance that God is moving things from confusion and discord to harmony and unity. His love and justice are gaining victory over hatred and violence, injustice and oppression. Even while we wait for such change to come we are assured of God's ultimate victory. The eye of faith sees that victory in the yellow rays of a new day.

PRAYER: O coming Christ bring justice and righteousness, mercy and love as in the yellow rays of a new day dawning. Amen

～ ～ ～ ～ ～ ～

DECEMBER 11

THE GOLDEN SUNLIGHT OF A NEW DAY

Blessed be the Lord God of Israel, for he has looked favorably on his people and redeemed them. He has raised up a mighty savior for us in the house of his servant, David.
—Luke 1:68-69

READ: Luke 1:59-80

In the story of the birth of John the Baptist as told in the first chapter of Luke, it is clear that this very special child would play an important role in the drama of God's salvation for Israel, and for all humankind as well. John was to be the herald of the King who was coming to save the world. "And you, child, will be called the prophet of the Most High; for you will go before the Lord to prepare his ways." (Luke 1:76)

The final color of the dawn is gold. The golden color stretches over the entire sky—clouds included. The dawn has reached its fulness. The sun is up. Both the color of gold and the image of the sun have long symbolized the King. And so it is that with the golden light of dawn the King of heaven and earth appears—Jesus Christ, the Lord and King of all creation. "By the tender mercy of our God, the dawn from on high will break upon us, to give light to those who sit in darkness, and in the shadow of death, to guide our feet into the way of peace." (Luke 1:78-79)

Let the golden light of each dawn which we experience symbolize the coming of Christ the King into our world each day. Let Advent be the time when we wait for the King of Light.

PRAYER: O coming Christ, I want you to be the sun of my soul, the King in my life, to rule and protect, and to vanquish all evil in the world.

~ ~ ~ ~ ~ ~

DECEMBER 12

GOOD ROOT STOCK

> "I am the vine, you are the branches. Those who abide
> in me and I in them bear much fruit, because apart from me
> you can do nothing.
>
> —John 15:5

READ: Isaiah 11:1-10 and John 15:1-11

When riding through London on a double decker bus, among the interesting sights are the rose trees, oftentimes in the center of symmetrical gardens in the front of houses. These are domestic roses four of five feet above ground growing out of a sturdy straight small tree trunk, the result of some careful grafting. Apparently domestic roses are typically the result of grafting tender rose branches onto good root stock. Similarly commercial orchards use healthy root stock onto which young fruit trees are grafted.

Baptism is the engrafting of a person onto good root stock. The Old Testament scriptures referred to the advent of the Messiah as the one coming from the root of Jesse, the father of King David. The New Testament recognizes Jesus as the one into whom the Christian is engrafted. The sign of this engrafting is baptism, marking the beginning of the new life in Christ.

The symbolism of root, vine and branch is full of implications for us. From the very beginning, as marked by our baptism, we are continually nourished with life-giving spiritual nutrients which come from Christ, our root. John, in giving us the image of the vine and the branches, sees Jesus as the Word made flesh. Certainly it is feeding upon the Word through the Bible which nourishes us so that we might blossom and bear fruit.

Engrafting into Christ brings us into close fellowship with all the other branches which comprise the church, Christ's body. Baptism is the sign of our welcome and entry into Christ's family. All Christians are thus brothers and sisters.

PRAYER: O Christ be my root, nourish me, let my life blossom, and may I bear good fruit for you. Amen

~ ~ ~ ~ ~ ~

DECEMBER 13

FAR AS THE CURSE IS FOUND

In those days Jesus came from Nazareth of Galilee and was baptized by John in the Jordan.

—Mark 1:9

READ: Mark 1:1-11

"When were you born again?" This is always an awkward question for those who have grown up in the church. One true answer to such a question is to give the date of your baptism, even if that was as an infant. Baptism marks the forgiveness of sins and the cleansing of a person for a new life in Christ, the washing away of the old and the beginning of the new.

Advent is a good time to remember our baptism. Baptism is a sign for us to rest easy in faith. God has provided for our forgiveness, which is always available to us. Baptism assures us that we don't have to do something great and good to atone for our sins. All we have to do is to admit our errors before God, and accept in faith his gracious pardon. What a good feeling this gives us about God, and about ourselves.

The question posed to us about the date of our being born again can threaten our certainty in the faith. If we can't point to a date we remember, we are given the impression that we lack something crucial, or worse yet, that we are not "saved." Remembering our baptism and what that means can reassure us that nothing is missing. In Baptism God has done it all through Christ's sacrifice. In Advent we celebrate the coming of such assurance.

In the familiar Christmas carol we sing "No more let sins and sorrows grow./ He comes to make his blessings flow/ Far as the curse is found."

PRAYER: O coming Christ, thank you for your promise of forgiveness and new birth. Amen

~ ~ ~ ~ ~

DECEMBER 14

DESPAIR INTO HOPE

Now faith is the assurance of things hoped for, the conviction of things not seen.

—Hebrews 11:11

READ: Hebrews 11:1-16

Late fall stretching into early December can be a time of desolation, at least in terms of nature, for everything appears to be dormant and asleep. The earth remains brown and gray except for snow. There is little sign of life—a depletion of hope, it seems. But we don't have to remain in such a negative frame of mind. For Christians, December is a time of profound hope because of Advent.

Advent is a season of hope, hope for a new beginning. Hope for seed-time and a harvest of good. How often we wish we had another chance. To do it all over again—right. Jesus Christ comes with that promise. With forgiveness for past mistakes, and guidance for a new start. His life, death, and resurrection give us faith to stake our lives on his new beginning for us. The faith he engenders in us is the basis for knowing that a new chance at life is ours in Christ. In this way Advent turns our despair into hope.

PRAYER: O coming Christ, bring to me a new start in life. Forgive me for my mistakes, indeed for my sin, and by your mercy place me on a new pathway. Amen

DECEMBER 15

PEACE BEYOND DISCORD

> Come now, let us argue it out, says the Lord: though your sins are like scarlet, they shall be like snow; though they are red like crimson, they shall become like wool.
> —Isaiah 1:18

READ: Isaiah 55:10-13

There is something very peaceful about a snowfall, especially when there is no wind. The silence and the hypnotic effect of the flakes gently floating to earth, the pure white covering, and the softness of the fluffy coating give one the impression of perfect peace. Often in the northern hemisphere the first full snowfall comes during Advent. Snow, as a sign of peace is doubly meaningful to the Christian during this season.

Isaiah uses snow to depict forgiveness; forgiven of sin we are whiter than snow, he said. Peace and forgiveness go together. Without forgiveness there can be no peace in our hearts. In fact it is often unforgiven sin which festers and causes us to be resentful and cantankerous—anything but peaceful—with each other. When we finally come to accept God's forgiveness and can feel good about ourselves, we find that we feel better about each other, and we are more apt to relate to each other in peace and harmony.

The snowfall in the Advent season symbolizes forgiveness and denotes peace. Advent is the season in which we look ahead to the ultimate coming of peace, when we are set right with God and with each other.

PRAYER: Prince of Peace, come into my heart, and bring me peace.
Amen

~ ~ ~ ~ ~

DECEMBER 16

MOURNING BECOMES JOY

Weeping may linger for the night, but joy comes with the morning.
—Psalm 30:5

"I have said these things to you so that my joy may be in you, and that your joy may be complete.
—John 15:11

READ: Psalm 30:1-5 And John 15:9-15

So much sorrow in our lives is connected with loss. We mourn the death of a loved one, or when we are plunged into deep sadness when a relationship is broken. When we are rejected by someone important to us we are grief stricken. The loss of physical or mental capacities in the course of life causes poignant sorrow. The Psalmist speaks of tears at nightfall. Anyone who has ever experienced grief over serious loss knows that often it is during the night that loneliness is most difficult to bear.

The onset of winter is like the falling of night, for its privations often keep us from frequent associations with those whom we love. There is thus something lonely about winter when the severity of the elements keeps us indoors for long periods of time.

But the Psalmist declares that joy comes in the morning, as many a lonely person can testify. The sunlight of a new day can make one's mourning turn to joy—at least momentarily.

Advent points to an eternal morning when the coming of Jesus Christ presents us with a new day, a day in which the mourning and sadness of our lives can become joy. Many Christian folk over the centuries have found that a relationship with Jesus Christ can go a long way in making up for whatever loss of relationship they may have mourned. With such a relationship with Jesus Christ, Wonderful Counselor, and Friend, our mourning becomes joy.

PRAYER: O coming Christ, bring daybreak to my life. Turn whatever sadness I have into gladness, my mourning into joy. Amen

~ ~ ~ ~ ~

DECEMBER 17

RAISED FROM DEATH TO LIFE

What you sow does not come to life unless it dies. And as for what you sow, you do not sow the body that is to be, but a bare seed . . .

—I Corinthians 15:36,37

READ: I Corinthians 15:20-22 and Luke 2:1-20

Winterbourne is a tiny rivulet of water which begins to run in the cold of winter when all else is still frozen. Christmas is an infant's cry of life in the night of human suffering, the birth of a child in the midst of the death of the aged. It is God's lively love coming to thaw the ice of frozen humanity. Christmas is winterbourne in the midst of winter. That is why for those of us living in the northern hemisphere it does not seem like Christmas unless there is snow.

The Christian church over the centuries has celebrated Christmas with such joy because of our resurrection faith. We know that Christ conquered death for us on Easter morn. Sometime between the years 274 and 336 in Rome, December 25 was chosen for the festival of the birth of Christ, presumably because December 25 was the winter solstice on which the birthday of the sun was observed by the Romans.

Thus, when the long nights of winter begin to turn toward the lengthening sun of summer, the winterbourne begins to run, we celebrate the birth of the Son of righteousness who comes to turn the long winter of human misery into the summer of God's grace when we are raised from death to life.

PRAYER: O coming Christ, raise me from whatever in me is sinful and dead, and cause me to rise to new heights of living with God's grace flowing in me. Amen

DECEMBER 18

A CHILD IS BORN

A child has been born for us, a son given to us; authority rests upon his shoulders . . .

—Isaiah 9:6

READ: Isaiah 9:2-7

It wasn't too uncommon in the ancient world for people who

yearned for a better life to anticipate the birth of a child-king, who would miraculously lead them into some new era of peace and prosperity. Thus it was that the prophet, Isaiah, spoke to the people of Judah about a future king, who would be born a child, destined to lead God's chosen people into a new golden age.

During Advent we look forward to the coming of the Child of Bethlehem, and like the people of Isaiah's time, we are eager to have that child become our ruler. We know from the gospel stories of Jesus that he is indeed the one to follow. In following Jesus we are assured that our lives are in tune with what God our Creator wants, for Jesus is the son of God, the king in God's new kingdom.

May the remaining days of December be our time to prepare our hearts for Christ's coming, and to yield our wills for his ruling.

PRAYER: O coming Christ, come and be my King, ruling my life with love and righteousness. Amen.

~ ~ ~ ~ ~ ~

DECEMBER 19

BECOMING CHILDREN

"Truly I tell you, unless your change and become like children, you will never enter the kingdom of heaven."
—Matthew 18:3

READ: Matthew 18:1-7

Many people say, "Christmas is for the children." On the surface this sounds nice, and makes us think of the wonder and excitement of children aglow with the lights of the Christmas tree reflecting upon their smooth young faces. And somehow the rest of us wish we could be children again.

The fact of the matter is that Jesus is asking us to become like children in order to accept his kingdom and his rule in our lives. He wants us to place ourselves in his care as a child would, eagerly and unashamedly to expect blessings from him as a child would, and in the innocense of childhood to acknowledge God as our Parent.

Christmas is for those who put away their own urge to rule others and their inflated pride, Only then do we have the eager openness with which to ask to be God's child. Christmas is for those who can kneel before the Babe of Bethlehem and ask him to be their Parent.

PRAYER: O coming Christ, take me by your hand that I may be your child. Amen.

DECEMBER 20

DARKNESS DISPELLED BY FIRE

> And by night with a pillar of fire, to give them light on the way which they should go.
> —Nehemiah 9:12

READ: John 1:1-9

December is the darkest of months. It is in December, toward the end of Advent, when the shortest day of the year occurs. "It's getting dark so early!" Is a common expression of the season. In our modern technological society the progressing darkness of this time of year presents no problem. We merely use more electricity. But to the ancients the night was a source of danger and confusion. It was not easy to light up much darkness in those days, to illuminate one's journey.

However, the Israelites were given direction for their wandering in the wilderness both night and day. The scriptural account refers to the "pillar of fire," which gave them light for their safe passage during the long nights of their journey. They affirmed that it was God who gave them this direction and protection on their way to the promised land.

During the long nights of our journey through life we also

need God's protection and guidance. We need light to dispel life's darkness. Christians believe, as John the Baptist declared, that Jesus Christ is the light to dispel darkness. In Advent we celebrate the coming of God's illumination into our dark world. That's why candles are so much a part of Advent, and in the Christmas celebrations throughout the season.

Through Christ we see life more clearly. He shows us the way to live, and by his light we are given protection from whatever might rob us of God's saving love. In Advent we look to the light which is coming into the world—Jesus Christ.

PRAYER: O coming Christ, illumine my pathway, enlighten my mind, brighten my life. Amen

~ ~ ~ ~ ~ ~

DECEMBER 21

A CHILD SHALL LEAD

And a little child shall lead them.
—Isaiah 11:6

READ: Isaiah 11:1-10

The coyote, long popular as a symbol of the old west, is not popular with the new west, so to speak. The coyote is a predator which is a danger to sheep. This concerns western ranchers. The reintroduction of the wolf into the Yellowstone ecosystem poses a similar threat to the lives of sheep in the area, especially lambs. Even close to town, sheep can be endangered by vicious dogs, supposedly domesticated. In contrast, notice that Isaiah prophecies a day when the wolf and the lamb will dwell together, as well as the leopard and the goat, the calf and the lion, and the cow and the bear.

In other words, peace is coming, a gift of God so great that it will extend to the world of nature. Christ is seen as the Prince of Peace, the little Child who shall lead us into a peaceable kingdom.

As you think of the many tensions and conflicts which make up your life, ponder the effect of the Christ child can have upon those pressure spots in your life. He will reconcile us to each other and keep us from doing harm to one another. He will take the predator instinct out of our lives. Such is the promise of Isaiah.

Let this season of Advent be a time when you allow the love of God to work its wonderful peacemaking effect upon your relationships with others. Pray also for the coming of peace among nations when the suicide bombs in the Middle East, and violent acts of terror throughout the world shall cease. Such prayer is not in vain, the promises of Isaiah assure us!

PRAYER: O, Prince of Peace, come into our lives this day and bring us together again with those whose lives may be at cross purposes with ours in any way. Amen.

~ ~ ~ ~ ~ ~

DECEMBER 22

OF SUCH BELONGS THE KINGDOM

But Jesus said, "Let the little children come to me, and do not stop them; for it is to such as these that the kingdom of heaven belongs.

—Matthew 19:14

READ: Matthew 19:13-15

Children are always being urged to act like adults, to behave in a grown-up fashion. From the standpoint of Jesus' words in this story in Matthew such a sudden transition into adulthood would be a shame, for Jesus is taking the child as a model for the adult to emulate. He is urging grown-ups to become like children in order to enter his kingdom. What does he mean by that?

It is the simple trustfulness of a child which should be our way of accepting God's offer of grace and love, forgiveness and salvation. We ought to accept on face value God's promise to lead us into a new life. Like a child who does not know where his mother or father leads, we must trust Christ to lead us into new pathways of life known only to God.

Toward the end of Advent we think of those who came to see the Christ child. The simple naivete of the shepherds, trusting the song of promise of the angels, left their flocks to come to the Christ child. In a strange way, when they came to pay homage to the Christ child they themselves became like little children. In that act of trustful homage, they entered the kingdom of heaven!

PRAYER: In humble and innocent trust, O God, I accept your love and power to lead me all the way into your kingdom. Through the Christ child. Amen.

~ ~ ~ ~ ~ ~

DECEMBER 23

BORN THY PEOPLE TO DELIVER

He (the Lord) will rejoice over you with gladness, he
will renew you in his love.

—Zephaniah 3:17

READ: Zephaniah 3:14-18 and I Peter 2:9-10

One's identity is a problem for many persons today. We speak of someone going through an identity crisis. Certain aspects of our lives give us our identity. "Tell me about yourself." "Well, first of all, I'm an office secretary." One's job or profession is usually first. Sometimes it is family that provides identity—what our children have accomplished, or who our parents were. Lots of times we are confused as to our truly meaningful identity. Much talk about identity crises has been popular in self-help books.

One of the significant promises of this season is that Jesus comes to us to give us a new IDENTITY. "Once you were not a people, but now you are God's people." (I Peter 2:10)

The Christian's identity is found in God's calling us to become a part of God's people—the church of Jesus Christ. This new identity gives you roots in God's creation and in Christ's call to discipleship. You are given a new work to do, a new profession to follow, that of proclaiming God's love through what you do and say. This new life in Christ gives you new family identity—brothers and sisters in Christ with a new Parent. Once a small child who had grown up in a Christian home and church was asked what she would do if something happened to her parents. Her reply was that her church would be her family and would take care of her.

The identity which Christ provides gives us a future—that is the ultimate victory with Christ and inclusion in the eternal and everlasting kingdom of God. What better identity could one ask for?

PRAYER: I thank you for my new name in Christ, for new work to do, a new family in which to live, and for a future filled with hope. In Christ. Amen.

~ ~ ~ ~ ~

DECEMBER 24

HAIL THE HEAVEN-BORN PRINCE OF PEACE

> While they were there, the time came for her to deliver her child. And she gave birth to her firstborn son.
>
> —Luke 2:6,7

READ: Isaiah 9:6 and Luke 1:46-55

There is a very special stillness about the night before Christmas. It is delightfully mystical. All the stores have finally closed. The blaring advertising has finally ceased. The frenzied preparations are over. Those who have traveled to be with family have arrived. And in the stillness of this night of nights our waiting has come to an end. In the blessed story, Joseph and Mary have arrived in Bethlehem and have come to the inn and they too are waiting for a few more moments. All is ready. All is quiet. It is a holy night.

This mystical feeling of quiet readiness symbolizes the coming of the Prince of Peace into our world and into our own lives. Jesus comes putting into perspective all of life's efforts, helping us achieve some measure of stability, and he provides us with a calmness which is most refreshing.

With the shutting of the shops and sunset on December 24th, Christmas has finally come!

"And suddenly there was with the angel a multitude of the heavenly host, praising God and saying, 'Glory to God in the highest heaven, and on earth peace among those whom he favors!'" (Luke 2:13-14)

PRAYER: In the holy stillness of this night make me ready for Christ to come into my life and my world. In him, I pray. Amen.

~ ~ ~ ~ ~ ~

DECEMBER 25

CHRISTMAS!

So they went with haste and found Mary and Joseph,
and the child lying in the manger.

—Luke 2:16

READ: Luke 2:1-20

The long wait for Mary and Joseph finally had come to a glorious end. Their first child was born. From that day onward their lives would be changed drastically. A birth in the family always changes things markedly. The entrance of another human being on the face of the earth is an event of wonder and importance. The coming of God in human form in the birth of Jesus is more wonderful and more important than any other event in human history.

And so our long wait for Christmas is over. Have you ever felt let down when Christmas finally comes? Or perhaps on the day after? Do not let that happen this year. Allow the birth of the baby Jesus to change things radically in your life. From this day onward allow him room in your life, to be a participant in every event and an influence upon your every decision. "And all who heard it were amazed at what the shepherds told them. But Mary treasured all these words and pondered them in her heart". (Luke 2:18-19)

Let us, like the shepherds, spend our days glorifying and praising God for all that we have heard and seen, as it has been told to us.

PRAYER: Come into my life, Lord Jesus, I pray. Come into our lives and stay! In Him Amen.

~ ~ ~ ~ ~

DECEMBER 26

LOVE

"For God so loved the world that he gave his only Son, so that everyone who believes in him may not perish but may have eternal life."

—John 3:16

READ: John 1:14, 29-34

More than anything else the coming of Christ is the coming of love into the world in a new and profound way. Jesus is the gift of God's love to us. He loved others in a way which was perfect and not at all self-seeking, as our love can so easily be. He inspires love for one another within the fellowship of his followers then and since—a fellowship of love not found in many other groupings of people.

Such love is expressed in a variety of ways at Christmastime. At its best, the giving of gifts is an act of love. Singing carols to shut-ins, sharing food with the hungry, exchanging of cards and messages with friends of years gone by, and the overall congeniality of the season all testify to the presence of love as the basic element of this season of Christmas

Because the giving of the Christ-child is seen as God's gift of love, so ought we to place in the lives of others our gift of love to them. Now that God has initiated the perfect gift of love for all time, our loving ought to be not only during this season but in all our days to come.

PRAYER: We thank you for your unlimited love for us in the gift of gifts—Jesus Christ, your Son, our savior. Because of him may I love others today and in my tomorrows as well. Through Christ. Amen.

DECEMBER 27

PAYING HIM HOMAGE

On entering the house, they saw the child with Mary
his mother; and they knelt down and paid him homage.
—Matthew 2:11

READ: Zechariah 2:11-13 and Matthew 2:1-2, 9-11

After the very last days of the Babylonian captivity of the people of Israel, the prophet, Zechariah, assured the people that once again they would have God's presence with them. In exile they felt separated from God, with whom they had felt close when they dwelled in Jerusalem. Now, forced to lived a long way from the Temple, they yearned for God's presence.

Many times in our lives we wish God would be near us, but we feel distant from God. God's gift of Jesus to us is the gift of God's presence in our midst. The promise is fulfilled. Now God is with us always.

The wise men came to the Christ Child from a region to the East, where the Babylonian captives had been held. They recognized in the child, Jesus, the presence of God. They knelt before him and paid him homage—they worshiped him. Now from wherever we come, out of whatever captivity we have been held, we kneel before the Christ, we pay him homage. We worship him. Our New Born King!

PRAYER: We sing and shout for joy, O God. You have come to us, and you will remain with us in Christ Jesus, Our Lord, and through your Holy Spirit. In Christ. Amen.

~ ~ ~ ~ ~

DECEMBER 28

A LIGHT TO REVEAL GOD'S LOVE

". . . my eyes have seen your salvation, which you have prepared in the presence of all your peoples, a light for revelation to the Gentiles and for glory to your people Israel."

—Luke 2:30-32

READ: Luke 2:22-35

As an important part of celebrating Jesus' birth, Mary and Joseph brought him to the Temple in Jerusalem for the appropriate rituals of birth. While there, a devout man named Simeon saw the child. He recognized in the child God's salvation for all the world. Simeon proclaimed his faith concerning Jesus—that this child would be a light to reveal God's will.

No better description of Jesus' life and ministry among us can be found than, that he is a light to reveal God's will. In his teaching, through his healing of suffering, in the kindness with which he dealt with friend and enemy alike, in his self-sacrifice upon the cross and in his preparation of the disciples for their task of carrying on the work, Jesus brought so perfectly to us the intention of God for the world. For Simeon to perceive all this at the time of Jesus' infancy is indeed a miracle of faith.

In a sense each new life given to us provides us with an overwhelming awareness of the possibilities in one tiny human life. As parents hold their child at baptism, the potential for that child to become a faithful and obedient servant of Christ is affirmed by the church. As each of us remembers his or her own baptism, we are called to re-commitment to such promises.

The birth of the Christ-child indeed brings all the light we shall ever need—the light of God's will for our lives. This is the message of Christmastide.

PRAYER: Now, Lord, you have fulfilled your promise of light to us in Christ. Let me live in his light. In Christ. Amen.

~ ~ ~ ~ ~ ~

DECEMBER 29

SOME BROUGHT GIFTS

On entering the house, they saw the child with Mary

his mother: . . . . Then, opening their treasure chests, they offered him gifts of gold, frankincense, and myrrh.

—Matthew 2:11

READ: Matthew 2:1-12

It is a very normal reaction to a significant event to bring a gift. A housewarming, a birthday, and anniversary, a retirement, even a death—all occasions when we are apt to bring gifts. The more valued the person or our relationship with him or her is, the more valued the gift we bring. Matthew tells us that the strangers from the east who came to see the child, Jesus, brought gifts of great value to offer to him. The valuable items they presented indicate how they valued this new king, born in Bethlehem. These people were the first of a long procession of faithful followers of Christ who have brought valuable gifts to him and to his mission. It would be impossible to calculate the amount of financial contributions Christians have given to the Christian enterprise since the days of the Wise Men! Great cathedrals, Christian hospitals, schools of all levels, art and music commissioned by patrons, as well as operating and capital expenses for churches and mission stations. The funds for these have been given as acts of worship to Christ, as were the gifts of gold, frankincense, and myrrh given to the child in Mary's arms. What homage has been paid to Jesus Christ in the two millennia since his birth!

What shall be our gift? How do we value Jesus? Of what value shall our gift to him be? Can we give him anything less than our very lives? He is the one who gave his life for us that we might have fuller, more meaningful lives.

What does it means to give one's life to Christ? It means involving him in every significant decision we make in such a way that we try to do what he wants at every point. Is is wanting to "have the mind of Christ," as Paul said.

PRAYER: Oh Christ, I give myself to you. Be present in my every thought and decision from this time onward! Amen

~ ~ ~ ~ ~ ~

DECEMBER 30

SHE SPOKE OF HIM TO EVERYONE

At that moment she came, and began to praise God
and to speak about the child to all who were looking for the
redemption of Jerusalem.

—Luke 2:38

READ: Luke 2:36-40

When we see something beautiful, or experience an outstanding event our normal reaction is to want to tell others about it. When we have been given unexpected news we simply want to tell others about it. When you meet someone who is especially striking in one way or another, you feel like telling others about your new acquaintance.

When the aging Anna saw Jesus at the time Mary and Joseph brought the child into the Temple she was so sure of his identity as God's special messenger to bring salvation, that she immediately began to tell everyone whom she met about him. Anna was the first witness to Christ. Hundreds of thousands of Christ's followers have been telling others about him in all the centuries since Anna.

Following Anna's example, may we find ourselves so taken with the good news of God's love in Christ that we are unable to keep the news to ourselves. May we become effective witnesses to the truth as revealed to us in Jesus Christ. One does not have to be an expert theologian to tell others how one feels about Jesus Christ. Anna wasn't theologically trained, but she spoke to everyone about Jesus.

PRAYER: Help me to share the faith you have given to me, O God, through Christ, the Lord of Life. Amen.

~ ~ ~ ~ ~ ~

DECEMBER 31

AT THE STROKE OF 12

Blessed be the name of the Lord from this time on and forevermore. From the rising of the sun to its setting the name of the Lord is to be praised.

—Psalm 113:2-3

READ: Psalm 113

Within earshot of Chicago's "Loop," where all the New Year's eve revelry was about to begin a gathering of Christian worshipers sat in a chapel of a large church building on Chicago's famed "Magnificent Mile." The service was designed to conclude at the stroke of 12, the very moment an old year was ending and a new year was about to begin. Just before the congregation rose and the organist began to accompany the singing of "Old Hundredth," the pastor leading the service announced, "As we hear the shouts and the bells, the noisemakers and the revelry of the crowds filling the corner of State and Randolf streets in the Loop, let us drown out their noise in the quietness of this sacred hour by singing our praises to God using the Doxology!"

And then the worshipers sang:

Praise God from whom all blessings flow;
Praise Him, all creatures here below;
Praise Him above, ye heavenly host;
Praise Him Father, Son, and Holy Ghost.
Amen."

As the last strains of the AMEN drifted upward from that Christian group who had come in off of the cold, windy streets of

Chicago, the noise of the crowd subsided, and the city resumed its usual din. Then the worshipers returned to their apartments beginning the new year with praise to God still lingering in their hearts.

What a way to end the year and to prepare for the new year. Forgiven for past mistakes, upheld by a knowledge of God's creative goodness in the present, and confidently facing future challenges with the sure and certain hope of God's continued grace. Surely that is to praise God from whom all blessings flow—at the stroke of 12!

PRAYER: Almighty God, Creator of all life, for forgiving love, and guiding grace, I give you thanks. For the blessed hope for a new year dawning I praise you, Father, Son, and Holy Ghost. Amen. And Amen!

~ ~ ~ ~ ~ ~

MAY YOU HAVE A HAPPY AND BLESSED NEW YEAR!